Manager's Guide
to Compliance

Manager's Guide
to Compliance

*Sarbanes-Oxley, COSO, ERM, COBIT,
IFRS, BASEL II, OMB A-123, ASX 10,
OECD Principles, Turnbull Guidance,
Best Practices, and Case Studies*

ANTHONY TARANTINO

WILEY

John Wiley & Sons, Inc.

Library of Congress Cataloging-in-Publication Data

Tarantino, Anthony, 1949-
  Manager's guide to compliance : Sarbanes-Oxley, COSO, ERM, COBIT, IFRS, BASEL II, OMB A-123, ASX 10, OECD principles, Turnbull guidance, best practices, and case studies / Anthony Tarantino.
      p. cm.
  Includes index.
  ISBN-13: 978-0-471-79257-4 (cloth)
  ISBN-10: 0-471-79257-8 (cloth)
   1. Accounting—Law and legislation—United States. 2. Auditing, Internal—Law and legislation—United States. 3. Disclosure of information—Law and legislation—United States. 4. Accounting—Standards. 5. Auditing, Internal—Standards. I. Title.
  KF1357.T37 2006
  346.73'06648--dc22

                                         2005034272

Printed in the United States of America

10 9 8 7 6 5 4 3 2 1

Dedicated
to
Ted and Allie

NOTE TO THE READER

In providing the information contained in this book, the author and contributors are not engaged in rendering legal or other professional advice and services. As such, this text should not be used as a substitute for consultation with professional, legal, or other competent advisers. All information is provided herein "as is."

Contents

PREFACE   XI
ACKNOWLEDGMENT   XVII

CHAPTER 1
U.S. SOX Section 401: Off-Balance Sheet Arrangements   1

CHAPTER 2
U.S. SOX Section 404: Internal Controls   21

CHAPTER 3
U.S. SOX Section 406: Code of Ethics   32

CHAPTER 4
U.S. SOX Section 409: Real-Time Reporting of Material Changes   35

CHAPTER 5
U.S. SOX Impact on Privately Held Companies and Nonprofits   39

CHAPTER 6
U.S. SOX Impact on Small U.S. Companies   44

CHAPTER 7
U.S. SOX Impact on Foreign Companies   49

CHAPTER 8
U.S. Government's Version of U.S. SOX: OMB Circular A-123   53

CHAPTER 9
U.S. Healthcare Efforts to Improve Internal Controls: U.S. HIPAA   69

CHAPTER 10
Bankers' and Insurers' Efforts to Improve Internal Controls   71

CHAPTER 11
Australia, Canada, and UK Efforts to Improve Internal Controls   79

CHAPTER 12
EU Efforts to Improve Internal Controls: OECD Principles   91

CHAPTER 13
Global GAAP (IFRS) and Global Reporting Language (XBRL)   96

CHAPTER 14
Compliance and Internal Controls Impact on Outsourcing   106

CHAPTER 15
Civil and Criminal Penalties for Noncompliance   108

CHAPTER 16
Business Penalties for Noncompliance: A Material Weakness   121

CHAPTER 17
Revenue Recognition Requirements: U.S. SAB 101 and 104   125

CHAPTER 18
Data Retention Requirements   135

CHAPTER 19
Compliance and Internal Control Software   139

CHAPTER 20
Auditing Internal Controls   147

CHAPTER 21
Best Practices in Internal Controls: Enterprise Risk Management   178

CHAPTER 22

Best Practices in Internal Controls: IT Risk Management & SDLC (NIST 800-30)   185

CHAPTER 23

Best Practices in Internal Controls: Mapping COBIT to COSO I, COSO II, & PCAOB   190

CHAPTER 24

Best Practices in Internal Controls: COBIT IT Control Objectives   194

CHAPTER 25

Best Practices in Compliance and Internal Controls: ASX 10 Principles   200

CHAPTER 26

Best Practices in Internal Controls: Segregation of Duties (SOD)   228

CHAPTER 27

Best Practices in Internal Controls: Case Studies   242

CHAPTER 28

Best Practices in Compliance Project Management   254

CHAPTER 29

Best Practices in Governance and Ethics   261

CHAPTER 30

Costs *versus* Benefits and the Business Reaction   266

APPENDIX A Frequently Asked P2P Questions   278

APPENDIX B Links to Referenced Organizations and Documents   290

GLOSSARY   292

INDEX   304

Preface

The massive U.S. corporate scandals of the last several years have led to a huge change in the way organizations are governed. At its heart was a failure of leadership, ethics, and morality on several levels, which led to a breakdown in investor confidence. The failures occurred among corporate executives, boards of directors, regulatory agencies, rating agencies, and the press. One could argue this was caused by a lack of virtue and a breaking of a social contract between organizations (public and private) and those who invest in and rely on them. These are age-old concepts. In his *Analects*, the great Chinese sage Confucius (551–479 B.C.) argued virtue was the key characteristic of superior leadership. Virtue provides a moral power that allows one to win a following without resorting to physical force and enables a leader to maintain good order. Mencius (372–289 B.C.), is often referred to as the second great Chinese sage, and he developed the notion of a social contract in which one rules by a mandate of heaven. If a leader broke the social contract, then his followers would be absolved of all loyalty and might be required to overthrow him. Enron, WorldCom, Parmalat, Ahold, and others broke the mandate of heaven in corporate America and Europe and exposed the lack of virtue in those entrusted with good corporate governance.

These events have spawned a move toward more robust compliance on a global level, which will require much improved internal controls and will change the nature of business in fundamental ways. The struggle for improved compliance is nothing new. Investors have always sought greater transparency as organizations have sought to limit transparency to protect competitive information. Scandals have always acted as a catalyst to force improved corporate governance and transparency. The South Sea Bubble scandal in the early 1700s fostered improved accounting standards in British companies. U.S. states began enacting blue-sky laws in the early 1900s as the result of shady stock promotions. Of course, the greatest reforms came as a result of the great stock market crash of 1929 and depression during the 1930s. This led to the passage of federal security legislation in 1933 and 1934 and the creation of the Securities and Exchange Commission (SEC).[1] Reforms have continued, but were greatly accelerated by scandals of the late 1990s. So there is little chance for a significant rollback in compliance requirements, especially when most investors do not place much faith in corporate boards to provide viable oversight. A Wall Street Journal/Harris poll found about two-thirds of investors expressing doubts in the ability of corporate boards of directors to provide effective oversight.[2]

Many skeptics have made analogies with Year 2000 (Y2K) and International Organization for Standardization (ISO) certifications, suggesting that this is only a passing fad or an American-based overreaction to Enron-type scandals. Though the argument about an overreaction has some merit, this is no passing fad. Though the U.S. Sarbanes-Oxley Act (SOX) has received the lion's share of attention, initiatives are underway in almost every global region and industry to improve transparency in financial reporting. In spite of ongoing complaints from U.S. companies above excessive compliance costs, the Wall Street Journal/Harris online poll found that most U.S. investors still believe corporate governance regulations remain too lenient. The same poll found only 6% of investors believing corporate governance to be too strict. This skepticism about the effectiveness of corporate governance has led nearly one-third of investors to reduce or to divest their stake in various companies due to concerns about the quality of their corporate governance.[3]

The reasons for the wave of compliance initiatives and the need for improved internal controls are simple. We are fast approaching a global marketplace in which investors will demand a level playing field in comparing financial results whether companies or industries are based in the United States, the European Union (EU), Russia, China, or other Third World countries. Privates and nonprofits are feeling the pressure to improve internal controls from their insurers and bankers if they want to get the most competitive rates. This is not

---

[1] John Emshwiller, "Opening the Books," *Wall Street Journal*, October 17, 2005.
[2] Becky Bright, "Investors Are Skeptical of Success of Sarbanes-Oxley, Poll Finds," Wall Street Journal/Harris On Line Poll, October, 14, 2005.
[3] Becky Bright, "Investors Are Skeptical of Success of Sarbanes-Oxley, Poll Finds," Wall Street Journal/Harris On Line Poll, October, 14, 2005.

to say bumps will not occur along the way. Years of sloppy business practices, weak internal and external audits, and lackluster enforcement will make this a painful process. In Third World countries where most businesses are family run and/or closely held, this will present additional challenges.

A major debate is underway as to whether mandatory government regulations with severe criminal and criminal penalties, such as SOX, are needed to improve governance and internal controls, or whether principles-based guidelines, advocated in Europe, will suffice. New York's Attorney General, Eliot Spitzer, has referenced President Teddy Roosevelt, who advocated 100 years ago that government alone must oversee marketplaces and that self-regulation was doomed to fail. "Teddy Roosevelt understood the marketplace . . . that in order to preserve dynamism in the marketplace there needed to be that force to ensure competition and a level playing field," he says. "That's the role we play on Wall Street. That's what we've done in terms of labor markets and the environment."[4]

The major U.S. scandals at Enron, Tyco, WorldCom, Riggs Banks, Fannie Mae, ImClone, HealthSouth, Marsh & McClennan, and European scandals at Ahold and Parmalat would suggest the futility of voluntary measures, but it is still early in the process and not yet clear if SOX will have the desired effect and the benefits will outweigh the costs. Post-SOX scandals such as Refco, the largest independent futures brokerage firm, will also raise the debate that all the detailed oversight and higher audit standards can still miss major corruption, in this case poor due diligence for Refco's August 2005 IPO.[5]

Today's managers face a growing challenge and dilemma in the global thrust to improve governance and compliance, which at its core requires robust internal controls. The dilemma comes in how to comply in a manner that does not punish operational efficiencies and competitiveness. This will be true for privately and publicly held companies throughout the globe and even for nonprofit institutions. Down to the U.S. state level (California's AB 1386 protects individual identities) and at federal government agency level (US OMB's A-128 applies SOX to federal agencies), compliance initiatives will become

---

[4]Michael Gormley, "Gangbuster to Governor? New York's Attorney General Starts Down a Familiar Path," Associated Press, Sunday, June 13, 2004.
[5]Julie Johnsson, "Chicago's Grant Thornton Sued Over Refco Scandal," *Chicago Business*, Oct. 13, 2005.

role models bound to spread to other U.S. states, local government agencies, and international governments.

The good news in global compliance efforts is the acceptance of COSO-like standards to improve internal controls. Improved internal controls are at the core of almost all compliance regulations. Though a healthy debate continues between the use of voluntary guidelines versus compulsory regulations, there is widespread acceptance for the need to improve internal controls using the Committee of Sponsoring Organizations (COSO) definition and approach. COSO used a commonsense approach to internal controls, which includes defining and categorizing the criticality of business processes, the risks associated with business processes, and the means to mitigate risks. The mitigation process includes assigning its owners, and then testing, auditing, and certifying the adequacy of controls.

We will begin with an introduction to SOX, which is technically called the Public Company Accounting Reform and Investor Protection Act of 2002. SOX was sponsored by Senator Paul Sarbanes (Democrat–Maryland), then chairman of the Committee on Banking, Housing and Urban Affairs in the Senate, and Representative Michael Oxley (Republican–Ohio), the Financial Services Committee chair in the House. It passed the Senate unanimously, won easy approval in the House, and President Bush signed it into law on July 30, 2002. The internal control provisions went into effect for larger companies in 2004. Smaller companies and foreign filers are given more time, with deadlines pushed from July 2005 to July 2007.

The SEC has delivered several final rulings defining its SOX inter- pretation. Based on the final rulings, the intent is to expand rather than to limit the reach of the act. William H. Donaldson, the former chairman of the SEC, made it clear in his September 2003 testimony, that SOX is essential in restoring investor confidence by providing transparency in financial reporting. He summarized the events of the 1990s and made an ominous comparison with the events of 1929: "The low points in this story are now household names, not just Enron, but also WorldCom, Tyco, Adelphia, and others. There was other serious misconduct as well, including in the once-celebrated IPO market, which in too many cases lacked both fairness and integrity. The cost of this corner cutting to investors has been enormous. While thankfully we have not witnessed the same intensity of human suffer- ing that came with the depression of the 1930s, the most recent down- turn in the market directly affected many more investors than the

1929 market crash, because many more individuals had much more of their savings invested in the stock market."[6]

We will provide a more detailed look at SOX Sections 401, 404, 406, and 409 and then discuss the impact of SOX on small and foreign filers, privates, and nonprofits. This will be followed by an overview of SOX-like legislation coming to U.S. federal agencies, Australia, Canada, and the UK. We will include a discussion of efforts to improve internal controls in the following industries: health (HIPPA), banking (GLB and Basel II), and insurers (Solvency II). The movement to create principles-based guidelines by the OECD and global Generally Accepted Accounting Principles (GAAP) by the IFRS will be compared to SOX and U.S. GAAP. The impact on outsourcing will include an explanation of the Statement on Auditing Standards No. 70 (SAS 70) audit process. The civil and criminal penalties for noncompliance will demonstrate the major changes brought about by the U.S. corporate scandals. Best practices in internal controls will be offered that include several case studies and the role technology can play in automating compliance. Finally, we will provide a cost versus benefits analysis. This text is designed to be an introductory guide and handbook for professionals in information technology (IT), operations, finance, and supply chain. It may be helpful to internal and external auditors but is not designed to provide a framework for the audit process. It may help regulators as a high-level overview of the many compliance and governance initiatives underway throughout the world. Finally, it may also be helpful to investors who seek to evaluate the merits of the compliance initiatives in mitigating risks in companies, industries, and regions they are considering.

Note: Throughout the text we have used auditing examples and case studies around the procure-to-pay (P2P) process since it is typically well understood by accounting, operations, and IT professionals.

Anthony Tarantino
April 2006

---

[6]Testimony Concerning Implementation of the Sarbanes-Oxley Act of 2002, by William H. Donaldson, Chairman U.S. Securities and Exchange Commission. Before the Senate Committee on Banking, Housing and Urban Affairs, September 9, 2003, http://www.sec.gov/news/testimony/090903tswhd.htm.

ACKNOWLEDGMENTS

The author gratefully acknowledges the following individuals for their invaluable input and expertise:

Koti Ancha, MSIE, Six Sigma Black Belt, Senior Program Manager, Supply Chain Strategy, Seagate Technology, Scotts Valley, CA. For assistance in providing case studies and general editing.

Mark Stebelton, CPA, Senior Program Manager, Compliance Softwares and SOX SME, Logical Apps, Irvine, CA. For sharing expertise, specifically regarding SAS 70.

Holly Tran, CISSP, CISM, MSEE, Manager, BearingPoint. For system security and compliance practice support.

Greg Henzel, MBA, Manager, BearingPoint. For contributions to mapping the following standards: COSO, ERM, and PCAOB.

Richard Marti, Manager, BearingPoint. For contributions to mapping the following standards: COSO, ERM, and PCAOB.

Shirley Cui, MSCS. For indexing and general editing support.

CHAPTER 1

U.S. SOX Section 401: Off-Balance Sheet Arrangements

INTRODUCTION[1]

Christopher Cox replaced William Donaldson as SEC Chairman in 2005. Since assuming his chairmanship, Cox has advocated a rethinking of regulations, arguing that they are overly complex and this complexity is partly to blame for the accounting scandals of the 1990s. Maybe the best evidence of this is the convoluted and confusing regulations and guidance around off-balance sheet (OBS) arrangements. This chapter will detail the current state of the U.S. regulations. It appears that the current regulations invite abuse and misunderstanding, and do not assure investors that Enron-type abuses are a thing of the past.

Section 401 of the Sarbanes-Oxley Act of 2002 requires the listing of off-balance sheet (OBS) arrangements, transactions, and obligations (including contingent obligations) that may have a material effect, current or future, on financial conditions, changes in financial results in operations, liquidity capital expenditures, capital resources, or significant components or revenues or expenses. The SEC final ruling requires the disclosure of "the nature and business purpose of the OBS arrangements, why and how they are needed in running a business." For those wondering why this is an area of concern, a one-word explanation should suffice—Enron. It was Enron's horrible abuse, and Arthur Andersen's blessing such OBS arrangements, that led to the most infamous and globally recognized scandal in a generation.

The problems stem from the complexity and resulting confusion in how to account for OBS arrangements. Unfortunately, the SEC has not simplified the process to the extent to preclude significant abuse.

Even a process as seemingly straightforward as procurement is given alternative interpretations. With U.S. GAAP's taking a rules-based approach (as opposed to principles-based as favored by the International Financial Reporting Standards (IFRS)), it is curious how rules and guidance can be issued which are not clear and straightforward. One cynical interpretation is that the complexity is by design serving those who make their living interpreting the regulations and those using the complexity of the regulations to minimize their tax exposure. A less cynical interpretation is that U.S. tax law continues to evolve to the point that even the brightest financial experts struggle in understanding it.

After reading this section, ask yourself if these regulations are straightforward enough to assure their consistent application by companies of all sizes and complexities and to avoid Enron-type abuses of the past.

The following are some simple examples of OBS obligations that may need to be accounted for:

- **Long-Term Purchase Agreements**: Common practice is to use long-term purchase agreements to assure a reliable source of supply for goods and services at the lowest price. Many companies are moving their direct material programs to Vendor/Supplier Managed Inventory (VMI) programs, which are controlled by long-term purchase agreements. Section 401 clearly requires a time-phased listing of obligations (Year 1, Years 2–3, etc.) in a tabular format specified by the SEC.
- **Cancellation and Restocking Charges**: Though the SEC is clear in defining the requirement to list time-phased obligations, restocking and cancellation charges are not mentioned specifically in Section 401 but are listed as new triggering events requiring an 8-K filing "any material early termination penalties" under Section 409. Most long-term agreements include such provisions. Though the SEC's intent is unclear, a company suffering a major downturn and paying restocking and/or cancellation charges will have trouble defending not listing these as OBS obligations.
- **Lease Agreements**: In addition to the aforementioned items, Capital and Operating Lease obligations should be listed as OBS obligations. Fees incurred due to early termination of agreements will need to be accounted for as well.

Even more complex is the requirement to account for contingent OBS obligations. The SEC provides an instruction "that a company must provide the disclosure required regarding off-balance sheet arrangements, whether or not the company is also a party to the transaction or agreement creating the contingent obligation arising under the off-balance sheet arrangement. In the event that neither the company nor any affiliate of the company is a party to the transaction or agreement creating the contingent obligation arising under the off-balance arrangement in question, the four-business-day period for reporting the event under this item would begin on the earlier of

- The fourth business day after the contingent obligation is created or arises, and
- The day on which an executive officer of the company becomes aware of the contingent obligation."

This has major ramifications for those enterprises that sell through channel partners with indirect channel sales agreements. OBS obligations may exist for consignment inventory, returns, rebate programs with volume incentives, warranty, special pricing agreements, and so on. Contingent OBS obligations may come into play for those who have outsourced manufacturing, distribution/logistics, and design.

Obviously stung by the terrible abuses of Enron, the SEC has laid out a comprehensive process for companies to explain OBS transactions and obligations.

The SEC's definition of OBS arrangements addresses certain guarantees that may be a source of potential risk to a company's future liquidity, capital resources, and results of operations, regardless of whether or not they are recorded as liabilities. The SEC has ruled that this may include "contracts that contingently require the guarantor to make payments to the guaranteed party based on another entity's failure to perform under an obligating agreement (e.g., a performance guarantee)."

Accounting for OBS arrangements is not enough. The SEC has ruled that companies will have to explain the nature and business purpose of such arrangements. "The disclosure should explain to investors why a company engages in off-balance sheet arrangements and should provide the information that investors need to understand the business activities advanced through a company's off-balance sheet arrangements. For example, a company may indicate that the arrangements enable the company to lease certain facilities rather than acquire them, where the latter would require the company to recognize a liability for the financing. Other possible disclosures under this requirement may indicate the off-balance sheet arrangement enables the company to obtain cash through sales of groups of loans to a trust; to finance inventory, transportation, or research and development costs without recognizing a liability; or to lower borrowing costs of unconsolidated affiliates by extending guarantees to their creditors."

The SEC requires companies to explain the impact on their "liquidity, capital resources, market risk support, credit risk support or other benefits. This disclosure should provide investors with an understanding of the importance of off-balance sheet arrangements to the company as a financial matter . . . . Together with the other disclosure requirements, companies should provide information sufficient for investors to assess the extent of the risks that have been transferred and retained as a result of the arrangements."

The SEC goes further. "In addition, the disclosure should provide investors with insight into the overall magnitude of a company's off-balance sheet activities, the specific material impact of the arrangements on a company, and the circumstances that could cause material contingent obligations or liabilities to come to fruition. Disclosure is required to the extent material and necessary to investors' understanding of

- The amounts of revenues, expenses, and cash flows of the company arising from the arrangements,
- The nature and total amount of any interests retained, securities issued and other indebtedness incurred by the company in connection with such arrangements, and
- The nature and amount of any other obligations or liabilities (including contingent obligations or liabilities) of the company arising from the arrangements that is, or is reasonably likely to become, material and the triggering events or circumstances that could cause them to arise."

DEFINITION OF OBS ARRANGEMENTS[2]

The SEC has defined the term OBS arrangement as "any transaction, agreement or other contractual arrangement to which an entity that is not consolidated with the company is a party, under which the company, whether or not a party to the arrangement, has, or in the future may have:

- Any obligation under a direct or indirect guarantee or similar arrangement,
- A retained or contingent interest in assets transferred to an unconsolidated entity or similar arrangement,
- Derivatives, to the extent that the fair value thereof is not fully reflected as a liability or asset in the financial statements, and
- Any obligation or liability, including a contingent obligation or liability, to the extent that it is not fully reflected in the financial statements (excluding the footnotes thereto)."

In particular, the proposals require a disclosure where the likelihood of the occurrence of a future event implicating an OBS arrangement or its material effect was higher than remote. As mentioned above, the SEC noted, "the disclosure threshold departed from the existing MD&A threshold, under which a company must disclose information that is 'reasonably likely' to have a material effect on financial condition, changes in financial condition or results of operations." While this is an improvement, there is still an ambiguity as to the dividing line between "reasonably likely" and "remote."

The SEC requires disclosure of enumerated items only "to the extent necessary to an understanding of the company's off-balance sheet arrangements and their effect on financial condition, changes in financial condition and results of operations." Specifically, the SEC requires a company to disclose

- "The nature and business purpose of the company's off-balance sheet arrangements;
- The significant terms and conditions of the arrangements;
- The nature and amount of the total assets and of the total obligations and liabilities of an unconsolidated entity that conducts off-balance sheet activities;
- The amounts of revenues, expenses and cash flows, the nature and amount of any retained interests, securities issued or other indebtedness incurred, or any other obligations or liabilities (including contingent obligations or liabilities) of the company

arising from the arrangements that are, or may become, material and the circumstances under which they could arise;

- Management's analysis of the material effects of the above items, including an analysis of the degree to which the company relies on off-balance sheet arrangements for its liquidity and capital resources or market risk or credit risk support or other benefits; and
- A reasonably likely termination or material reduction in the benefits of an off-balance sheet arrangement and any material effects."

The SEC specifies the need to account for "amounts of a company's known contractual obligations, aggregated by type of obligation and by time period in which payments are due." The SEC rejects requests to exclude "purchase orders and contracts for goods and services in the ordinary course of business." It requires "disclosure of the amounts of a company's purchase obligations without regard to whether notes, drafts, acceptances, bills of exchange, or other commercial instruments will be used to satisfy such obligations because those instruments could have a significant effect on the company's liquidity."

The SEC specifies that the categories of contractual obligations partly include

- Long-term debt obligations,
- Capital lease obligations,
- Operating lease obligations,
- Purchase obligations, and
- Other long-term liabilities reflected on the company's balance sheet under its Generally Accepted Accounting Principles (GAAP).

OBS ENTITIES[3]

In 2005, the SEC issued its "Report and Recommendations Pursuant to Section 401(c) of the Sarbanes-Oxley Act of 2002 On Arrangements with Off-Balance Sheet Implications, Special Purpose Entities, and Transparency of Filings by Issuers," which added much needed clarification and expanded examples for purchase orders, leases, derivatives, and contingent OBS obligations. The SEC's introduction underscores the complexity around OBS: "Issuers are involved in any number of contractual obligations, including debt obligations, retirement obligations, compensation agreements, leases, guarantees, derivatives, and obligations to purchase goods and services. In many cases, liabilities are recognized on the balance sheet at the inception of the contract, because one party has performed. For example, if an issuer borrows money, it recognizes a liability upon receipt of the funds. In other cases, liabilities are recognized as time passes, as in the case of interest related to the borrowed funds. In still other cases, contractual obligations remain off the balance sheet. Examples of these obligations may include operating leases, portions of obligations related to retirement plans, certain guarantees, and certain derivatives."

The 2005 SEC Report and Recommendations provide much needed additional background on OBS entities and obligations. The SEC's initial ruling was weak in providing examples and scenarios. "Companies have used off-balance-sheet entities responsibly and irresponsibly for some time. These separate legal entities were permissible under Generally Accepted Accounting Principles (GAAP) and tax laws so that companies could finance business ventures by transferring the risk of these ventures from the parent to the off-balance-sheet subsidiary. This was also helpful to investors who did not want to invest in these other ventures."

In a major understatement, the SEC noted in its 2005 Report that Enron and similar scandals have given OBS a bad reputation as something underhanded "or at least less than fully transparent. The insinuation is that something that should be on the balance sheet is not, and that the reporting issuer has designed the transaction or arrangement to produce that result. However, questions about whether items should be reflected on the balance sheet do not arise only when there is an attempt to deceive financial statement users."

The SEC defends OBS by noting that "many legitimate transactions generate such questions, and there are, of course, bounds as to what should be included on a balance sheet. It is this broader, more-inclusive question of the proper bounds of what should be included on the balance sheet" that are addressed in its 2005 Report. According to the SEC, the common characteristic of OBS is their creation of a condition "in which there may be a legal or economic nexus between the issuer and risks, rewards, rights or obligations not reflected (or not fully-reflected) on the balance sheet."

The SEC describes how OBS can refer to many things: including separate legal entities, i.e., separate companies of which the parent holds less than 100% ownership, or contingent liabilities such as letters of credit or loans to separate legal entities that are guaranteed by the parent. Under U.S. GAAP, these items can be excluded from the parent's financial statements, but usually they must be described in footnotes. Ironically, Enron did list their OBS arrangements, but their implications were missed by Arthur Andersen and the SEC.

While U.S. GAAP and U.S. tax laws do allow off-balance-sheet entities for valid reasons, they can be abused by those wishing to hide obligations and thus overstate earnings. In the case of Enron, OBS vehicles were used to grossly inflate financial results by fraudulently creating earnings to cover bad trades.

The SEC defines a balance sheet as portraying the financial position of an organization at a point in time. It is made up of three basic components:

1. Assets, which are 'probable future economic benefits obtained or controlled by a particular entity as a result of past transactions or events';
2. Liabilities, which are 'probable future sacrifices of economic benefits arising from present obligations of a particular entity to transfer assets or provide services to other entities in the future as a result of past transactions or events'; and
3. Equity, which is 'the residual interests in the assets of an entity that remains after deducting its liabilities.'"

Liabilities or Equity

Though the SEC's definition appears straightforward, many questions and issues exist in determining which items should be captured on the balance sheet. "Perhaps the most pervasive question is whether, in deciding which assets and liabilities to include in the balance sheet, one should look to those assets and liabilities legally controlled by an issuer or to those assets and liabilities that expose an issuer to risks and rewards. In most simple structures, these two approaches to analyzing the question produce similar answers as to whether or not to consolidate. However, more complex structures have developed in business practice for which these two different philosophies produce different answers."

Examples of off-balance obligations include purchase orders, leases, derivatives, and contingent OBS, which we will describe in greater detail.

PURCHASE ORDERS[4]

In its 2005 Report the SEC explains that a purchase obligation could be as simple as a standard one-time purchase order, or as complex as long-term contracts for goods and services for deliveries over an extended period. The major accounting and regulator issue is around the rights and obligations inherent in a contract, and when they take effect—upon signing, or later when performance against the contract occurs.

"Upon signing the contract, the purchaser could record an asset (e.g., 'inventory receivable') and a liability (e.g., 'Purchase Obligation'). The seller could also record an asset for the cash to be received and a liability reflecting its obligation to deliver the inventory. However, at this point in time, nothing has been delivered and no payment has been made. Nonetheless, one could argue that, even though no performance has occurred, the issuers have many of the same risks and rewards as if the exchange had already been completed, and thus should recognize the related assets and liabilities. Under this view, it could be argued that binding contracts give rise to assets and liabilities in advance of any performance under the contract."

This seems straightforward until the SEC explains the contrary view: "The contrary view is that assets and liabilities should only be recognized to the extent performance has occurred—that is, to the extent that one or both parties have carried out the actions (duties) agreed to in the contract, such as delivering or paying for the goods. Under this view, until some amount of performance has occurred on a contract, the buyer does not have an asset for the goods or services to be received nor a liability (i.e., a present obligation) to pay for them, and the seller does not have a recognizable asset for the right to collect the contractual payments." With this approach assets and liabilities would not be recorded "until some performance has occurred." For example, if the purchaser of the inventory paid for it in advance, the purchaser's obligation to pay would be considered performed, and the purchaser would at that time record an asset to recognize its right to receive inventory. "The latter view underlies the more common financial reporting treatment. Thus, signing a contract for the sale/purchase of goods generally does not result in the recognition of an asset or liability by either party." The problem with the SEC's explanation is that nothing is mentioned about the obligations in canceling the contract or purchase agreement.

The SEC explains exceptions to this approach. "Two of the major exceptions are addressed in separate sections of this report: leases and derivatives. In yet other cases, while the assets and liabilities related to an unperformed contract are not separately recognized, losses embedded in those contracts are recognized. This so called 'loss contract' accounting is required when an issuer has committed to purchase inventory at prices that ensure a loss on resale of that inventory, and when a long-term construction contract is expected to result in a loss."

In January 2002, the SEC released FR-61, "Commission Statement about Management's Discussion and Analysis of Financial Condition and Results of Operations," which described the views of the Commission regarding certain disclosures that should be considered by issuers, including disclosures about contractual obligations and commercial commitments. This guidance was updated in the 2003 revision by the Commission of Item 303(A) (4) of Regulation S-K. Item 303(A) (4) requires disclosures about certain OBS arrangements, including certain contractual obligations. Specifically, these new rules require tabular disclosure in Management Discussion and Analysis (MD&A) of contractual obligations, including open purchase orders, which will result in future cash payments.

This disclosure is intended to provide financial statement users with information about unrecognized and recognized obligations. Though the disclosures do not provide information about the related assets to be received as a result of those cash payments, the disclosures are an attempt to portray contractual obligations broadly.

OBS Issues in Accounting for Contractual Obligations

The SEC provides for ways to account for unperformed contractual obligations. "For example, all contractual rights and obligations could be recognized as assets and liabilities. This would recognize the fact that once an entity enters into a firm contract to buy or sell something, the entity is generally subject to many of the same risks and rewards as if the transaction had already been completed. For example, once an issuer has entered into a firm fixed-price contract to purchase inventory, future declines in the value of that inventory affect the issuer. Similarly, once an issuer has agreed to sell inventory for a particular price, future decreases in the value of that inventory do not affect the issuer."

Unfortunately, the SEC's guidance may provide too many options and add to the confusion in how to account for OBS arrangements: "However, to the extent neither party to a contract has performed, each party's rights and obligations are, at least implicitly, contingent upon the other party's. As such, some assert the rights and obligations in the contract do not qualify as assets and liabilities because they do not result from past transactions. Others believe that, because the rights and obligations are contingent upon one another, they should be accounted for only as a group, that is, the 'unit of account' would be the contract as a whole, rather than the assets and liabilities individually. In this analysis, the assets and liabilities would be offset against one another. Assuming the contract represents an exchange of equal values, the values of the assets and liabilities would likely net to zero, thus effectively resulting in no impact on the balance sheet. Although standard-setters have almost invariably determined that such unperformed contracts should not result in the recording of assets and liabilities, the basis for these decisions is not always stated. For example, as mentioned above, losses on certain contractual commitments, such as inventory purchases and construction contracts are required to be recognized before performance occurs. Conceptually, the loss in these contracts might be viewed as akin to an asset impairment loss, even though the rights in these contracts have not previously been reported as assets."

The SEC Report and Recommendations does discuss the potential confusion: "Another potentially confusing aspect of accounting for loss contracts is that the accounting is applied far beyond the situations specifically addressed in the accounting guidance. Although this guidance specifically applies to very narrow classes of transactions, issuers and auditors have often applied it by analogy to other unperformed contractual obligations. These analogies have been applied sporadically, meaning that losses inherent in some unperformed contracts are recorded, while others are not."

LEASES[5]

In its 2005 "Report and Recommendations Pursuant to Section 401(c) of the Sarbanes-Oxley Act," the SEC defines leases as follows: "A lease is a contractual obligation that allows assets owned by one party to be used by another party, for specified periods of time, in return for a payment or series of payments. Assets that are commonly leased include automobiles, airplanes, buildings and other real estate, machinery, computer equipment, and many other tangible assets . . . ." SFAS No. 13, Accounting for Leases (issued in 1976), provides the basic guidance for leases. "Leases that transfer most of the benefits and responsibilities of ownership to the party using the asset may be economically similar to sales with attached financing agreements." This is recognized in SFAS No. 13, which states that "a lease that transfers substantially all of the benefits and risks incident to the ownership of property should be accounted for as the acquisition of an asset and the incurrence of an obligation by the lessee and as a sale or financing by the lessor. Otherwise, the lease should be accounted for as a rental contract. We concentrate on the case where an issuer is the lessee, that is, where the issuer is the party using the asset, as this is the scenario most likely to result in no elements of the lease or leased asset being on the balance sheet."

Capital and Operating Leases

The SEC explains the difference between rental leases and capital leases: "Leases can transfer control of the asset from the lessor to the lessee for as much of the asset's life as desired, and can also transfer as many of the risks and rewards of ownership as desired. Leasing transactions can take many forms and include many different terms. Yet, despite this diversity in leasing arrangements, all leases receive one of two opposing accounting treatments; either the lease is treated as if it were a sale or as if it were a rental. If 'most' of the risks and rewards of ownership are transferred to an issuer leasing an asset, the lease is treated as a sale of the entire asset by the owner (i.e., the lessor) and a purchase of an asset financed with debt by the issuer using the asset (referred to as the 'whole-of-the-asset' approach). This kind of lease is called a 'capital lease'. In these cases, the lessor removes the cost of the asset from its balance sheet and reports a sale of the asset for proceeds equal to the present value of the required lease payments, plus the expected remaining value of the leased asset at the end of the lease term. The issuer using the asset records the asset and a related liability for the present value of the required lease payments on its balance sheet. If the lease does not transfer sufficient risks and rewards to the lessee to be treated as a sale and purchase, it is instead treated like a rental contract. This kind of lease is called an 'operating lease'. In this case, the owner of the asset retains the asset on its balance sheet and records lease rental revenue (as well as depreciation, property taxes, etc.) in its income statement on a period-by-period basis. The issuer using the asset does not record the asset, or a related liability for the future contractual rental payments, on its balance sheet, but records leasing expense in its income statement, also on a period-by-period basis. SFAS No. 13 specifies that a lease is a capital lease if:

- The lease transfers ownership to the issuer (i.e., the lessee) using the asset by the end of the lease term;
- The lease contains an option whereby the issuer can purchase the leased property at a price sufficiently lower than the expected fair value of the leased property at the end of the lease term; or the term of the lease is equal to or greater than 75% of the estimated economic life of the leased property; or
- The present value of the minimum lease payments to be made by the issuer is equal to or greater than 90% of the fair value of the leased property.

The SEC does discuss the potential confusion and potential for errors in accounting for leases: "While in the majority of cases the evaluation of whether these criteria have been met is straightforward, in certain circumstances it can be challenging, as leases sometimes contain contingent or variable payment requirements, optional term extensions, and other clauses that affect the calculations under one or more of the tests described above. However, such determinations are very important, as they can completely change the accounting for the lease. The identification of which agreements should be accounted for as leases, and thus subject to the tests listed above, is also challenging in some situations. In order to reduce the chances of like arrangements being accounted for differently, the accounting guidance defines leases by their characteristics, not by their label. Thus, any contract, or portion of a contract, that meets the definition of a lease must be accounted for as one. While most leases are indeed explicitly identified as such, some are not. The accounting guidance also includes extensive disclosure requirements for leases. These requirements vary based upon the type of lease and whether the issuer is the lessor or lessee."

OBS Issues in Accounting for Leases

Compliance Week reported in its May 2005 issue that lease-related problems accounted for about one quarter of April's material weaknesses, up from 10% in March. Many of these stemmed from a letter by the SEC's chief accountant, Donald T. Nicolaisen, to a professional accounting group. The letter was written after a wave of restatements to correct lease-related accounting errors, reiterated the rules. According to *Compliance Week*: "The letter focused on three issues related to lease accounting: depreciation of the costs to improve leased property, how to recognize periods of free or reduced rent, and how to account for landlord incentives to make improvements."

The SEC explains that OBS issues arise from the contractual obligations that leases impose and "whether to record the rights and obligations inherent in the contracts as assets and liabilities when neither party to the contract has performed. With respect to leases, however, the question is really how to assess whether performance has occurred. As noted above, the current lease accounting standards focus on a determination as to which party to a lease agreement has the risks and rewards of ownership of the leased asset. This, in turn, determines whether the owner is deemed to have sold the asset and whether the issuer using the asset is deemed to have purchased the asset. As a consequence of this approach, the issuer leasing the asset will either recognize the entire leased asset on its books and a liability for all of its contractually required payments, or it will recognize no asset and no liability. The lease accounting guidance either treats the contract as if all of the performance occurs at the beginning of the lease, or as if none of it does. The intention is to treat those leases that are economically equivalent to sales as sales, and to treat other leases similar to service contracts. This approach, while a significant improvement from previous lease accounting, which rarely if ever required recognition of a capital lease, does not allow the balance sheet to show the fact that, in just about every lease, both parties have some interest in the asset, as well as some interest in one or more financial receivables or payables . . . . The 'all-or-nothing' nature of the guidance means that economically similar arrangements may receive different accounting, if they are just to one side or the other of the bright line test. For example, most would agree that there is little economic difference between a lease that commits an issuer to payments equaling 89% of an asset's fair value vs. 90% of an asset's fair value. Nonetheless, because of the bright-line nature of the lease classification tests, this small difference in economics can completely change the accounting. Conversely, economically different transactions may be treated similarly."

The SEC does acknowledge the complexity and potential for errors: "The significant amount of structuring of leases also makes analyzing potential changes to the lease guidance very difficult. Indeed, the current accounting guidance, which is criticized by many, would likely be held in much higher regard were it being applied to the lease arrangements that existed when it was debated and created. Changes in lease terms in response to the accounting guidance have caused undue focus on the weaknesses of the guidance. The fact that lease structuring based on the accounting guidance has become so prevalent will likely mean that there will be strong resistance to significant changes to the leasing guidance, both from preparers who have become accustomed to designing leases that achieve various reporting goals, and from other parties that assist those preparers."

DERIVATIVES[6]

In its 2005 "Report and Recommendations Pursuant to Section 401(c) of the Sarbanes-Oxley Act," the SEC references Robert L. McDonald, (Derivatives Markets, 2003) to explain derivatives as "simply a financial instrument (or even more simply, an agreement between two people) which has a value determined by the price of something else. For example, a stock option contract derives its value, at least in part, from the price of the underlying stock; similarly, a gold futures contract derives its value from the price of the underlying gold; an interest rate swap derives its value from the underlying interest rates . . . Derivatives permit issuers to mitigate and take on risk, and also to select which risks they want to retain and manage, and which they want to shift to others willing to bear them. For example, a manufacturer that requires oil as an input to production is exposed to the risk of an oil price increase. If oil prices do increase, cost of production increases and the manufacturer's profitability may suffer. Such an issuer may choose to contract with another party to effectively fix the price it will pay for oil at some future date through a "forward" contract. In this case, the issuer has "hedged" its exposure, and is protected from the negative economic effects of an adverse change in oil prices . . . . Of course, locking in a price through such a forward contract also precludes any cost savings the issuer might have experienced from a beneficial change in oil prices."

The current accounting guidance for derivatives has been in effect since 2001. It was a much needed update to an outdated accounting standard that the SEC maintains did not keep pace with changes in global financial markets and related financial innovations. According to the SEC, the current financial reporting for derivatives centers around three main issues:

1. Should derivative contracts be recognized on issuer balance sheets?
2. Should the changes in the value of derivative contracts be recognized in the income statement?
3. How should the overall sensitivity of the issuer to changes in important variables be conveyed?

Accounting for Derivatives

The SEC explains the accounting for derivatives as follows: "In general SFAS No. 133 requires that derivatives be recorded as assets or liabilities on the balance sheet at fair value, and re-measured each period with changes in fair value reflected in earnings. In part, the rationale for this approach was FASB's view that recognizing derivatives on the balance sheet based on measurements other than fair value was generally less relevant and understandable. For example, if historical cost were used to measure derivatives, many would be reported at a value of zero because no payment is made at the inception of the contract (e.g., most forward contracts)."

Hedge Accounting

The SEC explains hedge accounting of derivates as follows: "Many issuers utilize derivative instruments to hedge their exposure to certain economic risks. When a derivative is used to hedge an exposure, the value of the derivative should have an inverse relation to the value of the exposure it is hedging." The SEC notes that the core principle under SFAS No. 133 is to recognize changes in the value of derivatives in the income statement, but it also provides for an exception to address potential timing differences in recognizing offsetting gains and losses. "These timing differences occur in part because GAAP utilizes a 'mixed-attribute' approach where some items are recognized at historical cost, others at the lower of cost or market, and still others at fair value. As a consequence, changes in the value of a derivative may not be reflected in earnings at the same time as changes in the value of the hedged exposure unless hedge accounting is used."

CONTINGENT OBS OBLIGATIONS[7]

In its 2005 Report on Section 401, the SEC describes contingent OBS obligations as "situations where uncertainty exists about whether an obligation to transfer cash or other assets has arisen and/or the amount that will be required to settle such obligation." Examples include an organization which is:

- A party in a lawsuit and any payment is contingent upon the outcome of a settlement or an administrative or court proceeding;
- Providing a warranty for goods and services sold in which payment is contingent on the number of items that actually become defective and qualify for benefits under the warranty
- Acting as a guarantor on a loan for another organization and payment is contingent on whether the other organization defaults.

All these are examples of contingent OBS that present the potential for confusion, errors, and fraud. The issue is what, if any, liability should be recognized before such contingencies are resolved. The SEC notes that SFAS No. 5, Accounting for Contingencies, provides guidance for contingent OBS treating them in one of three ways. To begin with, a decision is made as to whether the loss itself is deemed "probable" to occur and whether the loss amount is estimable. Recognition of a liability is required if the loss is deemed probable and estimable.

No contingent OBS liability is recognized on a balance sheet, but financial reporting must note the existence of the potential loss if it is probable but the amount is not easily estimated, or if the loss is reasonably possible, but not probable. Of course the thresholds for "reasonable" and "probable" are not easily quantified and very much open to interpretation, which will be discussed in the next section.

The SEC acknowledges the lack of a consensus in how to handle OBS issues: "In contrast to the SFAS No. 5 approach, some recent accounting guidance requires that certain obligations that include contingencies be recognized at fair value. Under a fair value approach, the degree of uncertainty associated with a contingent liability is reflected in the measurement of the liability, rather than in the determination of whether a liability is recognized."

OBS Issues in Accounting for Contingent Obligations and Guarantees

The key issue in contingent liabilities is how to account for uncertainty. The SEC notes, "If uncertainty is taken into account in the recognition of liabilities . . . the balance sheet will report those liabilities that are highly likely to reduce cash or other assets available for distribution to shareholders. In addition, the items on the balance sheet would be reported at the amount most likely to be paid or received."

But the SEC acknowledges that this treatment creates several issues: "First, while the SFAS No. 5 accounting results in the recording of a liability that reflects the most likely payment, the balance sheet reflects information about only that outcome. Information about the other potential outcomes is ignored for the purpose of recording the liability. While disclosures in the notes to the financial statements might help to provide this information, in practice those disclosures are rarely detailed enough to allow an investor to take into account multiple possible loss outcomes."

It is ironic that the SEC is so open in admitting to potential for abuse and errors in its treatment of contingent OBS. The SEC acknowledges the problems in relying on what may be a subjective management analysis of whether a loss is probable. This makes the audit process very difficult as well.

The SEC's Section 401 Report discusses their long-term advocacy of improvements in OBS reporting. Some of this is the obvious embarrassment over the Enron scandal in which OBS and SPEs were used to hide a majority of the firm's debt. The outrageous abuse of OBS arrangements and obligations and its certification by Arthur Andersen stand as one of the most embarrassing failures in regulations in U.S. corporate history. Ironically, the SEC does not reference any comments it made advocating improvements in OBS accounting prior to Enron.[8]

Sadly, after all the reports and recommendations by the SEC, there is little to prevent the continued abuse of OBS and SPEs. The rules are so complex that unethical companies have a great deal of weasel room to hide problems and inflate earnings. For ethical organizations, the rules are open to conflicting interpretations for even processes as straightforward as purchasing.

ENDNOTES

1. This section extensively quotes and references the SEC's "Report and Recommendations Pursuant to Section 401(c) of the Sarbanes-Oxley Act of 2002 On Arrangements with Off-Balance Sheet Implications, Special Purpose Entities, and Transparency of Filings by Issuers."

2. This section extensively quotes and references the SEC's "Report and Recommendations Pursuant to Section 401(c) of the Sarbanes-Oxley Act of 2002 On Arrangements with Off-Balance Sheet Implications, Special Purpose Entities, and Transparency of Filings by Issuers."

3. This section extensively quotes and references the SEC's "Report and Recommendations Pursuant to Section 401(c) of the Sarbanes-Oxley Act of 2002 On Arrangements with Off-Balance Sheet Implications, Special Purpose Entities, and Transparency of Filings by Issuers."

4. This section extensively quotes and references the SEC's "Report and Recommendations Pursuant to Section 401(c) of the Sarbanes-Oxley Act of 2002 On Arrangements with Off-Balance Sheet Implications, Special Purpose Entities, and Transparency of Filings by Issuers."

5. This section extensively quotes and references the SEC's "Report and Recommendations Pursuant to Section 401(c) of the Sarbanes-Oxley Act of 2002 On Arrangements with Off-Balance Sheet Implications, Special Purpose Entities, and Transparency of Filings by Issuers."

6. This section extensively quotes and references the SEC's "Report and Recommendations Pursuant to Section 401(c) of the Sarbanes-Oxley Act of 2002 On Arrangements with Off-Balance Sheet Implications, Special Purpose Entities, and Transparency of Filings by Issuers."

7. This section extensively quotes and references the SEC's "Report and Recommendations Pursuant to Section 401(c) of the Sarbanes-Oxley Act of 2002 On Arrangements with Off-Balance Sheet Implications, Special Purpose Entities, and Transparency of Filings by Issuers."

8. SEC "Report and Recommendations Pursuant to Section 401(c) of the Sarbanes-Oxley Act of 2002 On Arrangements with Off-Balance Sheet Implications, Special Purpose Entities, and Transparency of Filings by Issuers."

CHAPTER 2

U.S. SOX Section 404: Internal Controls

INTRODUCTION[1]

No area of U.S. SOX has generated more interest and controversy than Section 404, which calls for the creation and maintenance of viable internal controls. Over the decades, the SEC has ruled that internal controls include policies, procedures, training programs, and other processes beyond financial controls. The SEC has defined internal controls to include "the safeguarding of assets against unauthorized acquisition, use, or disposition." Companies will need to document and test the adequacy of these internal process controls as well. The SEC has looked to the Committee of Sponsoring Organizations (COSO) for its understanding of internal controls. COSO's concept of internal controls is gaining acceptance as a global standard. According to COSO, internal control is a process, affected by an entity's board of directors, management, and other personnel, designed to provide reasonable assurance regarding the achievement of objectives in the following categories:

- Effectiveness and efficiency of operations
- Reliability of financial reporting
- Compliance with applicable laws and regulations

  Key concepts within the COSO framework include:

- Internal controls are an ongoing process, a means to an end, and not an end in themselves.
- Internal controls are affected by people at all levels of an organization and not just policies and procedures and their documentation.

- Internal controls will never eliminate risks but can provide a reasonable assurance that controls are in place to mitigate risks.[2]

The following are examples of inadequate internal controls that may need to be identified with corrective actions:[3]

- **Disparate Financial and Planning Systems:** Many companies use disparate financial and planning systems to run their businesses. This may include several Enterprise Resource Planning (ERP), Customer Relationship Management (CRM), Logistics, and Financial Systems. Compounding the problem is that outputs from these disparate systems are typically keyed into spreadsheets manually without access or revision controls. The resulting errors have resulted in misstatements in financial reporting.
- **Reconciliations of Intercompany Accounts Not Performed on a Timely Basis:** Many organizations process a significant number of routine intercompany transactions on a regular basis. Many individual intercompany transactions are immaterial and primarily relate to balance sheet activity, for example, cash transfers between business units to finance normal operations. Though a formal management policy typically requires a monthly reconciliation of intercompany accounts and confirmation of balances between business units, many times no process is in place to guarantee the performance of these procedures. As a result, detailed reconciliations of intercompany accounts may not be performed on a timely basis, leading to errors in financial reporting.
- **Poor Physical and Logical Control of Assets:** Many companies have substantial amounts of capital equipment, which is often not physically or logically controlled in a timely manner. Extreme examples include transactions following the actual movement of assets by weeks or even months, inaccurate assessment of the condition and value of capital equipment, and poor inventory accuracies creating the double misery of excess inventories and critical shortages.
- **Poor Purchase and Customer Order Visibility:** Many companies do a poor job of maintaining the visibility of valid open purchase and customer commitments. The best evidence is an examination of open commitments with a historical or past due date. In many

cases, these past due items are bogus and the result of sloppy order maintenance. Lack of maintenance on the purchasing side can result in the accumulation of several months' worth of past due items and represent significant and bogus cash requirements, frustrating finance's efforts to forecast cash flows. Lack of maintenance on the customer side can result in a major misrepresentation of sales backlogs.

- **Poor Customer and Supplier Master Control:** Inadequate control of customer and supplier masters is a common problem in many organizations. This can be caused by the failure to adopt and rigorously maintain naming conventions, with the result that the same supplier or customer is listed many times, with different names and identity numbers. The failure to identify that W.W. Grainger, Grainger Inc., Grainger Incorporated, and Grainger Corp. are the same supplier will frustrate efforts to achieve the most complete pricing.

- **Poor Item/Parts Master Control:** The increasing trend toward mergers, acquisitions, and facility consolidations has often resulted in the same items unknowingly listed under several different item or part numbers. A related problem is the failure to cross-reference items with the same form, fit, and function. The result is the double misery of excess inventories and item shortages.

- **Inventory Write-Offs:** Poor practices around forecasting, trading partner collaboration, and end-of-life product management often result in excess and obsolete inventory being written off. Many companies struggle in projecting the magnitude of these write-offs. Companies will need to demonstrate that they have implemented formal internal controls to minimize and forecast the impact of end-of-life product cycles.

- **Poor Understanding of Supply Base and Spend:** Many companies have not evaluated their supply base as to the most significant commodities and their corresponding key suppliers. As a consequence, they have not adequately sourced and negotiated these critical commodities on a strategic and systematic manner, and thus are paying premium prices over the marketplace. External auditors are beginning to question these practices and investors will be unforgiving when examples of poor sourcing and contract practices become public knowledge.

- **Modifications to Standard Sales Contract Terms Not Reviewed to Evaluate Impact on Timing and Amount of Revenue Recognition:** Organizations commonly use standard sales contract but then allow sales personnel to modify the terms of the contract. The nature of these modifications can affect the timing and amount of revenue recognized. Many times organizations do not have adequate procedures in place to review sales contract modifications in a timely manner. These modifications could result in revenue recognition errors and misstatements even with management's regular review of contract gross margins. This could rise to the threshold of a material weakness for the following reasons: The magnitude of a financial statement misstatement resulting from this deficiency would reasonably be expected to be material, individual sales transactions are frequently material, and gross margin can vary significantly with each transaction (which would make compensating detective controls based on a reasonableness review ineffective).[4]
- **Violations of Segregation of Duties (SOD):** Many organizations have been lax in maintaining the segregation of duties among responsibilities which are inherently in conflict with one another. Such violations of SOD would include access to create suppliers, create purchase orders, receive purchase orders, and pay invoices for purchase orders once they are received.[5]

The SEC will not permit a company to claim adequate internal controls under Section 404 until all material weaknesses reported have been resolved and a viable corrective action plan has been documented.

In its final ruling, the SEC noted " . . . it was recognized that internal control is a broad concept that extends beyond the accounting functions of a company. Early attempts to define the term focused primarily on clarifying the portion of a company's internal control that an auditor should consider when planning and performing an audit of a company's financial statements. However, this did not improve the level of understanding of the term, nor satisfactorily provide the guidance sought by auditors. Successive definitions and formal studies of the concept of internal control followed."

The SEC final ruling referenced the enactment of the Foreign Corrupt Practices Act (FCPA) in 1977, which required companies "to devise and maintain a system of internal accounting controls sufficient to provide reasonable assurances that

- Transactions are executed in accordance with management's general or specific authorization;
- Transactions are recorded as necessary (1) to permit preparation of financial statements in conformity with generally accepted accounting principles or any other criteria applicable to such statements, and (2) to maintain accountability for assets;
- Access to assets is permitted only in accordance with management's general or specific authorization; and
- The recorded accountability for assets is compared with the existing assets at reasonable intervals and appropriate action is taken with respect to any differences."[6]

The SEC final ruling referenced the Treadway Commission, a 1985 private-sector initiative formed to study American financial reporting systems. "In 1987, the Treadway Commission issued a report recommending that its sponsoring organizations work together to integrate the various internal control concepts and definitions and to develop a common reference point." The COSO of the Treadway Commission undertook an extensive study of internal control to establish a common definition that would serve the needs of companies, independent public accountants, legislators and regulatory agencies, and to provide a broad framework of criteria against which companies could evaluate the effectiveness of their internal control systems.

In 1992, COSO defined internal control as a process, effected by an entity's board of directors, management and other personnel, and designed to provide reasonable assurance regarding the achievement of objectives in three categories:

1. Effectiveness and efficiency of operations
2. Reliability of financial reporting
3. Compliance with applicable laws and regulations

COSO further stated that internal control consists of

- Control environment, activities, policies
- Risk assessment, functions, plans

- Control activities, projects, procedures
- Information and communication, initiatives, processes
- Monitoring, systems[7]

DEFINITION OF INTERNAL CONTROLS[8]

The SEC's final rules define "internal control over financial reporting" as a "process designed by, or under the supervision of, the company's principal executive and principal financial officers, or persons performing similar functions, and effected by the company's board of directors, management and other personnel, to provide reasonable assurance regarding the reliability of financial reporting and the preparation of financial statements for external purposes in accordance with generally accepted accounting principles and includes those policies and procedures that:

- Pertain to the maintenance of records that in reasonable detail accurately and fairly reflect the transactions and dispositions of the assets of the company;
- Provide reasonable assurance that transactions are recorded as necessary to permit preparation of financial statements in accordance with generally accepted accounting principles, and that receipts and expenditures of the company are being made only in accordance with authorizations of management and directors of the company;
- Provide reasonable assurance regarding prevention or timely detection of unauthorized acquisition, use, or disposition of the company's assets that could have a material effect on the financial statements."

Under the final rules, a company's annual report must include "an internal control report of management that contains:

- A statement of management's responsibility for establishing and maintaining adequate internal control over financial reporting for the company;
- A statement identifying the framework used by management to conduct the required evaluation of the effectiveness of the company's internal control over financial reporting;

- Management's assessment of the effectiveness of the company's internal control over financial reporting as of the end of the company's most recent fiscal year, including a statement as to whether or not the company's internal control over financial reporting is effective. The assessment must include disclosure of any "material weaknesses" in the company's internal control over financial reporting identified by management. Management is not permitted to conclude that the company's internal control over financial reporting is effective if there are one or more material weaknesses in the company's internal control over financial reporting; and
- A statement that the registered public accounting firm that audited the financial statements included in the annual report has issued an attestation report on management's assessment of the company's internal control over financial reporting."[9]

SOX made a major change in internal controls by holding chief executive officers (CEOs) and chief financial officers (CFOs) personally and criminally liable for the quality and effectiveness of their organization's internal controls.[10] Part of the process is to attest to the public that an organization's internal controls are effective. Internal controls can be expected to provide only a reasonable assurance, not an absolute assurance, to an entity's management and board. An organization must ensure that its financial statements comply with Financial Accounting Standards (FAS) and International Accounting Standards (IAS) or local rules via policy enforcement and risk avoidance methodology called "Internal Control." There must be a system of checks and balances and of defined processes that lead directly from actions and transactions reporting to an organization's owners, investors, and public hosts.

According to COSO, Internal Control is comprised of five inter-related components:

1. **Control Environment:** For each business process, an organization needs to develop and maintain a control environment including categorizing the criticality and materiality of each business process, plus the owners of the business process.
2. **Risk Assessment:** Each business process comes with various risks. A control environment must include an assessment of the risks associated with each business process.

3. **Control Activities:** Control activities must be developed to manage, mitigate, and reduce the risks associated with each business process. It is unrealistic to expect to eliminate risks completely.

4. **Information and Communication:** Associated with control activities are information and communication systems. These enable an organization to capture and exchange the information needed to conduct, manage, and control its business processes.

5. **Monitoring:** The internal control process must be continuously monitored with modifications made as warranted by changing conditions.[11]

DOCUMENTATION OF INTERNAL CONTROLS[12]

No one form of documentation is specified by SOX (Section 404) or other compliance initiatives, but at a minimum, documentation should provide reasonable support for the following:

- Design of controls over relevant financial statement assertions
- How significant transactions are initiated, recorded, processed, and reported
- Identification of where material misstatements could occur
- Identification of controls designed to prevent or detect fraud
- Controls over period-end financial reporting processes
- Controls over safeguarding of assets
- Results of management's testing and evaluation

Typically, organizations rely on Microsoft Windows® Office software to support documentation requirements:

- MS Project
- Excel
- Visio

These are used to document controls for:

- Narratives
- Flowcharts
- Risk/control matrices

Best practices in documenting Internal Control include the use of

- Electronic work and approval flows
- Risk management tools
- Event management tools
- Document management tools

Of these best practices, deploying a document management tool should be given the highest priority. These tools are readily available and include access and revision controls within a central repository for all applicable documentation.

Best practices would include the replacement of uncontrolled spreadsheets. PriceWaterhouseCooper's (PWC's) 2004 white paper "The Use of Spreadsheets: Considerations for Section 404 of the Sarbanes-Oxley Act" makes a compelling argument for eliminating uncontrolled spreadsheets in preparing and presenting financial findings. This will be a painful process for financial folks who have grown up using spreadsheets at sophisticated levels. The problems stem from the uncontrolled nature of spreadsheets (poor security, no version control, poor or nonexistent training and documentation) and the inability to prevent errors in their use (no independent testing).[13]

Computer World's May 24, 2004, article notes that "Anecdotal evidence suggests that 20% to 40% of spreadsheets have errors. . ."[14] but recent audits of 54 spreadsheets found that 49 (or 91%) had errors, according to research by Raymond R. Panko, a professor at the University of Hawaii.[15] The *Journal of Property Management* on July 1, 2002, stated, "30 to 90 percent of all spreadsheets suffer from at least one major user error. The range in error rates depends on the complexity of the spreadsheet being tested. In addition, none of the tests included spreadsheets with more than 200 line items where the probability of error approaches 100 percent."[16]

According to PWC, spreadsheets have resulted in material events and financial restatements and have been used to perpetuate fraud. Therefore, they represent significant risks, which are difficult to mitigate. PWC noted the example of a utility company that suffered a $24 million fraud through the manipulation of spreadsheets.

Section 404 has stressed even well run organizations to standardize, document, train, and test the key controls in running their businesses. In many cases, internal controls have been neglected for many years, or have become disparate through multiple mergers and acquisitions. In spite of the many complaints about the cost of complying with Section 404, many of these cleanup activities are long overdue. Organizations have typically been well aware of the need to improve internal controls, but could not create a business case to fund the activities until the 404 forced them to act. The costs of these cleanup activities have been disproportionably high for smaller companies, but the SEC has recently proposed guidelines to reduce these costs (discussed in Chapter 6).

ENDNOTES

1. This section references and extensively quotes the SEC's Final Rule: Management's Reports on Internal Control Over Financial Reporting and Certification of Disclosure in Exchange Act Periodic Reports, 17 CFR PARTS 210, 228, 229, 240, 249, 270 and 274 [RELEASE NOS. 33-8238; 34-47986; IC-26068; File Nos. S7-40-02; S7-06-03] RIN 3235-AI66 and 3235-AI79.
2. COSO Key Concepts Web Page.
3. Parts of this section copied with permission from the publisher, Institute for Supply Management™, "The Impact of Sarbanes On Supply Management," by Anthony Tarantino, *Inside Supply Management*™, April 2004, 15:4, 6.
4. Example from the SEC: www.sec.gov/rules/pcaob/34-49544-appendixd.pdf.
5. Example from the SEC: www.sec.gov/rules/pcaob/34-49544-appendixd.pdf.
6. Anti-Bribery and Books & Records Provisions of the Foreign Corrupt Practices Act Current Through Pub. L. 105-366 (November 10, 1998) United States Code, Title 15. Commerce and Trade, Chapter 2b—Securities Exchanges.
7. Internal Control-Integrated Framework Executive Summary, COSO web site.
8. This section references and extensively quotes the SEC's Final Rule: Management's Reports on Internal Control Over Financial Reporting and Certification of Disclosure in Exchange Act Periodic Reports, 17 CFR PARTS 210, 228, 229, 240, 249, 270

and 274 [RELEASE NOS. 33-8238; 34-47986; IC-26068; File Nos. S7-40-02; S7-06-03] RIN 3235-AI66 and 3235-AI79.

9. SEC Press Release: SEC Implements Internal Control Provisions of Sarbanes-Oxley Act; Adopts Investment Company R&D Safe Harbor, 2003-66, May 27, 2003.

10. SOX SEC Final Rule, Management's Reports on Internal Control Over Financial Reporting and Certification of Disclosure in Exchange Act Periodic Reports, 17 CFR PARTS 210, 228, 229, 240, 249, 270 and 274, RELEASE NOS. 33-8238; 34-47986; IC-26068; File Nos. S7-40-02; S7-06-03.

11. Internal Control-Integrated Framework Executive Summary, COSO web site.

12. This section references and extensively quotes the SEC's Final Rule: Management's Reports on Internal Control Over Financial Reporting and Certification of Disclosure in Exchange Act Periodic Reports, 17 CFR PARTS 210, 228, 229, 240, 249, 270 and 274 [RELEASE NOS. 33-8238; 34-47986; IC-26068; File Nos. S7-40-02; S7-06-03] RIN 3235-AI66 and 3235-AI79.

13. PWC 2004 White Paper, "The Use of Spreadsheets: Considerations for Section 404 of the Sarbanes-Oxley Act."

14. *Computer World*, "Spreadsheet Overload? Spreadsheets Are Growing Like Weeds, but They May Be a Liability in the Sarbanes-Oxley Era," by Alan Horowitz, May 24, 2004.

15. "What We Know About Spreadsheet Errors," by Raymond R. Panko, University of Hawaii College of Business Administration, January 2005.

16. "Coming Up Short: Database Management Systems Help Solve Spreadsheet Shortcomings," *Journal of Property Management*, July-Aug 2002.

CHAPTER 3

U.S. SOX Section 406: Code of Ethics

Section 406 of SOX requires disclosure whether an enterprise "has adopted a code of ethics for its chief executive office and its senior financial officers, or persons performing similar functions" and requires an explanation if they have not adopted such a code of ethics. Section 406 states that a separate code may be created for different types of positions. Though the section does not require the code of ethics to apply to lower-level directors and managers, the SEC final ruling states: "The instruction also clarifies that the provisions of the company's code of ethics that address the elements listed in the definition and apply to those officers may be part of a broader code that addresses additional issues and applies to additional persons, such as all executive officers and directors of the company."[1]

Most organizations have a code of ethics that all new hires are required to sign, but most organizations do not do much in the way of training and educating in some of the more complex areas such as conflicts of interest. Section 406 imposes this code on senior executives. Common sense and a best practices approach would strongly suggest applying a compliance-minded code of ethics to all those who influence the processes associated with procure-to-pay (P2P), order-to-cash, general accounting, and system administration. This would include whistleblower requirements that prohibit remaining silent when potential violations occur. In too many cases, good and ethical people were aware of wrongdoing but feared to speak up. Remaining silent in such a situation should be made a violation of the code of ethics and made a cause for termination.

Hundreds of whistleblower actions have been filed since the enactment of SOX Section 806. "In the 30 months since enactment, more than 400 whistleblower complaints have been filed with Occupational Safety and Health Administration (OSHA). The agency's goal is to attempt to complete SOX investigations within 60 days of receiving the complaint. As a result, corporate employers are given only 21 days to respond. In some cases, OSHA investigations have languished for more than 12 months. . . . The unfortunate employer seeking to challenge an OSHA reinstatement order has limited options. Regulations permit the employer to move to stay a reinstatement order before the Department of Labor's Office of Administrative Law Judges (OALJ). Yet to prevail, the employer must show a substantial likelihood that it will ultimately prevail (though it has not had the opportunity to conduct any discovery), and that reinstatement would cause irreparable harm to the employer as a safety or a security risk."[2]

Maybe the best argument for updating codes of ethics is as a defense against the rising number of whistleblower actions that are being filed against U.S. corporations. This must include a viable means for employees, contractors, and external auditors to report abuse without fear of retaliation. The Enron scandal broke with the whistleblower activities by Arthur Andersen employees, a contractor to Enron.

The National Whistleblower Center web site (www.whistleblowers .org) provides an overview of the major changes in whistleblower protections. "Unlike most whistleblower laws, the SOX's whistleblower protection provisions are not limited to providing a legal remedy for wrongfully discharged employees. In addition to containing employment-based protections for employee whistleblowers, the law contains four other provisions directly relevant to whistleblower protection. First, the law requires that all publicly traded corporations create internal and independent 'audit committees.' As part of the mandated audit committee function, publicly traded corporations must also establish procedures for employees to file internal whistleblower complaints, and procedures which would protect the confidentiality of employees who file allegations with the audit committee . . . . Second, the SOX sets forth new ethical standards for attorneys who practice before the Securities and Exchange Commission (SEC). This law, and the SEC's implementing regulations, require attorneys, under certain circumstances, to blow the whistle on their employer or 'client.' . . . Third, the SOX amended the federal obstruction of justice statute and criminalized retaliation against whistleblowers who provide 'truthful information' to a 'law enforcement officer' about the 'commission or possible commission of any Federal offense.' This provision of the SOX was not limited in its application to publicly traded corporations; it covers every employer nationwide . . . . Fourth, Section 3(b) of the SOX contains an enforcement provision concerning every clause of the SOX. This section states that 'a violation by any person of this Act [i.e., the SOX] . . . shall be treated for all purposes in the same manner as a violation of the Securities Exchange Act of 1934.' This section grants jurisdiction to the SEC to enforce every aspect of the SOX, including the various whistleblower-related provisions. It also provides for criminal penalties for any violation of the SOX, including the whistleblower-related provisions."[3]

A viable code of ethics with the appropriate training and management support should be considered an essential component of internal controls, core to SOX Section 404 and virtually all other compliance initiatives. This must include an independent and powerful ombudsman process that is responsible to the board of directors, not to a "C-level" executive.[4]

ENDNOTES

1. SEC, 17 CFR PARTS 228, 229 and 249, [RELEASE NOS. 33-8177; 34-47235; File No. S7-40-02] RIN 3235-AI66, Disclosure Required by Sections 406 and 407 of the Sarbanes-Oxley Act of 2002, Jan. 24, 2003.
2. Mary E. Pivec, *Legal Times,* "Whistleblower Protection Pitfalls," April 18, 2005.
3. The Sarbanes-Oxley Act ("SOX"): Legal Protections for Corporate Whistleblowers, Stephen M. Kohn, National Whistleblower Center web site.
4. SEC Final Rule, 17 CFR PARTS 228, 229 and 249, [RELEASE NOS. 33-8177; 34-47235; File No. S7-40-02] RIN 3235-AI66, Disclosure Required by Sections 406 and 407 of the Sarbanes-Oxley Act of 2002.

CHAPTER 4

U.S. SOX Section 409: Real-Time Reporting of Material Changes

INTRODUCTION[1]

Section 409 requires a "real-time issuer disclosure . . . on a rapid and current basis" or the reporting of material events, which affects financial reporting. The Securities and Exchange Commission (SEC) had proposed "timely" and "real-time" to mean two working days, but a great deal of negative feedback has increased the period to four days. The 8-K form will continue to be used for this process. The number of events requiring an 8-K form has been increased by eight, including off-balance sheet (OBS) obligations. Once a company declares a material event, it must document a permanent corrective action, before it can claim to have adequate process controls under Section 404. Filing 8-K forms will continue to be through the Electronic Data Gathering, Analysis, and Retention (EDGAR) system. The SEC describes EDGAR as follows: "For the past several years, the EDGAR electronic filing system has enabled domestic public companies to file their documents with the Commission from anywhere in the world within significantly shortened timeframes. These documents are now available to the public through EDGAR on a real-time basis."[2] The changes in the 8-K form were effective August 23, 2004.[3]

Events that may rise to the threshold of requiring the filing of an 8-K form under Section 409 include[4]

- **Late Supplier Deliveries:** A key supplier, especially in an outsourced environment, misses delivery dates and jeopardizes major customer shipments. If the missed shipments are material, i.e., they impact financial results, they need to be reported via the 8-k form.

- **Enterprise Resource Planning (ERP) System Crashes:** A company replaces and consolidates various legacy ERP/planning systems with a Tier One ERP system. On the conversion ("Go Live") date, various glitches shut down the system, disrupting shipments for a few days. If the impact is material, an 8-K form may need to be filed.
- **Poor Inventory Accuracy:** A company takes its annual physical inventory after a series of system and physical location changes. The resulting adjustments show the inventory to be financially overstated with significant quantity imbalances. If the changes in the inventory levels are material, they need to be reported.
- **Major Cancellation Charges:** A downturn in business compels a company to cancel its orders to its primary outsourced supplier. If the supplier's cancellation and early termination charges affect the financial results for the quarter, they need to be reported via the 8-K form.

It will be difficult, in the best of circumstances, to obtain the needed information, collaborate with needed resources within and outside of an organization, and decide if an event rises to the threshold of Section 409. The SEC has made it clear that a company cannot identify a material weakness and claim to have internal controls.

The real-time disclosures under Section 409 must be in plain English and may "include trend and qualitative information and graphic presentations, as the Commission determines, by rule, is necessary or useful for the protection of investors and in the public interest."

Currently, companies must provide the SEC with an 8-K form within five business days if their companies issue an earnings release. Traditionally, companies often follow up an earnings release by dishing up important new details in a conference call. Typically, chief financial officers (CFOs) have used these conference calls to report additional good news. The five-day 8-K requirement is not expected to produce many ripples. What will cause a major change from the status quo is the requirement to issue 8-Ks in real time when something big and unexpected happens.

DEFINITION OF REAL-TIME REPORTING OF MATERIAL CHANGES[5]

Under Section 409, companies must report material changes in the financial or operating condition of the company "on a rapid and current basis," which has been interpreted to mean four working days. The SEC has expanded the number of events that will trigger an 8-K filing. Currently, The SEC lists nine specific events, including a change in control, a significant acquisition, or a bankruptcy. To that, the SEC proposes adding 11 triggering events:

1. Entry into a material agreement not made in the ordinary course of business
2. Termination of a material agreement not made in the ordinary course of business
3. Termination or reduction of a business relationship with a customer that constitutes a specified amount of the company's revenues
4. Creation of a direct or contingent financial obligation material to the company
5. Events triggering a direct or contingent financial obligation material to the company, including any default or acceleration of an obligation
6. Exit activities including any material write-off or restructuring
7. Any material impairment
8. A change in a rating agency decision, issuance of a credit watch, or change in a company outlook
9. Movement of the company's securities from one national securities exchange or interdealer quotation system of a registered national securities association to another, delisting of the company's securities from an exchange or quotation system, or a notice that a company does not comply with a listing standard
10. Notice to the company from its currently or previously engaged independent accountant that the independent accountant is withdrawing a previously issued audit report or that the company may not rely on a previously issued audit report
11. Any material limitation, restriction, or prohibition, including the beginning and end of lockout periods, regarding the company's employee benefit, retirement, and stock ownership plans

After much discussion, the SEC has excluded from the 8-K reporting requirement

- Letters of Intent, even if they contain binding elements such as confidentiality agreements and
- Contract terminations as a result of a normal "expiration of the agreement on its stated termination date or as a result of completion by all parties of their obligations."

ENDNOTES

1. This section references and extensively quotes the SEC's "Additional Form 8-K Disclosure Requirements and Acceleration of Filing Date," 17 CFR PARTS 228, 229, 230, 239, 240 and 249, RIN 3235-AI47, March 25, 2004.
2. SEC, "Important Information About EDGAR," /info/edgar/regoverview.htm, July 2, 2003.
3. SEC 17 CFR PARTS 210, 229, 240 and 249, [RELEASE NOS. 33-8128; 34-46464; FR-63; File No. S7-08-02] RIN 3235-AI33, Acceleration of Periodic Report Filing Dates and Disclosure Concerning Website Access to Reports.
4. Parts of this section copied with permission from the publisher, "The Impact of SOX and Corporate Governance on IT," by Anthony Tarantino, Cutter Consortium, April 2004, Vol. 7, No. 18.
5. This section references and extensively quotes the SEC's "Additional Form 8-K Disclosure Requirements and Acceleration of Filing Date," 17 CFR PARTS 228, 229, 230, 239, 240 and 249, RIN 3235-AI47, March 25, 2004.

CHAPTER 5

U.S. SOX Impact on Privately Held Companies and Nonprofits

With two notable exceptions, SOX affects only American publicly traded companies and regulates what boards must do to ensure auditors' independence from their clients. It creates and defines the role of the Public Company Accounting Oversight Board (PCAOB), a new entity empowered to enforce standards for audits of public companies. The two provisions affecting private entities:

1. SOX explains processes for electing competent audit committee members and for ensuring adequate reporting procedures are in place.
2. SOX calls for regulations, and closes most of the loopholes, for all enterprises—for-profit and nonprofit—relating to document destruction and whistleblower protection.[1]

Forward-looking privates and nonprofits will look at SOX as a best practice and find it advantageous to take a proactive approach in demonstrating good corporate governance as a means to assure donors, bankers, insurers, and various government agencies that they are operating in an efficient and ethical manner. Robert Half, in its white paper, "The Impact of Sarbanes-Oxley on Private Business," July 2003, summarizes what the leaders are doing as best practices:

- Adopting internal audit functions that mimic public companies
- Imposing a formal code of ethics

- Reforming their boards to include independent members and financial experts
- Restricting consulting services provided by their audit firms to avoid potential conflicts of interest, adopting a formal code of ethics
- Providing formal certifications of financial information and enhancing accounting competencies[2]

BoardSource and The Independent Sector in their 2003 white paper "The Sarbanes-Oxley Act and Implications for Non-profit Organizations" stated: "While nearly all of the provisions of the bill apply only to publicly traded corporations, the passage of this bill should serve as a wake-up call to the entire nonprofit community. If non-profit leaders do not ensure effective governance of their organizations, the Government may step forward and also regulate non-profit governance. Indeed, some state attorneys general are already proposing that elements of the Sarbanes-Oxley Act be applied to non-profit organizations."[3]

Robert Half's white paper provides valuable insights into the impact of SOX on public interest entities, or nonprofits, such as colleges, charities, hospitals, churches, labor unions, professional associations, etc. According to Robert Half, forward-thinking privates and nonprofits are adopting SOX provisions to demonstrate that their practices are consistent with publicly held companies. The leaders will view these reforms as an opportunity to improve internal control and governance processes. "Firms that respond by adopting some degree of voluntary compliance can better position themselves for establishing strong business credit and obtaining major financing. In addition, they are able to enhance relationships and credibility with key stakeholders, since a variety of constituencies increasingly expects firms to uphold a solid reputation for openness and integrity."

Half's white paper lists pressures from third parties on privates and nonprofits to comply:

- Those that rely heavily on lenders or insurers.
- Those doing business with government entities.
- Indiana has added SOX requirements to its Requests For Proposals (RFPs).
- New York and California have adopted aggressive requirements.

- Several other states have similar legislation pending.
- Those that report to federal regulatory agencies—the FDIC has already issued guidelines for smaller banks to adopt reforms.
- Those that are planning to go public.
- Those that consider themselves acquisition targets.

Section 404's reporting requirements do apply to those private companies with public debt including certifications by executives and internal controls.

A 2003 Robert Half survey reported 58% of 1,400 Chief Financial Officers (CFOs) from privately held businesses said their companies are responding to accounting regulations by implementing new practices. Among those who cited a specific action,

- 44% are reviewing or changing current accounting procedures.
- 36% are creating or expanding the internal audit function.
- 23% are hiring an independent firm for consulting work.
- 8% are restructuring executive compensation plans.
- 2% are taking some other action.[4]

There will be an impact on supply base management. Publicly held enterprises may insist that their privately held trading partners voluntarily comply, especially if they are the recipients of long-term agreements for critical goods and services. This will provide confidence that these trading partners are efficiently and ethically run organizations as well as providing their investors that they have a stable and reliable supply base.

PriceWaterhouseCooper's (PWC's) Spring 2005 survey of nonprofit healthcare providers found that "about two-thirds of large non-public and not-for-profit health systems intend to comply with part or all of its standards. Good governance would suggest internal audit work with management to evaluate adopting the more significant elements of The Act related to control documentation and the testing for effectiveness."[5]

Paul Mickly, writing in the April 2005 issue of *Washington Business Journal*, notes that the whistleblower protection of SOX applies to private companies as well as public companies and that nearly half of the U.S. states are considering mini-versions of SOX, which will expand whistleblower protection. SOX creates civil and criminal penalties for retaliation against whistleblowers. "The civil provision has already produced a wave of litigation, with more than 300 charges filed since July 2002. In some respects, it is narrowly tailored: It protects only people who were employed by or otherwise working for publicly traded companies. Significantly, an administrative law judge has ruled that the civil provision applies to employees of private companies that are subsidiaries of publicly held companies. And the civil remedy applies to 'contractors and subcontractors' of publicly traded companies, regardless of whether the contractors and subcontractors are themselves publicly traded. (Alleged reprisal against employees of Arthur Andersen, a subcontractor to Enron, helped spur enactment of Sarbanes-Oxley.)"[6]

Mickly notes implications exist for companies that seek to go public in that they will be "pressured from their funding sources and potential acquirers to establish governance and compliance protocols that will pass muster if they, in fact, become public . . . . These implications may affect privately held companies even assuming Sarbanes-Oxley does not apply directly. But the statute does have direct application to private companies in the provisions protecting whistleblowers from retaliation." But the parallel and criminal provisions of the whistleblower provisions have a much broader sweep according to Mickly: "Whoever knowingly, with the intent to retaliate, takes any action harmful to any person, including interference with the lawful employment or livelihood of any person, for providing to a law enforcement officer any truthful information relating to the commission or possible commission of any federal offense, shall be fined under this title [$250,000] or imprisoned for not more than 10 years, or both." Significantly, this provision applies to "any person in any sector of the economy, whether associated with a public company or a private one."[7]

Historically, criminal enforcement of whistleblower provisions has been uncommon, but the legal and political climate has changed dramatically. Mickly notes: "But the reach of the law is so broad and the opportunity for ambitious prosecutors to make a name for themselves so clear, that one dare not ignore the potential for criminal liability. And in some jurisdictions, private civil claims may be fashioned under the theory of 'wrongful discharge' in violation of public policy . . . . The potential for mischief is great. An employee anticipating that he or she will suffer adverse action in his/her employment can effectively preempt the process by reporting some element of truthful information about any matter governed by federal law and then effectively be insulated because of the company's apprehension over the prospect of criminal sanctions or possibly wrongful discharge litigation."

Finally, privately held companies and nonprofits will find their independent auditors conditioned and toned by their publicly held clients to follow SOX-based protocols and disciplines, and they will be much more demanding and detailed than in the past.

ENDNOTES

1. Foley and Lardner White Paper, "The Impact of Sarbanes-Oxley on Private Companies," March 2005.
2. Robert Half White Paper, "The Impact of Sarbanes-Oxley on Private Business," July 2003.
3. BoardSource and The Independent Sector, White Paper, "The Sarbanes-Oxley Act and Implications for Non-profit Organizations," 2003.
4. Robert Half White Paper, "The Impact of Sarbanes-Oxley on Private Business," July 2003.
5. PWC's Internal Audit Newsletter, "The Top Industry Issues Facing Healthcare Organizations Today," spring 2005.
6. Paul Mickly, "Private Cos. Not Off the Hook for Sarbanes-Oxley," *Washington Business Journal*, April 8, 2005.
7. Paul Mickly, "Private Cos. Not Off the Hook for Sarbanes-Oxley," *Washington Business Journal*, April 8, 2005.

CHAPTER 6

U.S. SOX Impact on Small U.S. Companies

Small companies were initially defined by the SEC for purposes of the Sarbanes-Oxley Act as those with a public float under $75 million. (Public float is the number of common shares of an issuer, or the market value of the number of shares, that are available for trading by the public. Shares held by corporate insiders or affiliated companies are not included in the public float.) Due to major criticism from U.S. small businesses, the SEC has delayed small company SOX compliance twice—currently July 2007. The delay allowed the SEC the time to address a major flaw in the initial recommendations around Section 404—that a one-size-fits-all approach to internal control regulations will cause severe economic hardship on smaller companies.

The original SEC estimations of the cost to comply with Section 404 have proven to be grossly understated. The projected cost estimates for the smallest companies continue to rise to the point where they would force many out of business—a $1 million hit to the bottom line. The concerns became so great in 2004 that the deadline was extended an additional year to July 2006. In August 2005, an SEC advisory committee on small public companies recommended another one-year extension to July 15, 2007.[1] Small companies were given some minor relief as to the level of detail they would need to provide, but the SEC was initially unwilling to acknowledge the need for special treatment for small companies, referencing the Treadway Commission report indicating corporate fraud was more prevalent in small companies.[2]

The growing concerns led to the creation of an SEC elite advisory committee to recommend changes in the Section 404 internal control process for small and very small companies. The Preliminary Report of the Internal Controls Subcommittee to the Advisory Committee on Smaller Public Companies was published on December 7, 2005.[3] While the report is preliminary and not yet formally adopted, the SEC will likely approve its recommendations.

The subcommittee recommended a major change in SEC's definition of small companies with the creation of a three-tier approach. The first tier is made up of microcap companies representing the bottom 1% of market capitalization (about $100 to $125 million) or about 50% of all public U.S. companies. These microcap companies would be exempt from U.S. SOX 404 provisions altogether but would still have to declare material weaknesses and comply with all other SEC regulations including Section 302. The second tier is made up of small companies with a capitalization representing about 6% of all U.S. companies (under $700 million) or about 7,000 public companies in the United States. These companies would be allowed to perform their own audits, free of external auditors.

The Preliminary Report acknowledged some fundamental differences between small and large companies:

- Small companies tend to rely on the daily interaction of management as opposed to large companies, which tend to rely on more complex formal controls and systems.
- The quality of key managers is more critical in small companies due to lack of more complex formal controls and systems.
- While management's daily interaction can be very effective, it is not easily documented or tested by auditors.
- Audit Standard No. 2 (AS2), introduced by the PCAOB in early 2005, may be overkill for smaller companies and not intended as guidance for management.
- Small companies typically rely more heavily on manual controls than automated controls.
- COSO's 2005 guidance for small companies, relying on Audit Standard No. 2, is not practical to the point of being deployable.

The Preliminary Report also graphically portrays the large financial burden imposed on small companies and warns that it will hurt capital formation and entrepreneurship.

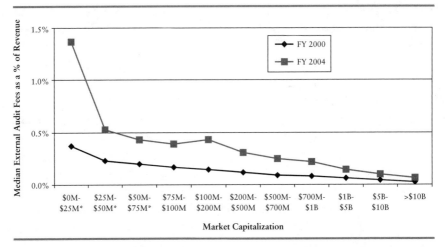

EXHIBIT 6.1   Median External Audit Fees as a Percent of Revenue[4]

Recommendations in the Preliminary Report include:

- Scaling back substantive testing designed to find material weaknesses
- Integrating financial auditing and the internal control auditing
- Not treating all restatements as material weaknesses, acknowledging that accounting complexities are the cause of many restatements
- Determining materiality on an annual, rather than on a quarterly, basis
- Reducing IT control testing as it is a major cause of excessive costs
- Rethinking of Audit Standard No. 2 or creating audit standard more suitable to small companies

One solution for small companies may lie in compliance technology—the automation of controls with application and database softwares. Judith Burns, in January 11, 2005, *Dow Jones Newswires,* quoted COSO Chairman Larry Rittenberg. Rittenberg noted that software programs and automation may be one way for smaller firms to meet the demands. Rittenberg expects COSO to consider other ways to help smaller companies comply with the law, not duck it. "Small businesses are at risk if they don't have good controls and we've got to accept that," said Rittenberg. But, he added, "there may be alternative ways to achieve the same objectives."[5] COSO was formed in 1985 to make recommendations on how companies and auditors might identify and attack fraudulent financial reporting. The group consists of the American Institute of Certified Public Accountants (AICPA), the American Accounting Association, Financial Executives International, the Institute of Management Accountants, and the Institute of Internal Auditors.[6]

The ongoing debate over the treatment of small companies helps to reinforce the assessment popular in Europe that the Sarbanes-Oxley Act was and remains a major overreaction to American corporate scandals. The changes in the regulations and suggested changes make it difficult for entrepreneurs to determine the viability of going or staying public. The Preliminary Report appears to be a realistic approach, but the best advice to the SEC may be to make up its mind once and for all, so small businesses can plan ahead.

There is also a major dilemma in the treatment of small companies and some lessons for other regulatory agencies debating how to best handle small companies. While it is valid to make adjustments in regulations to accommodate small companies, the SEC's Preliminary Report does not provide adequate protection to investors to where they can invest in smaller companies with the same assurance as larger companies. There is no warning label on small company stocks and investors would be foolish to trust rating agencies and investment firms given their spotty track record ranging from Enron to Refco. The SEC is the controlling agency and should develop a simple means for investors to evaluate companies based on their internal controls. It could be as simple as an ABC rating, with an "A" rating for large companies that are fully audited, a "B" rating for small companies performing their own internal audits, and "C" for the microcap companies exempt from Section 404 controls. It should not be a convoluted rating system that small investors cannot easily decipher.

ENDNOTES

1. Tammy Whitehouse, "Relief on 404, Filing Schedule In Store for Small Cos.," *Compliance Week*, Aug. 16, 2005.
2. The Treadway Commission's COSO Research: "Fraudulent Financial Reporting: 1987–1997—An Analysis of U.S. Public Companies. Section I. Executive Summary and Introduction,"

http://www.coso.org/publications/executiv_summary_fraudulent_financial_reporting.htm.

3. The SEC's Preliminary Report of the Internal Controls Sub-committee to the Advisory Committee on Smaller Public Companies, Preliminary as of 12-7-2005.
4. Background Statistics: Market Capitalization of Public Companies; August 2, 2005; SEC Office of Economic Analysis.
5. Judith Burns, *Dow Jones Newswires,* January 11, 2005.
6. COSO home page, www.COSO.org.

CHAPTER 7

U.S. SOX Impact on Foreign Companies

In March 2005, The Securities and Exchange Commission (SEC) announced an extension of the compliance dates for "non-accelerated filers and foreign private issuers in complying with SOX."[1] The new deadline to comply with the internal control over financial reporting requirements is for its first fiscal year ending on or after July 15, 2006. This is a one-year extension from the previously established July 15, 2005, compliance date for nonaccelerated filers and foreign private issuers.[2] As discussed in Chapter 6, the SEC proposed on December 7, 2005, to separate its treatment of foreign filers from small U.S. companies with a new approach for microcap and small companies, but has yet to address any additional changes for foreign filers.

In March 2005, Donald T. Nicolaisen, the SEC's Chief Accountant, said, "The Section 404 requirements are among the most important parts of the Sarbanes-Oxley Act, and I encourage public companies to devote the necessary resources to make sure those requirements are implemented effectively. I don't underestimate the effort this will require for smaller companies and foreign private issuers, but this extension will provide additional time for those issuers to take a good hard look at their internal controls, as the Act contemplates."[3] The extension also gave the SEC time to come up with a more cost-effective approach to internal controls for small U.S. companies and foreign filers.

Alan L. Beller, Director of the Division of Corporation Finance, added, "Section 404 reporting has the long-term potential to substantially improve the reliability of financial reporting. It is already having that effect for companies with the vast majority of U.S. market capitalization. Given the burdens in designing and implementing Section 404 compliance for smaller and non-U.S. companies, this extension strikes the right balance. Companies should use the extension not to delay but to improve the quality of their efforts."[4]

The SEC considered the particular challenges facing nonaccelerated filers and foreign private issuers in determining to grant these extensions. Many foreign companies are facing regulatory and reporting challenges in addition to internal control reporting as companies incorporated in a European Union (EU) member country are required to prepare their financial statements for 2005 in accordance with new International Financial Reporting Standards (IFRS).

Business Week's Beth Carney on December 15, 2004, reported about 300 European companies with equity or debt traded in the United States were required to report to the SEC. "Yet a few with dual listings on European and U.S. stock exchanges are reevaluating whether it makes sense to be listed in the U.S. at all. Some companies that are undergoing cost-cutting programs, such as British online-travel group Lastminute and German software company Lion Bioscience (LEON), already have initiated the process to withdraw from U.S. stock exchanges." A delegation of leading European companies including "Cadbury Schweppes (CSG), Siemens (SI), and BASF (BF), met in 2004 with the then SEC Chairman William Donaldson to lobby for rule changes that would ease the burden. According to the Confederation of British Industry (CBI), the trade group that organized the Anglo-German delegation, the main complaint was the increased cost of complying with US SOX's new regulations."[5]

Rising compliance costs are reducing the advantages of listing on a U.S. exchange as U.S.-based institutional investors become more willing to buy shares on European markets. For online travel group, LastMinute, which had fewer than 5% of its shares in the form of NASDAQ-traded American Depository Receipts (ADRs), the advantages did not out weigh the costs. It announced plans to de-list in July of 2004, but this became a moot point when LastMinute was acquired by Sabre Holdings in July 2005.[6]

According to *Business Week*'s Carney, it is unlikely U.S. markets will witness a major "exodus of international companies in the near future, and not only because many continue to want access to the world's largest pool of market capital. Currently, even if outfits leave an exchange, they are still required to report to the SEC until they can prove that their U.S. shareholders number less than 300. For many companies, this can be close to impossible."[7]

SOX is bound to reduce the number of new listings for both European companies and companies from developing countries, which may start looking to European stock exchanges for their dual listings. Carney gives the example of Air China, the largest air carrier in China, which has opted to list on Hong Kong and London stock exchanges. "It was able to use the same prospectus in both locations because the regulatory requirements are so similar." Typical of the sticker shock are the comments by the pharmaceutical giant, AstraZeneca International. Paul Grant, in the Feb. 3, 2005 issue of *Accountancy Age,* quotes Jon Symonds, AstraZeneca International's chief financial officer (CFO), who has admitted it will cost "tens of millions" of dollars for the company to comply with SOX. He admitted that there were benefits but the SOX was like "using a sledgehammer to crack a nut." But Symonds acknowledged that "AstraZeneca would not abandon the U.S. market" under any circumstances.[8]

In the same article, Symonds stated that, "At least 60 European companies, including 25 from the UK, are set to withdraw their US listings because of Sarbanes-Oxley, according to comments made by CBI director general Sir Digby Jones last week. The figure would be even larger if not for the 300-shareholder rule that the Securities and Exchange Commission has imposed. Companies cannot deregister from the SEC, and thus avoid Sarbanes-Oxley, unless they have fewer than 300 US shareholders."[9]

In April 1, 2005, WebCPA PFP briefs, "Foreign Investors and Analysts Vague on SOX 404 Impact," reported that most foreign investors understand little about US SOX 404. The article references the PWC survey of investors and analysts who cover U.S.-listed companies. PWC found that "just 60 percent of analysts and investors in Europe, and a scant 40 percent in Japan, admit to having some knowledge of SOX 404." Only 25% "claimed to have a good grasp of how Section 404 will affect mergers and acquisitions." Ironically, "Nine in 10 analysts and investors in Asia, where awareness is lowest, said that they would be very likely to sell or mark down shares in a company that was the subject of a negative disclosure . . . ."[10]

As other regulatory requirements come into force with Basel II, Solvency II, the Organization for Economic Cooperation and Development (OECD) Principles, and the IFRS's standardized Generally Accepted Accounting Principles (GAAP), the negative reactions to SOX will undoubtedly reside. The majority of complaints stem from the internal control provisions of Section 404, but almost all of these new regulations will include a COSO framework to improve internal controls. The main difference will be the harsh criminal penalties that U.S. SOX imposes.

ENDNOTES

1. SEC Press Release, "Extension of Compliance Dates for Non-Accelerated Filers and Foreign Private Issuers Regarding Internal Control Over Financial Reporting Requirements," 2005-25, March 2, 2005.
2. SEC Press Release, "SEC Votes to Propose Changes in Filing Deadlines and Accelerated Filer Definition; Postpone 404 Compliance Date for Nonaccelerated Filers; Propose Issuing Section 28(e) Interpretive Guidance, 2005-134," Sept. 21, 2005.
3. SEC Press Release, "Extension of Compliance Dates for Non-Accelerated Filers and Foreign Private Issuers Regarding Internal Control Over Financial Reporting Requirements," 2005-25, March 2, 2005.
4. Extension of Compliance Dates for Non-Accelerated Filers and Foreign Private Issuers Regarding Internal Control Over Financial Reporting Requirements for Immediate Release, 2005-25, Washington, D.C., March 2, 2005.
5. Beth Carney, "Foreign Outfits Rue Sarbanes-Oxley," *BusinessWeek*, December 15, 2004.
6. LastMinute.com Press Release, July 20, 2005.
7. Beth Carney, "Foreign Outfits Rue Sarbanes-Oxley," *BusinessWeek*, December 15, 2004.
8. Paul Grant, "AstraZeneca Faces Huge Sarbox Hit," *Accountancy Age*, Feb. 3, 2005.
9. Paul Grant, "AstraZeneca Faces Huge Sarbox Hit," *Accountancy Age*, Feb. 3, 2005.
10. WebCPA, "Foreign Investors and Analysts Vague on SOX 404 Impact," April 1, 2005.

CHAPTER 8

U.S. Government's Version of U.S. SOX: OMB Circular A-123

OVERVIEW OF OMB CIRCULAR A-123[1]

The Office of Management and Budget (OMB) issued Circular A-123, defining management's responsibility for internal control in federal agencies. OMB Circular A-123 goes into effect in FY2006. To anyone in the public sector familiar with the SOX Section 404, this seems like déjà vu all over again. Compliance will be mandatory starting October 1, 2005, and the new regulations apply to agencies subject to the Chief Financial Officers Act of 1990 (CFO Act). The new rules govern "everything that generates entries into your financial statement," OMB Controller Linda Springer told *Federal Computer Week* shortly before the Circular was released. The Circular emphasizes that internal controls should be "an integral part of the entire cycle of planning, budgeting, management, accounting, and auditing" and not "an isolated management tool." [2]

This is a sensible move. The federal government would have a difficult time defending a "Do as I say and not as I do" approach to controls, especially with the huge financial and legal burden SOX has placed on corporate America. As with SOX, federal managers are required to provide an annual assessment of the effectiveness of internal controls over financial reporting to taxpayers who get a clearer picture of how tax dollars are being spent. Circular A-123 "ensures Congress and the public that the Federal Government is committed to safeguarding its assets and providing reliable financial information." [3]

David Perera, in *Federal Computer Week*, notes that "A group of government financial officers, auditors and OMB officials first proposed the now-mandatory regulations by comparing government controls with section 404 of the Sarbanes-Oxley Act. Committee members decided that if more exacting controls are a good thing for companies, it made sense to parallel them on the federal side, said Elliot Lewis, assistant inspector general at the Labor Department."[4]

The changes intend to strengthen the credibility of the annual agency management assessments of financial status the government is required to produce under the Federal Managers' Financial Integrity Act. The revised circular states that those assessments will now be due 45 days after the end of the fiscal year.

In response to the new internal control requirements for publicly traded companies detailed in Section 404 of SOX, the federal government reexamined existing internal control requirements for federal agencies. Circular A-123 and the statute it implements, the Federal Managers' Financial Integrity Act of 1982 (FMFIA), are at the center of federal requirements to improve internal control. Circular A-123, last revised in June 1995, reflects policy recommendations developed by a joint committee of representatives from the Chief Financial Officer Council (CFOC) and the President's Council on Integrity and Efficiency (PCIE).[5]

The policy changes have two major goals:

1. To strengthen the requirements for conducting management's assessment of internal control over financial reporting.
2. To emphasize the need for agencies to integrate and coordinate internal control assessments with other internal control-related activities.

The attachment (Appendix A) to Circular A-123

- Defines management's responsibilities related to internal control,
- Defines the process for assessing internal control effectiveness, and
- Requires a summary of the significant changes in internal controls.

Circular A-123 provides updated internal control standards and new specific requirements for conducting management's assessment of the effectiveness of internal control over financial reporting (Appendix A). It emphasizes the need for integrated and coordinated internal control assessments to synchronize all internal control-related activities.

The wording of Circular A-123 is in line with SOX Section 404. In the past, the OMB used the term "management controls." This wording has been changed to "internal controls" to "better align with the currently accepted standards for internal control and current terminology."

The standards in Circular A-123 use terminology and an approach right out of the COSO framework:

- Control environment
- Risk assessments
- Control activities
- Definition of materiality
- Corrections of material weaknesses

This is a summary of A-123's requirements:

- It requires internal controls to be "cost-effective," "identify needed improvements," and "take corresponding corrective action." It recommends establishing a senior assessment team, which at least oversees the assessment process.
- It requires the controls over financial reporting to be documented and requires the assessment process of the controls over financial reporting to be documented.
- It requires a management assurance statement about the effectiveness of internal controls with corrective actions, if applicable.
- It provides a noncompliance clause that permits OMB to require an agency to obtain an audit opinion over the internal controls over financial reporting if the agreed-upon deadlines for corrective actions are continuously not met.

The following can be viewed as a mission statement by the OMB for all federal agencies:

Management has a fundamental responsibility to develop and maintain effective internal control. The proper stewardship of Federal resources is an essential responsibility of agency managers and staff. Federal employees must ensure that Federal programs operate and Federal resources are used efficiently and effectively to achieve desired objectives. Programs must operate and resources must be used consistent with agency missions, in compliance with laws and regulations, and with minimal potential for waste, fraud, and mismanagement. Management is responsible for developing and maintaining effective internal control. Effective internal control provides assurance that significant weaknesses in the design or operation of internal control, that could adversely affect the agency's ability to meet its objectives, would be prevented or detected in a timely manner. Internal Control—organization, policies, and procedures—are tools to help program and financial managers achieve results and safeguard the integrity of their programs.

A NEW FEDERAL APPROACH TO INTERNAL CONTROL AND RISK MANAGEMENT[6]

Under Circular A-123, internal controls must exist which are "applicable to agency operations." These internal controls assure the proper accounting in preparing accounts with reliable financial and statistical reports, which maintain accountability over the assets.

The OMB calls for a fundamental change in how agencies look at internal controls:

Instead of considering internal control as an isolated management tool, agencies should integrate their efforts to meet the requirements of the FMFIA with other efforts to improve effectiveness and accountability. Thus, internal control should be an integral part of the entire cycle of planning, budgeting, management, accounting, and auditing. It should support the effectiveness and the integrity of every step of the process and provide continual feedback to management.

Following a COSO/SOX terminology and approach, the OMB cautions federal managers to "carefully consider the appropriate balance between controls and risk in their programs and operations. Too many controls can result in inefficient and ineffective government; agency managers must ensure an appropriate balance between the strength of controls and the relative risk associated with particular programs and operations." In weighing costs versus benefits, the OMB notes that "the benefits of controls should outweigh the cost.

Agencies should consider both qualitative and quantitative factors when analyzing costs against benefits."

The goal is that the "appropriate internal controls should be integrated into each system established by agency management to direct and guide its operations. Internal control applies to program, operational, and administrative areas as well as accounting and financial management." Generally, identify and implement the specific procedures necessary to ensure effective internal control. Determining how to assess the effectiveness of those controls is left to the discretion of the agency head.

The OMB advises that agency managers have a "clear, organized strategy with well-defined documentation processes that contain an audit trail, verifiable results, and specify document retention periods so that someone not connected with the procedures can understand the assessment process."

Circular A-123 specifies that internal controls are an integral component of an organization's management providing reasonable assurance that the following objectives are being achieved:

- Effectiveness and efficiency of operations
- Reliability of financial reporting
- Compliance with applicable laws and regulations

As with SEC rulings over the decades, the OMB takes a broad view of internal control, noting that it includes the

- Plan of organization,
- Methods and procedures adopted by management to meet its goals, and
- Processes for planning, organizing, directing, controlling, and reporting on agency operations.

These internal control standards and the definition of internal control are based on a Government Accountability Office (GAO) Green Book.[7]

As in the public sector, the OMB warns that instituting internal controls is no guarantee that waste and fraud will be eliminated but notes that it "is a means of managing the risk associated with Federal programs and operations. Managers should define the control environment (e.g., programs, operations, or financial reporting) and then perform risk assessments to identify the most significant areas within that environment in which to place or enhance internal control."

Risk assessment is a critical step in the process to determine the extent of controls. After significant areas are identified, control activities should be implemented. Continuous monitoring and testing should help identify poorly designed or ineffective controls and should be reported upon periodically. Management is responsible for redesigning or improving those controls, communicating the objectives of internal control, and ensuring the organization is committed to sustaining an effective internal control environment.

FEDERAL STANDARDS FOR INTERNAL CONTROLS[8]

The OMB provides guidelines in management oversight. "To ensure senior management involvement, many agencies have established their own senior management council, often chaired by the agency's lead management official, to address management accountability and related issues within the broader context of agency operations." Relevant issues for such a council include ensuring the agency's commitment to an appropriate system of internal control; actively overseeing the process of assessing internal controls, including nonfinancial as well as financial reporting objectives; recommending to the agency head which control deficiencies are material to disclose in the annual FMFIA report; and providing input for the level and priority of resource needs to correct these deficiencies.

To meet these objectives, management is responsible for developing and maintaining internal control activities that comply with the following COSO-based standards:

- Control Environment
- Risk Assessment
- Control Activities
- Information and Communications
- Monitoring

Control Environment

The control environment is the organizational structure and culture created by management and employees to sustain organizational support for effective internal control. When designing, evaluating, or modifying the organizational structure, management must demonstrate its commitment to competence in the workplace.

Within the organizational structure, management must

- Define areas of authority and responsibility;
- Appropriately delegate the authority and responsibility throughout the agency;
- Establish a suitable hierarchy for reporting;
- Support appropriate human capital policies for hiring, training, evaluating, counseling, advancing, compensating and disciplining personnel;
- Uphold the need for personnel to possess and maintain the proper knowledge and skills to perform their assigned duties as well as understand the importance of maintaining effective internal control within the organization.

The organizational culture is crucial within this standard. The culture should be defined by management's leadership in setting values of integrity and ethical behavior. The culture is affected by the relationship between the organization and central oversight agencies and Congress. Management's philosophy and operational style set the tone within the organization. Management's commitment to establishing and maintaining effective internal control should cascade down and permeate the organization's control environment, aiding in the successful implementation of internal control systems.

Risk Assessment

Management should identify internal and external risks that may prevent the organization from meeting its objectives. When identifying risks, management should take into account relevant interactions within the organization as well as with outside organizations. When identifying risks, management should consider previous findings such as auditor identified, internal management reviews, or noncompliance with laws and regulations. Identified risks should then be analyzed for their potential effect or impact on the agency.

Control Activities

Control activities include policies, procedures, and mechanisms to meet agency objectives. Examples include proper segregation of duties that include separate personnel with authority to authorize a transaction, process the transaction, and review the transaction; physical controls over assets such as limited access to inventories or equipment; proper authorization; and appropriate documentation and access to that documentation.

Internal control needs to be in place over information systems, general and application controls. General control applies to all information systems such as the mainframe, network and end-user environments. It includes agency-wide security program planning, management, control over data center operations, and system software acquisition and maintenance. Application control should be designed to ensure transactions are properly authorized and processed accurately and that the data are valid and complete. Controls should be established at an application's interfaces to verify inputs and outputs, such as edit checks. General and application controls over information systems are interrelated, and both are needed to ensure complete and accurate information processing. Due to the rapid changes in Information Technology (IT), controls must adjust to remain effective.

Information and Communications

Information should be communicated to relevant personnel at all levels within an organization. The information should be relevant, reliable, and timely. An agency must communicate with outside organizations as well, whether providing information or receiving it. Examples include receiving updated guidance from central oversight agencies; management communicating requirements to the operational staff;

and operational staff communicating with the information systems staff to modify application software to extract data requested in the guidance.

Monitoring

Monitoring the effectiveness of internal control should occur in the normal course of business. In addition, periodic reviews, reconciliations or comparisons of data should be included as part of the regular assigned duties of personnel. Periodic assessments should be integrated as part of management's continuous monitoring of internal control, which should be ingrained in the agency's operations. If an effective continuous monitoring program is in place, it can level the resources needed to maintain effective internal controls throughout the year.

Deficiencies found in internal control should be reported to the appropriate personnel and management responsible for that area. Identified deficiencies, through internal review or by an external audit, should be evaluated and corrected. A systematic process should be in place for addressing deficiencies.

INTERNAL CONTROL OVER FINANCIAL REPORTING

Internal control over financial reporting should assure the safeguarding of assets from waste, loss, unauthorized use, or enterprise resource planning (ERP) system appropriation. Control assures compliance with laws and regulations pertaining to financial reporting. Financial reporting includes annual financial statements of an agency as well as other significant internal or external financial reports.

An agency needs to determine the scope of financial reports that are significant (i.e., which reports are included in the assessment of internal control over financial reporting). In addition to the annual financial statements, significant reports might include quarterly financial statements; financial statements at the operating division or program level; budget execution reports; reports used to monitor specific activities such as specific revenues, receivables, or liabilities; reports used to monitor compliance with laws and regulations such as the Anti-Deficiency Act; and so on. See Exhibit 8.1.

EXHIBIT 8.1 Summary of A-123 Reporting Requirements

Area	Definition	Reporting
Control Deficiency (FMFIA Section 2 and internal control over financial reporting)	▪ Control deficiencies exist when the design or operation of a control does not allow management or employees, in the normal course of performing their assigned functions, to prevent or detect misstatements on a timely basis. ▪ A design deficiency exists when a control necessary to meet the control objective is missing or an existing control is not properly designed, so that even if the control operates as designed the control objective is not always met. ▪ An operation deficiency exists when a properly designed control does not operate as designed or when the person performing the control is not qualified or properly skilled to perform the control effectively.	Internal to the organization and not reported externally. Progress against corrective action plans should be periodically assessed and reported to agency management.

Area	Definition	Reporting
Reportable Condition (FMFIA Section 2 and internal control over financial reporting)	**FMFIA overall**—A control deficiency, or combination of control deficiencies, that in management's judgment should be communicated because they represent significant weaknesses in the design or operation of internal control that could adversely affect the organization's ability to meet its internal control objectives. **Financial reporting**—A control deficiency, or combination of control deficiencies, that adversely affects the entity's ability to initiate, authorize, record, process, or report external financial data reliably in accordance with generally accepted accounting principles such that there is more than a remote likelihood that a misstatement of the entity's financial statements, or other significant financial reports, that is more than inconsequential will not be prevented or detected.	Internal to the organization and not reported externally. Progress against corrective action plans should be periodically assessed and reported to agency management.

(continued)

EXHIBIT 8.1 Summary of A-123 Reporting Requirements (Continued)

Area	Definition	Reporting
Material Weakness (FMFIA Section 2 and internal control over financial reporting)	Instances in which financial management systems do not substantially conform to financial systems requirements. Financial management systems include both financial and financially related (or mixed) systems.	Nonconformances and a summary of corrective actions to bring systems into conformance shall be reported to OMB and Congress through the PAR (Management Report for Government Corporations). Progress against corrective action plans should be periodically assessed and reported to agency management.
Nonconformance (FMFIA Section 4)	Instances in which financial management systems do not substantially conform to financial systems requirements. Financial management systems include both financial and financially related (or mixed) systems.	Nonconformances and a summary of corrective actions to bring systems into conformance shall be reported to OMB and Congress through the PAR (Management Report for Government Corporations). Progress against corrective action plans should be periodically assessed and reported to agency management.

GOVERNING LAWS AND ENFORCEMENT

There is one major difference between OMB Circular A-123 and SOX. SOX creates severe criminal and civil penalties for chief executive officers (CEOs) and chief financial officers (CFOs) who file fraudulent financial reports. A-123 has no such provisions. There are existing criminal statues covering fraud and there may well be administrative penalties since agencies are required to report on material weaknesses and corrective actions to prevent their re-occurrence.

Two federal statues constitute the governing laws for A-123:

1. **Federal Managers' Financial Integrity Act (FMFIA):** The FMFIA requires agencies to provide a statement of assurance annually regarding the effectiveness of management, administrative, and accounting controls, and financial management systems. Core to FMFIA is maintaining integrity and accountability in all programs and operation. The reasons are as follows:

   ■ It is critical for good government.

   ■ It demonstrates responsible stewardship over assets and resources in our care.

   ■ It ensures high quality, responsible leadership.

   ■ It ensures the sound delivery of services to customers.

   ■ It maximizes desired program outcomes.[9]

2. **Federal Financial Management Improvement Act of 1996 (FFMIA):** The FFMIA builds upon and complements the CFO Act, the Government Performance and Results Act, and the Government Management Reform Act. The FFMIA requires that federal agencies:

   ■ Conform to the government-wide Standard General Ledger;

   ■ Comply with all applicable federal accounting standards;

   ■ Establish financial management systems that support full disclosure of federal financial data, including the full costs of federal programs and activities;

- Include an auditor's statement regarding compliance with these provisions; and

- Establish a remediation plan for areas of an agency not in compliance with these requirements.[10]

SUMMARY

Extending the SOX approach processes and terminology to the federal government was a logical decision. Just as with the SEC's oversight of publicly held corporations, Circular A-123 requires federal agencies to be more accountable for the timeliness and accuracy of their financial reporting. In the process, they become more efficient and effective. The OMB, just like the SEC, made the creation and maintenance of a strong internal control infrastructure a key objective for federal agencies in achieving their missions and program results through improved accountability, identifying internal control weaknesses, and taking related corrective actions.

Circular A-123 has public sector ramifications far beyond federal agencies. States and local municipalities will feel pressure to adopt similar measures to assure taxpayers that their money is being managed well. The need for strong internal controls down to the municipality level can be seen in the City of San Diego, California, now referred to by some comedians as Enron by the Sea. The *Wall Street Journal* (*WSJ*) reported that the city faces a $1.1 billion shortfall in its pension plan, $15 million in legal and audit fees, at least five separate investigations, and a city government in chaos with its mayor and other city officials forced from office. The *WSJ* notes that the strict corporate regulatory environment is now spilling over to other financial institutions, even down to the city level.[11] The combination of local politics and poor and inconsistent regulatory oversight will increase pressure to impose SOX-like and A-123-like controls.

Compliance Week reports concerns that federal government may extend A-123 regulations down to contractors. Given the growing outsourcing trends and the huge funds at stake, this may be inevitable. Jim Taylor of the Department of Commerce noted that the shock to federal agencies and their contractors may not be nearly as dramatic as that to public companies. Government agencies and their contractors have been tightly regulated for many years. [12]

Many European Union (EU) member nations have higher tax rates than in the United States to support broad social programs. It would make sense for them to watch the first-year experiences of the federal agencies and then consider their own measures to improve internal controls.

ENDNOTES

1. This section extensively references and quotes the OMB's Circular A-123 and its Appendix A, issued under authority of the Federal Managers' Financial Integrity Act of 1982 as codified in 31 U.S.C. 3512.
2. Linda Springer, Federal e-Newsletter #383, January 12, 2005.
3. OMB Memo, Linda M. Springer, Memorandum to the Chief Financial Officers, Chief Operation Officers, Chief Information Officers, and Program Managers, "Subject: Revisions to OMB Circular A-123, Management's Responsibility for Internal Control, Dec. 21, 2004.
4. David Perera, "Sarbanes-Oxley for Feds Arrives," *Federal Computer Week*, Jan. 6, 2005.
5. The Circular is issued under the authority of the Federal Managers' Financial Integrity Act of 1982 as codified in 31 U.S.C. 3512.
6. This section extensively references and quotes the OMB's Circular A-123 and its Appendix A, issued under authority of the Federal Managers' Financial Integrity Act of 1982 as codified in 31 U.S.C. 3512.
7. GAO, Green Book, "Standards for Internal Control in the Federal Government," Nov. 1999.
8. This section extensively references and quotes the OMB's Circular A-123 and its Appendix A, issued under authority of the Federal Managers' Financial Integrity Act of 1982 as codified in 31 U.S.C. 3512.

9. Federal Managers' Financial Integrity Act of 1982, P.L. 97-255 (H.R. 1526).

10. Office of Federal Financial Management, Federal Financial Management Improvement Act (FFMIA) of 1996.

11. Deborah Solomon, "Lost City: After Pension-Fund Debacle, San Diego Is Mired In Problems," *Wall Street Journal*, October 10, 2005.

12. Matt Kelly, "Government Agencies Face New Internal Control Standards," *Compliance Week*, Sept. 2005.

CHAPTER 9

U.S. Healthcare Efforts to Improve Internal Controls: U.S. HIPAA

The Health Insurance Portability and Accountability Act (HIPAA) will improve internal controls and present major challenges to the U.S. health industry. U.S. HIPAA's goals include lowering costs and making administrative transactions more secure, efficient, and patient oriented. HIPAA seeks to enhance the privacy and security of individuals' health information. HIPAA creates requirements to address transaction standards, code sets, identifiers, privacy, and security—both electronic and physical. The requirements require any organization that electronically stores or sends patient information to retool how it handles health data, and to address privacy and security regardless of the form in which individually identifiable health information is stored or transmitted.

HIPAA imposes greater regulation over data transfer, storage, and reporting. Various federal and state agencies including the Office of Civil Rights will likely increase their monitoring to assess an organization's level of compliance with the various HIPAA requirements. A formal assessment of HIPAA compliance should be a mandatory part of any internal audit plan. Improved internal controls will need to include information systems and physical access to printed documents and records.

Steve Weil, CISSP, CISA, in his article, "The Final HIPAA Security Rule—Conducting Effective Risk Analysis," explains that risk analysis is a critical requirement of HIPAA's Security Rule. The Security Rule requires organizations to "conduct an accurate and thorough assessment of the potential risks and vulnerabilities to the confidentiality, integrity, and availability of electronic protected health information held by the covered entity." The rule further states that "the required risk analysis is also a tool to allow flexibility for entities in meeting the requirements of this final rule." "Risk" is the likelihood that a specific threat will exploit certain vulnerability, and the resulting impact of that event. "Risk analysis," the starting point in an overall risk management process, is a systematic and analytical approach that identifies and assesses risks and provides recommendations to reduce risk to a reasonable and appropriate level. This process will enable senior management to understand their organization's risks to Electronic Protected Health Information (EPHI) and to allocate appropriate resources to reduce and correct potential losses."[1]

ENDNOTES

1. Steve Weil, "The Final HIPAA Security Rule—Conducting Effective Risk Analysis," HIPPAAdvisory web site: www.hipaadvisory. com/Action/security/riskanalysis.htm.

CHAPTER 10

Bankers' and Insurers' Efforts to Improve Internal Controls

BASEL II IMPROVES BANKING'S INTERNAL CONTROLS[1]

In 2004, the Central Bank governors and the heads of bank supervisory authorities in the Group of Ten (G10) countries published a new framework for capital adequacy called "The International Convergence of Capital Measurement and Capital Standards: A Revised Framework." This is commonly known as Basel II since the meetings took place in Basel, Switzerland. The first Basel Accord, published in 1988, set standards for capital requirements because banking regulators well understood that weaknesses in internal controls presented major risks to banking on a global level.

The Basel II Framework builds on the 1988 Accord, setting out the details for adopting more risk-sensitive minimum capital requirements for banking organizations and including:

- A framework for banks to assess the adequacy of their capital and the adequacy to support their risks
- A framework for banks to strengthen market discipline by enhancing the transparency in banks' financial reporting

The Basel Committee intends for the new framework to be available for implementation in member jurisdictions by year-end 2006. The most advanced approaches to risk measurement will be available for implementation by year-end 2007, allowing banks and supervisors to benefit from an additional year of impact analysis or parallel capital calculations under the existing and new rules.

There are many parallels between Basel II's "Pillar 2" and the internal controls provisions of SOX Section 404. Both are built on a Committee of Sponsoring Organizations (COSO) framework and are designed to prevent the failure of major internal controls and include the means to identify and mitigate risks.

Sections 744 and 745 cover the internal control review process: "The bank's internal control structure is essential to the capital assessment process. Effective control of the capital assessment process includes an independent review and, where appropriate, the involvement of internal or external audits. The bank's board of directors has a responsibility to ensure that management establishes a system for assessing the various risks, develops a system to relate risk to the bank's capital level, and establishes a method for monitoring compliance with internal policies. The board should regularly verify whether its system of internal controls is adequate to ensure well-ordered and prudent conduct of business."

"The bank should conduct periodic reviews of its risk management process to ensure its integrity, accuracy, and reasonableness. Areas that should be reviewed include:

- Appropriateness of the bank's capital assessment process given the nature, scope and complexity of its activities;
- Identification of large exposures and risk concentrations;
- Accuracy and completeness of data inputs into the bank's assessment process;
- Reasonableness and validity of scenarios used in the assessment process; and
- Stress testing and analysis of assumptions and inputs."

Sections 751 and 752 cover the assessment of the control environment: "Supervisors should consider the quality of the bank's management information reporting and systems, the manner in which business risks and activities are aggregated, and management's record in responding to emerging or changing risks. In all instances, the capital level at an individual bank should be determined according to the bank's risk profile and adequacy of its risk management process and internal controls. External factors such as business cycle effects and the macroeconomic environment should also be considered."

BASEL II VERSUS SOX

In his article for *Global Risk Regulator*, Tim Leech compares the two accords in terms of their effectiveness and concludes that Basel II is more effective in six out of seven criteria. Leech compared: "the role of the board of directors; the regulator's role; the role of management; internal and external audit; reporting requirements; incentives to comply and timeliness of solution . . . . Basel II clears all but one of seven major hurdles, ranging from the role of directors to incentives to comply, where SOX stumbles from a lack of clarity. Only on timelines does SOX have the advantage. Sarbanes is already law, whereas Basel II's timetable remains under threat." Significantly, Leech also warns that the COSO Framework on which SOX relies is outdated. SOX and the SEC "encourages companies to use the COSO control criteria as reporting criteria. This now dated and somewhat obsolete control framework was never intended as a scoring grid for pass/fail analysis and is not well suited to objectively grade the quality of a company's external disclosure system."[2]

BASEL II IN THE AMERICAS

Tom Barkley reported in the *Wall Street Journal* (*WSJ*) on April 27, 2005, "Mexican Regulator Raises Bank Disclosure Requirements," that Mexico was improving the transparency of the financial reporting for its banks and other credit providers. The improvements are in accordance with the Basel II accords and "attempt to boost transparency and accountability, the National Banking and Securities Commission released more stringent requirements for publishing financial details, making data available online, and strengthening the independence of external auditors."

Barkley noted, "The requirements include publishing quarterly and annual financial data, reporting results signed by the chief executive and internal accounting officials, as well as summaries of shareholder resolutions . . . . In addition, financial firms must now publish such information on the Internet, according to the commission."[3]

Ironically, though Mexico and other Latin American nations have accelerated their efforts to improve controls, the United States has sought to delay Basel II adoption. Campion Walsh reported in *WSJ*, in April 29, 2005, "U.S. Bank Regulators Delay Basel II Proposal," that U.S. bank regulators had delayed the implementation of Basel II. "Previously, U.S. regulators have set a target of January 2008 to begin implementation of the accord, which is expected to allow large, well-capitalized banks and others that can show adequate risk management to hold less regulatory capital for loans . . . ."

The U.S. regulators said their industry survey raised more questions than anticipated, and that "Additional work is necessary to determine whether these results reflect differences in risk, reveal limitations of (the study), identify variations in the stages of bank implementation efforts (particularly related to data availability), and/or suggest the need for adjustments to the Basel II framework, the regulators said . . . . The U.S. bank agencies said they remain committed to moving ahead with Basel II while retaining other measures affecting bank reserves, including prompt corrective action and leverage requirements. The delay in the Basel II proposal is meant to ensure any changes support safety and soundness, good risk management and the strength of the U.S. bank sector, they said."[4]

The U.S. delay in adopting Basel II is unfortunate and will frustrate the effort to create a level playing field for the world's financial initiations and hurt American competitiveness. The delay demonstrates the limitations of voluntary measures as opposed to strict and mandatory deadlines with strong penalties for failure. Not only are Mexico and other Latin American countries pushing ahead on Basel II, they are also embracing the International Financial Reporting Standards (IFRS) movement toward a global Generally Accepted Accounting Principles (GAAP), and the Organization for Economic Cooperation and Development's (OECD's) Principles.

SOLVENCY II IMPROVES INSURERS' INTERNAL CONTROLS[5]

The European Commission's (EC's) Financial Services Action Plan (FSAP) creates major challenges for insurance carriers with a new solvency regime known as "Solvency II." It is currently planned to be adopted in October 2006. Capital markets are demanding greater stability and clarity in the measurement of solvency. While improving solvency requirements, the European commission believes that the rules for banks and insurers should be harmonized in that many of their product offerings are overlapping and consolidating. Solvency II takes a three-pillar approach similar to the three-pillar approach that Basel II applies to the banking industry.

Each of the three pillars of Solvency II will be affected by the risks that an insurer writes. The minimum capital required by Pillar I will reflect the risks the insurer runs, and Pillar II encourages a proactive attitude to the management of those risks. Pillar III will allow observers to compare the approach that different insurers are taking to risk. For instance, an insurer with a greater risk appetite should carry a higher capital requirement for the same credit rating.

Solvency II requires the following risk and control environment:

- An obligation to introduce an early risk warning system
- The presentation of future risks in a status report
- Periodic audits by company accountants
- The creation of internal control systems initiated by the Federal Financial Services Supervisory Authority

Solvency II requires a risk strategy with the following requirements:

- Creating an effective reporting system
- Installing early warning and monitoring tools
- Changing existing internal risk management processes so they can be measured against the new requirements (Pillar II)

COMMON ELEMENTS OF BASEL II AND SOLVENCY II

Basel II and Solvency II will require banks and insurers to rethink their existing risk management strategies in that many of them do not have systems to quantify and mitigate risks. Basel II and Solvency II take a three-pillar approach in which one pillar calls for enhanced internal controls including risk management as a means to promote transparency in financial reporting. As banks and insurers are required to manage risks, they will reward their customers who can demonstrate robust internal controls with, respectively, lower capital costs and lower rates.

THE GRAMM-LEACH-BLILEY FINANCIAL MODERNIZATION ACT (GLB)[6]

The Gramm-Leach-Bliley Financial Modernization Act of 1999 imposes financial privacy requirements on financial institutions including insurers, and it requires companies to give consumers privacy notices that explain the institutions' information-sharing practices. In turn, consumers have the right to limit some sharing of their information. The Federal Trade Commission (FTC) is charged with enforcing the act in situations where federal and state banking agencies and the SEC are not the controlling agencies.

One of the most significant procure-to-pay issues that come into play with the GLB Act is caused by the outsourcing of consumer data collection and aggregation processes to third-party providers such as LexisNexis, ChoicePoint, and Acxiom. These providers suffered major security breaches in 2004 and 2005 in which the consumer information was stolen with numbers now totaling over one million individual thefts. These major and well-publicized security breaches have increased demand for greater government controls. They call into question the validity and thoroughness of the Statement on Auditing Standards No. 70 (SAS 70) process and competency of those performing the audits.

A company's obligations under the GLB Act depend on whether the company has consumers or customers who obtain its services. A consumer is an individual who obtains or has obtained a financial product or service from a financial institution for personal, family, or household reasons. A customer is a consumer with a continuing relationship with a financial institution. Generally, if the relationship between the financial institution and the individual is significant and/or long-term, the individual is a customer of the institution. For example, a person who gets a mortgage from a lender or hires a broker to get a personal loan is considered a customer of the lender or the broker, but a person who uses a check-cashing service is a consumer of that service.

The difference between consumers and customers is important because only customers are entitled to receive a financial institution's privacy notice automatically. Consumers are entitled to receive a privacy notice from a financial institution only if the company shares the consumers' information with nonaffiliated companies with some exceptions. Customers must receive a notice every year for as long as the customer relationship lasts.

The privacy notice must be given to individual customers or consumers by mail or by in-person delivery; it may not, say, be posted on a wall. Reasonable ways to deliver a notice may depend on the type of business the institution is in: for example, an online lender may post its notice on its web site and require online consumers to acknowledge receipt as a necessary part of a loan application.

The privacy notice must be a clear, conspicuous, and accurate statement of the company's privacy practices; it should include what information the company collects about its consumers and customers, with whom it shares the information, and how it protects or safeguards the information. The notice applies to the "nonpublic personal information" the company gathers and discloses about its consumers and customers; in practice, that may be most or all of the information a company has about them. For example, nonpublic personal information could be information that a consumer or customer puts on an application; information about the individual from another source, such as a credit bureau; or information about transactions between the individual and the company, such as an account balance. Indeed, even an individual being a consumer or customer of a particular financial institution is nonpublic personal information. But information that the company has reason to believe is lawfully public, such as mortgage loan information in a jurisdiction where that information is publicly recorded, is not restricted by the GLB Act.

Other important provisions of the GLB Act affect how a company conducts business. For example, financial institutions are prohibited from disclosing their customers' account numbers to nonaffiliated companies when it comes to telemarketing, direct mail marketing, or other marketing through e-mail even if the individuals have not opted out of sharing the information for marketing purposes.

ENDNOTES

1. This section references and extensively quotes the Central Bank Governor's and Group of 10's, "International Convergence of Capital Measurement and Capital Standards: A Revised Framework," (Known as Basel II) Sections 744 and 755, June 26, 2004.
2. Tim Leech, "Basel II vs. Sarbanes-Oxley: Which Wins?" *Global Risk Navigator*, October 2003.

3. Tom Barkley, "Mexican Regulator Raises Bank Disclosure Requirements," *Wall Street Journal*, April 27, 2005.

4. Campion Walsh, "US Bank Regulators Delay Basel II Proposal," *Wall Street Journal*, April 29, 2005.

5. This section references and quotes from the European Commission's Financial Services Action Plan: Progress and Prospects Expert Group on Insurance and Pensions, Final Report, May 2004.

6. This section extensively references the Gramm-Leach-Bliley Financial Modernization Act of 1999, Subtitle A: Disclosure of Nonpublic Personal Information 15 U.S.C. § 6801-6809, and Subtitle B: Fraudulent Access to Financial Information 15 U.S.C. § 6821-6827.

CHAPTER 11

Australia, Canada, and UK Efforts to Improve Internal Controls

AUSTRALIA'S ASX 10 PRINCIPLES OF GOOD CORPORATE GOVERNANCE[1]

Australia has taken an approach to corporate governance and improved internal controls that should be considered a role model in that it provides guidance based on best practices for 10 key process areas. Companies may choose not to follow the recommended best practices, but must explain why. Formed in August 2002, the Australian Stock Exchange (ASX) Corporate Governance Council brought together 21 professional and business groups with the mission "to develop and deliver an industry-wide, supportable, and supported framework for corporate governance which could provide a practical guide for listed companies, their investors, the wider market and the Australian community . . . . The size, complexity and operations of companies differ, and so flexibility must be allowed in the structures adopted to optimize individual performance. That flexibility must, however, be tempered by accountability—the obligation to explain to investors why an alternative approach is adopted—the 'if not, why not?' obligation. The enhancement of corporate accountability and the adoption of this framework for reporting is a major evolution in corporate governance practice in Australia. The impact on Australian companies must not be underestimated."

The guideline approach takes into consideration that a checklist and one-size-fits-all approach is unrealistic, something that the Securities and Exchange Commission (SEC) and Public Company Accounting Oversight Board (PCAOB) only acknowledged in the spring of 2005. According to the ASX March 2003 introduction, "it states aspirations of best practice for optimizing corporate performance and accountability in the interests of shareholders and the broader economy. If a company considers that a recommendation is inappropriate to its particular circumstances, it has the flexibility not to adopt it, a flexibility tempered by the requirement to explain why. Companies are encouraged to use the guidance provided by this document as a focus for re-examining their corporate governance practices and to determine whether and to what extent the company may benefit from a change in approach, having regard to the company's particular circumstances. There is little value in a checklist approach to corporate governance that does not focus on the particular needs, strengths, and weaknesses of the company. The Council recognizes that the range in size and diversity of companies is significant and that smaller companies may face particular issues in attaining all recommendations from the outset. Performance and effectiveness can be compromised by material change that is not managed sensibly. Where a company is considering widespread structural changes in order to meet best practice, the company is encouraged to prioritize its needs and to set and disclose best practice goals against an indicative timeframe for meeting them."

Disclosure requirements

"Companies are required to provide a statement in their annual report disclosing the extent to which they have followed these best practice recommendations in the reporting period.[2] Where companies have not followed all the recommendations, they must identify the recommendations that have not been followed and give reasons for not following them. Annual reporting does not diminish the company's obligation to provide disclosure."[3]

What disclosures are necessary?

"It is only where a recommendation is not met or where a disclosure requirement is specifically identified that a disclosure obligation is triggered. Each recommendation is clearly identified as such. The commentary and guidance that follows each recommendation does not form part of the recommendation. It is provided to assist companies to understand the reasoning for the recommendation,

highlight factors which may be relevant for consideration, and make suggestions as to how implementation might be achieved."

Where should disclosure be made?

"Specific guidance is given at the end of each principle as to what disclosure the company is required or encouraged to make and where. In some cases, the company is required to set out the relevant disclosure in a separate corporate governance section of the annual report. Where the Corporations Act requires particular information to be included in the directors' report, the company has the discretion to include a cross-reference to the relevant information in the corporate governance section of the annual report rather than replicating that information." According to Australia's Treasury Department it is the responsibility of company boards of directors to certify that a company's financial statements comply with accounting standards, and provide an accurate view of its financial condition. The Corporations Act provides for a broad fiduciary responsibility of directors. The Act also requires auditors to form an opinion as to whether a company's financial statements comply with accounting standards and provide a view of its financial condition.[4]

What is the disclosure period?

"The change in reporting requirement applies to the company's first financial year commencing after 1 January 2003. Accordingly, where a company's financial year begins on 1 July, disclosure will be required in relation to the financial year 1 July 2003–30 June 2004 and will be made in the annual report published in 2004. Companies are encouraged to make an early transition to the best practice recommendations and are requested to consider reporting by reference to the recommendations in their corporate reporting this year."

What disclosures are necessary?

"It is only where a recommendation is not met or where a disclosure requirement is specifically identified that a disclosure obligation is triggered. Each recommendation is clearly identified as such. The commentary and guidance that follows each recommendation does not form part of the recommendation. It is provided

to assist companies to understand the reasoning for the recommendation, highlight factors which may be relevant for consideration, and make suggestions as to how implementation might be achieved."

Where should disclosure be made?

"Specific guidance is given at the end of each principle as to what disclosure the company is required or encouraged to make and where. In some cases, the company is required to set out the relevant disclosure in a separate corporate governance section of the annual report. Where the Corporations Act requires particular information to be included in the directors' report, the company has the discretion to include a cross-reference to the relevant information in the corporate governance section of the annual report rather than replicating that information."

CANADA'S 52-109 AND 52-111[5]

In reaction to growing corporate scandals in the United States and Europe, Canada is enacting its own version of SOX, which goes into effect beginning in 2006. Known as Ontario Securities Commission, Multi-Lateral Instrument 52-109 (similar to SOX Section 302) and Multi-Lateral Instrument 52-111 (similar to SOX Section 404), it parallels the provisions of SOX and follows a COSO framework.

Canada's 52-111 embraces the COSO framework and SOX Section 404 approach, covering:

- Control Environments
- Risk Assessments
- Control Activities
- Definition of Materiality
- Corrections of Material Weaknesses

52-111 provides the following definitions that closely parallel U.S. SOX and COSO:

- **Internal control audit report:** "means a report in which a participating audit firm expresses an opinion, or states that an opinion cannot be expressed, concerning management's assessment of the effectiveness of an issuer's internal control over financial reporting."

- **Internal control over financial reporting:** " . . . means a process designed by, or under the supervision of, the issuer's chief executive officer and chief financial officer, or persons performing similar functions, and effected by the issuer's board of directors, management and other personnel, to provide reasonable assurance regarding the reliability of financial reporting and the preparation of financial statements for external purposes in accordance with the issuer's GAAP and includes those policies and procedures that: (a) pertain to the maintenance of records that in reasonable detail accurately and fairly reflect the transactions and dispositions of the assets of the issuer, (b) provide reasonable assurance that transactions are recorded as necessary to permit preparation of financial statements in accordance with the issuer's GAAP, and that receipts and expenditures of the issuer are being made only in accordance with authorizations of management and directors of the issuer, and (c) provide reasonable assurance regarding prevention or timely detection of unauthorized acquisition, use or disposition of the issuer's assets that could have a material effect on the annual financial statements or interim financial statements."
- **Internal control report:** " . . . means a report of management that describes management's assessment of the effectiveness of an issuer's internal control over financial reporting."

52-111 requires that for any company trading on a Canadian stock exchange, company management must file an internal control report with its annual report. This report must contain

- An acknowledgment of the company's legal responsibility to establish and maintain adequate internal controls over its financial reporting;
- Conclusions as to the effectiveness of these internal controls over financial reporting based on managements' year-end evaluation of them (management assertion); and
- A report from the company's external auditors attesting to management's assessment: this report becomes an integral part of that company's published financial statements.

Specifically, Part 2 of 52-111, "Management's Assessment of Internal Control Over Financial Reporting," specifies the following to support robust internal controls:

■ "**2.1 Annual evaluation of effectiveness of internal control over financial reporting:** The management of an issuer must evaluate, with the participation of the issuer's chief executive officer and chief financial officer, or in the case of an issuer that does not have a chief executive officer or a chief financial officer, persons performing similar functions to a chief executive officer or chief financial officer, the effectiveness of the issuer's internal control over financial reporting as of the end of a financial year."

■ "**2.2 Control framework for evaluation:** (1) Management must base its evaluation of the effectiveness of an issuer's internal control over financial reporting on a suitable control framework. (2) A suitable control framework must be established by a body or group that has followed an open and transparent process, including providing the public with an opportunity to provide comments, when developing the control framework."

■ "**2.3 Evidence:** (1) An issuer must maintain evidence to provide reasonable support for management's assessment of the effectiveness of the issuer's internal control over financial reporting. (2) An issuer must maintain the evidence required under subsection (1) in a manner that will ensure the trustworthiness and readability of the information recorded. (3) The evidence required under subsection (1) must be maintained for the same period that the accounting records for the financial year to which the evidence relates are maintained in accordance with the Income Tax Act (Canada)."

■ "**2.4 Filing of internal control report:** An issuer must file an internal control report separately but concurrently with the filing of its annual financial statements and annual MD&A."

■ "**2.5 Form and content of internal control report:** (a) An internal control report must include: a statement of management's responsibility for establishing and maintaining adequate internal control over financial reporting for an issuer; (b) a statement identifying the control framework used by management to evaluate the effectiveness of the issuer's internal control over financial reporting; (c) management's assessment of the effectiveness of the issuer's internal control over financial reporting as of the end of the issuer's financial year, including a statement as to whether the internal control over financial reporting is effective; (d) disclosure of any material weaknesses in the issuer's internal control over financial reporting identified by management; (e) a statement that the participating audit firm that audited the issuer's annual financial statements has issued an internal control audit report; (f) disclosure of any limitations in management's assessment of the effectiveness of the issuer's internal control over financial reporting extending into a joint venture or a variable interest entity in which the issuer has a material interest; and (g) disclosure of any limitations in management's assessment of the effectiveness of the issuer's internal control over financial reporting extending into a business that was acquired by the issuer during the financial year."

The effective dates depend on the market capitalization of a given company:

- Over $500,000,000—June 30, 2006
- Over $250,000,000—June 29, 2007
- Over $75,000,000—June 29, 2008
- Under $75,000,000—June 29, 2009

THE UK'S TURNBULL GUIDANCE AND COMBINED CODE[6]

The Combined Code on Corporate Governance was published in July 2003, by the Financial Reporting Council and incorporates the Internal Control: Guidance for Directors on the Combined Code known as the Turnbull Guidance. The Turnbull Guidance predates SOX by three years (first published in 1999),[7] and the SEC has referenced the Turnbull Guidance as a suitable framework for judging the effectiveness of internal controls. It goes into effect in January 2006.

The Turnbull Guidance aims to help non-U.S. companies that are SEC registered, referred to as "SEC registrants," who have elected to adopt the Turnbull Guidance as a framework for SOX Section 404 purposes. The Turnbull Guidance describes the requirements of SOX Section 404 and identifies those parts of the Turnbull Guidance most relevant when complying with that section.

The Guidance uses terminology consistent with a COSO/SOX framework requiring management to evaluate:

- "The effectiveness . . . of internal control over financial reporting
- The framework on which management's evaluation of internal control over financial reporting is based;
- Any change in the issuer's internal control over financial reporting . . . that has materially affected . . . the issuer's internal control over financial reporting;
- An assessment, as of the end of the most recent fiscal year of the issuer, of the effectiveness of the internal control structure and procedures of the issuer for financial reporting; and
- A statement of the responsibility of management for establishing and maintaining an adequate internal control structure and procedures for financial reporting."

The term *internal control over financial reporting* is defined within the Turnbull Guidance, in terms very similar to U.S. SOX and COSO, as a process designed by, or under the supervision of, the issuer's principal executive and principal financial officers, or persons performing similar functions, and effected by the issuer's board of directors, management and other personnel, to provide reasonable assurance regarding the reliability of financial reporting and the preparation of financial statements for external purposes in accordance with GAAP and includes those policies and procedures that:

- Pertain to the maintenance of records that in reasonable detail accurately and fairly reflect the transactions and dispositions of the assets of the issuer;
- Provide reasonable assurance that transactions are recorded as necessary to permit preparation of financial statements in accordance with GAAP, and that receipts and expenditures of the issuer are being made only in accordance with authorizations of management and directors of the issuer; and
- Provide reasonable assurance regarding prevention or timely detection of unauthorized acquisition, use, or disposition of the issuer's assets that could have a material effect on the financial statements.

In its introduction, the October 2005 revised code discusses the importance of internal control and risk management, the objectives of the guidance, and internal control requirements:

The Importance of Internal Control and Risk Management

1. *A company's system of internal control has a key role in the management of risks that are significant to the fulfillment of its business objectives. A sound system of internal control contributes to safeguarding the shareholders' investment and the company's assets.*

2. *Internal control (as referred to in paragraph 19) facilitates the effectiveness and efficiency of operations, helps ensure the reliability of internal and external reporting and assists compliance with laws and regulations.*

3. *Effective financial controls, including the maintenance of proper accounting records, are an important element of internal control. They help ensure that the company is not unnecessarily exposed to avoidable financial risks and that financial information used within the business and for publication is reliable. They also contribute to the safeguarding of assets, including the prevention and detection of fraud.*

4. *A company's objectives, its internal organization and the environment in which it operates are continually evolving and, as a result, the risks it faces are continually changing. A sound system of internal control, therefore, depends on a thorough and regular evaluation of the nature and extent of the risks to which the company is exposed. Since profits are, in part, the reward for successful risk-taking in business, the purpose of internal control is to help manage and control risk appropriately rather than to eliminate it.*

Objectives of the Guidance

This guidance is intended to reflect sound business practice whereby internal control is embedded in the business processes by which a company pursues its objectives; remain relevant over time in the continually evolving business environment; and enable each company to apply it in a manner, which takes account of its particular circumstances.

The guidance requires directors to exercise judgment in reviewing how the company has implemented the requirements of the Combined Code relating to internal control and reporting to shareholders thereon.

The guidance is based on the adoption by a company's board of a risk-based approach to establishing a sound system of internal control and reviewing its effectiveness. This should be incorporated by the company within its normal management and governance processes. It should not be treated as a separate exercise undertaken to meet regulatory requirements.

Internal Control Requirements of the Combined Code

Principle C.2 of the Code states that "The board should maintain a sound system of internal control to safeguard shareholders' investment and the company's assets."

1. *Provision C.2.1 states that "The directors should, at least annually, conduct a review of the effectiveness of the group's system of internal control and should report to shareholders that they have done so. The review should cover all material controls, including financial, operational and compliance controls and risk management systems."*

2. *Paragraph 9.8.6 of the UK Listing Authority's Listing Rules states that in the case of a listed company incorporated in the United Kingdom, the following items must be included in its annual report and accounts:*

   ● *A statement of how the listed company has applied the principles set out in Section 1 of Combined Code, in a manner that would enable shareholders to evaluate how the principles have been applied;*

   ● *A statement as to whether the listed company has: complied throughout the accounting period with all relevant provisions set out in Section 1 of the Combined Code; or not complied throughout the accounting period with all relevant provisions set out Section 1 of the Combined Code and if so, setting out: (i) those provisions, if any, it has not complied with; (ii) in the case of provisions whose requirements are of a continuing nature, the period within which, if any, it did not comply with some or all of those provisions; and (iii) the company's reasons for non-compliance.*

3. *The Preamble to the Code makes it clear that there is no prescribed form or content for the statement setting out how the various principles in the Code have been applied. The intention is that companies should have a free hand to explain their governance policies in the light of the principles, including any special circumstances which have led to them adopting a particular approach.*

4. *The guidance in this document applies for accounting periods beginning on or after 1 January, 2006, and should be followed by boards of listed companies in:*
   - *assessing how the company has applied Code Principle C.2;*
   - *implementing the requirements of Code Provision C.2.1;*
   - *and reporting on these matters to shareholders in the annual report and accounts.*

   For the purposes of this guidance, internal controls considered by the board should include all types of controls including those of an operational and compliance nature, as well as internal financial controls.

ENDNOTES

1. This section extensively references and quotes the Australian Stock Exchange's "ASX Corporate Governance Council Principles of Good Corporate Governance and Best Practice Recommendations," March 2003, http://www.asx.com.au/corporategovernance.
2. ASX Listing Rule 4.10.3: Introduced 1/7/96. Origin: Listing Rule 3C(3)(e), 3B(2C). Amended 1/7/97, 1/7/98, 1/9/99, 30/9/2001. Cross reference: Listing rules 5.6 and 19.11A.
3. ASX Listing Rule 3.1: Compliance and Policy Rules, Exposure Draft, July 2002.
4. The Australian Government, Treasury, Part 10: Enforcement Issues, 2002
5. This section extensively references and quotes the Alberta Security Commissions Notice and Request for Comments on Multilateral Instrument 52-111, Reporting on Internal Control Over Financial Reporting, Feb. 4, 2005.
6. This section references and extensively quotes the Institute of Chartered Accountants in England & Wales, "Financial Reporting Council Internal Control, Revised Guidance for Directors on the Combined Code," October 2005, www.icaew.co.uk/internalcontrol. "All material from Internal Control Revised Guidance for Directors on the Combined Code and the Turnbull Guidance as an Evaluation Framework for the Purposes of Section 404(a) of the Sarbanes-Oxley Act is reproduced with the kind permission of the UK Financial Reporting

Council. For further information please visit www.frc.org.uk or call +44 (0)20 7492 2300."

7. The Institute of Chartered Accountants in England & Wales Internal Control, "Guidance for Directors on the Combined Code," September 1999. "All material from Internal Control Revised Guidance for Directors on the Combined Code and the Turnbull Guidance as an Evaluation Framework for the Purposes of Section 404(a) of the Sarbanes-Oxley Act is reproduced with the kind permission of the UK Financial Reporting Council. For further information please visit www.frc.org.uk or call +44 (0)20 7492 2300."

EU Efforts to Improve Internal Controls: OECD Principles

INTRODUCTION TO THE OECD[1]

The Organization for Economic Cooperation and Development (OECD) describes itself as "a group of 30 member countries sharing a commitment to democratic government and the market economy. With active relationships with some 70 other countries . . . it has a global reach . . . . The OECD plays a prominent role in fostering good governance in the public service and in corporate activity. It helps governments to ensure the responsiveness of key economic areas with sectoral monitoring."

OECD efforts to improve transparency in corporate transactions predate SOX by at least four years. In a 1998 workshop on combating bribery, the introduction noted that disclosure and transparency in corporate transactions means "sound accounting and auditing measures and internal company control, and is important because it goes to the heart of confidence in the financial integrity of companies, and thence to the efficient functioning of capital markets . . . . It is identified as important in both the OECD Convention and the Inter-American Convention Against Bribery (IAC)."

The introduction to the OECD Principles explains why good corporate governance is essential even in family run and closely held companies: "The degree to which corporations observe basic principles of good corporate governance is an increasingly important factor for investment decisions. Of particular relevance is the relation between corporate governance practices and the increasingly international character of investment. International flows of capital enable companies to access financing from a much larger pool of investors.

If countries are to reap the full benefits of the global capital market, and if they are to attract long-term 'patient' capital, corporate governance arrangements must be credible, well understood across borders and adhere to internationally accepted principles. Even if corporations do not rely primarily on foreign sources of capital, adherence to good corporate governance practices will help improve the confidence of domestic investors, reduce the cost of capital, underpin the good functioning of financial markets, and ultimately induce more stable sources of financing."

The relevant provision in the OECD Convention (Section 8) imposes obligations that are similar to SOX: "To prohibit the establishment of off-the-book accounts, the making of off-the-books or inadequately identified transactions, the recording of non-existent expenditures, the entry of liabilities with incorrect identification of their object, as well as the use of false documents, by companies subject to those laws and regulations, for the purpose of bribing foreign public officials or of hiding such bribery." Measures to increase transparency will include:

- Adequate accounting requirements
- Independent external audit
- Internal company controls

The revised OECD principles of corporate governance have taken a principles-based approach to corporate governance based on good standards rather than mandatory compliance mandated by SOX. The OECD argues that its Principles of Corporate Governance have done the following good things:

- Since 1999, they have played an important role in the development of national codes and principles.
- They have become a world standard.
- They have served as an effective framework for stimulating and organizing the debate about corporate governance in a wide range of countries including in many emerging market economies.

And unlike SOX, the Principles have been successful because they are only principles, allowing countries to adapt them to suit local circumstances and issues.

The OECD leaders have noted that "that EU and US perspectives to the value-added of the principles are different due to different degrees of ownership concentration and certain rights of stakeholders. The US is slow to grasp that other countries have different problems. The EU has different sets of problems, for example, related to CEO/chairman split. There is no OECD consensus on the latter. It is a good practice in some countries and very much depends on country variables. The OECD didn't follow the level of prescription as the EU did in its action plan . . . . Regarding regulatory competition, countries are already willing to raise their standards in response or pressure to different interest groups. Hence, that might be a good thing."

The OECD Principles have advanced in three main areas:

1. Ensuring an effective corporate governance framework
2. Ensuring the effective exercise of ownership
3. Ensuring means to deal with conflicts of interest

According to the OECD, "the corporate governance framework should promote transparent and efficient markets, be consistent with the rule of law and clearly articulate the division of responsibilities among different supervisory, regulatory, and enforcement authorities." An effective corporate governance framework comprises effective collaboration among governments, regulators, and stock exchanges in addition to private parties. In countries where codes and principles are part of the framework and a substitute for legal or regulatory provisions, their status including compliance mechanisms and sanctions should be specified.

Some elements such as insider trading perhaps should be a criminal offense (though for many countries, this is only recent), but other outcomes (e.g., what are regarded as desirable features of a corporate governance system) might best be left to individual contractual freedom so long as this exists through professional associations, codes and principles, and so forth.

BENCHMARKING IN THE OECD PRINCIPLES

The OECD has introduced the intriguing concept of using benchmarking and governance metrics, available from the Standard &

Poor's (S&P's) Corporate Governance Services, to provide investors and regulators with the ability to compare corporations. Nick Brady, in the Second Meeting of the EU's Corporate Governance Reform Task Force, described how benchmarking and metrics could work. The S&P's Corporate Governance Services "provides independent assessments of governance structures and practice worldwide. Assessments can be provided to companies on a confidential basis, can be encapsulated in a public governance score, or can be undertaken confidentially on behalf of financial market participants, for example regulators or investors . . . . In the post-January 2004 period, Governance Services are part of S&P Ratings. They provide governance assessments and corporate governance evaluations and scores. Approximately 100 assignments have been done to date in US, UK, France, Germany, Italy, Spain, Hungary, Russia, China, India, Indonesia, Brazil, Japan, Korea, Hong Kong, and Switzerland."[2]

Brady, reflecting on whether governance can be scored or benchmarked, noted, "governance structures and philosophies differ globally. Different countries are characterized by a different degree of concentration of ownership. There are different corporate governance focuses, i.e., shareholder versus broader stakeholder focus, legal and cultural dimensions vary in areas such as chairman/CEO split, one tier versus two tiered boards and quarterly reporting. Moreover, governance is not a one-size-fits-all concept. It must appreciate local specificities, ownership structures, and legal traditions. The Anglo-American governance is not the only answer."[3]

In regard to corporate governance scores, they are voluntary, that is, they are requested by companies that want to benchmark and improve corporate governance standards and to communicate these standards to investors, directors' and officers' insurers,[4] and other stakeholders.

The scores have an equity investor focus. The Corporate Governance Scoring is as follows: CGS-1 (very weak) to CGS-10 (very strong). The scoring is calculated based on company analytical structures encompassing:

- Ownership structure and external influences
- Shareholder rights and stakeholder relations
- Transparency, disclosure, and audit
- Board structure and effectiveness

A detailed confidential diagnostic report and a score are issued on the basis of public information, regulatory filings, nonconfidential information, and interviews with senior management and directors. The summary report can be published if client requests.

ENDNOTES

1. The Organization for Economic Develop and Cooperation, "The OECD Principles of Good Corporate Governance," 2004.
2. Nick Brady, in the Second Meeting of the EU's Corporate Governance Reform Task Force, September 30, 2004.
3. Nick Brady, in the Second Meeting of the EU's Corporate Governance Reform Task Force, September 30, 2004.
4. Director and Insurers directors and officers of both public and private corporations are fiduciaries in the EU, United States, and other countries, and as such, may face both civil and criminal liabilities for acts they perform on behalf of the corporation. Companies often provide directors and officers with insurance coverage called a Directors' and Officers' Insurance Policy (D&O Policy), which generally covers their potential liability for defense and settlement costs.

CHAPTER 13

Global GAAP (IFRS) and Global Reporting Language (XBRL)

INTERNATIONAL FINANCIAL REPORTING STANDARDS (IFRS)[1]

Effective January 1, 2005, all European Union (EU) companies that have shares traded on any EU-regulated market were required to prepare consolidated financial statements in accordance with International Financial Reporting Standards (IFRS). Member nations may elect to extend the IFRS to private companies as well. Seven thousand EU companies are using the IFRS. Firms that are listed in the United States have until 2007 to convert. In doing this, the EU will meet its goal of significantly and sustainedly improving the depth, efficiency, and liquidity of European capital markets. The UK has been a strong supporter of the IFRS as a replacement for its UK GAAP. Australia, Canada, Russia, and Japan are moving toward the IFRS as well.

BearingPoint's 2003 White Paper explains the profound impact of IFRS: "The introduction of IFRS as the European wide reporting standard will improve performance analysis of and comparability between companies. The sourcing of capital in the European market will subsequently be easier, more transparent, and more competitive. High-level portfolio management will also be better facilitated."

BearingPoint also describes the impact of Basel II: "Basel II's effects on the industry as a debtor to the financial services sector have been hotly debated over the past year. It is inevitable, however, that Basel II will have considerable consequences for corporate financial strategies and management. Small and Medium Size Enterprises (SMEs), in particular, will face performance criteria, which will become increasingly difficult to meet."[2]

The rating system is also undergoing major changes. The corporate scandals of the 1990s demonstrated the ineffectiveness of the major credit agencies in detecting corporate failures, even a few days prior to their insolvencies. The EU is leading an effort to transform the roles of rating agencies as well as their underlying structure to support a global harmonization of standards and ratings.[3]

As the BearingPoint White Paper notes, successfully implementing the IFRS will be difficult: "As recent events have shown, US GAAP has encountered problems due to their own complexity, making comprehension of the essential developments of a firm very difficult for financial analysts. At the same time, short-term, shareholder oriented corporate governance leads to ever increasing performance pressures, which are often alleviated through complex accounting methods. The imperfect habit of pro forma reporting severely undermines the objective of one reliable accounting and reporting standard."

While the EU has made a major leap forward with the IFRS, the lack of an overall governing authority like the U.S. Securities and Exchange Commission needs to be addressed to provide the assurances that regulations are being applied consistently. BearingPoint notes that several European companies claim full IFRS compliance, but in reality still fall short. "That the new international standards are still in a developmental stage is also shown in the fact that there still exists a strong tendency in the EU for IFRS to reflect national characteristics. Though ardently debated, only a European authority equivalent to the United States' SEC will guarantee a sufficient adherence to IFRS throughout the EU's 15—and soon to be 25—member countries."

BearingPoint's White Paper provides a comprehensive analysis of the issues in converting from national/local GAAPs to the IFRS. "Changes in IFRS/US GAAP will lead to a continuing shift from retrospective to present and prognostic valuation. At the same time, options, pensions, and financial instruments' accounting and valuation will become more complex. The third characteristic of change is the accounting and valuation of immaterial assets, which are expected to become increasingly complex over the coming years and reflect the transformation of the services and knowledge industry. All these developments will have a profound impact on valuation volatility and accuracy. More sophisticated methods will demand better reporting processes and, subsequently, new methods and systems in reporting and controlling."

Changes in Financial Reports

The BearingPoint White Paper discusses the changes in financial reports. "The conversion from local GAAP to IFRS/US GAAP reporting can have substantial and lasting effects on an organization's financial reports. But it can also have a reverse effect on a company's product structure portfolio. The type and scope of conversion depend on the industry sector and the specific business transactions of a company. The decisive basis for identifying all the relevant issues is a preliminary analysis of not only the most important accounting differences which will appear after a transfer to IFRS/US GAAP, but also their anticipated effects on the company's reports and the resulting financial figures. An example is the balance sheet representation under IFRS/US GAAP of long-term contract productions. According to IFRS, revenues from construction contracts are to be recognized earlier under the matching principle than is the case with most local GAAP standards. After considering and adopting an ideal accounting strategy, a company must set specific bookkeeping and transfer guidelines. This is the only way of ensuring that an organization's accounting strategy and reporting is uniformly and precisely applied and reporting risks are reduced."

International Accounting Standards 39 (IAS 39)

BearingPoint explains the added risk coming under IAS 39 in that it will become more "difficult to make accurate and prospective portfolio and implementation decisions that are flexible enough to accommodate for last minute changes in the respective standards. The key to managing this problem is a very sophisticated product definition model that even in the course of a conversion can accommodate for expected or potential changes in accounting standards."

Harmonizing External and Internal Reporting

BearingPoint notes the major change requiring harmonization of external (legal) and internal (management) reporting and controlling. "Under most local GAAPs, management reporting is fairly decoupled from legal reporting principles. Under international accounting and reporting standards, with its focus on present and pro forma market values, internal performance criteria have to be closely aligned to external reporting criteria. Otherwise, as is unfortunately the situation with a number of companies, operative business continues along its well-trodden tracks with little concern for adverse effects of the resulting decisions and transactions on the corporate balance sheet."

Increased IT Requirements

BearingPoint notes the increased demand on a variety of information systems that will come with IFRS conversion. "The following operations need special consideration:

- Collection of data and notes
- Validation and adjustment of external and internal data
- Full reporting process mapping
- Detailed reports
- Filing processes (e.g., 20-F, 6-K)
- Low-level, ad hoc analysis
- Integrated reporting and controlling dialogue"

There will also be greater demand for near real-time and prognostic reporting at a detailed level. "The increasingly complex accounting and reporting of immaterial assets will deepen the reporting spectrum. All these factors will lead to a rapid increase in overall reporting and controlling complexity, which has to be considered when defining reporting strategies." The current state of financial reporting systems is typically fragmented with multiple disparate legacy systems. Frequently, uncontrolled spreadsheets without version and access controls are used to aggregate critical financial information.

SUMMARY

The debate between U.S. GAAP with its rules approach and the IFRS and its principle approach continues.

U.S. GAAP is proving to be too complex and confusing to support viable financial analysis. This complexity has helped companies to mask financial and operational problems. The IFRS has its own problems and growing pains. The lack of an SEC-type regulatory authority in the EU nations will frustrate the standardization of financial reporting. While many member nations claim full IFRS compliance, much of their reporting still reflects local GAAP practices and characteristics. Only a SEC-type of authority will be able to enforce consistent adherence throughout the current 15 member nations, and the soon to be 25 member nations. Such an SEC-type authority will also need a very strong chairman who will be widely accepted as guiding light and financial guru.

The Financial Accounting Standards Board (FASB) and the International Accounting Standards Board (IASB) had been committed to working with each other and converging U.S. accounting standards and IFRS, with the ultimate goal being one set of high-quality global accounting standards, herein referred to as global generally accepted accounting principles, or Global GAAP. But, in October 2005, the European Commission (EC) declared its intent to at least temporarily drop its requirement that U.S. public companies listed in the EU follow the IFRS. Though this saves companies money in the short term, this will frustrate the goal of a global accounting standard, such as the IFRS. In reverse, foreign companies could get the same exemption here in the United States.

Thomas Kostigen, writing in MarketWatch.com, explains the differences between the rules-based American approach and the principles-based EU approach: "The U.S. system ostensibly allows for more loopholes because it permits corporations to seek alternative accounting methodologies while still adhering to rules . . . . For example, a U.S. company, while maintaining generally accepted accounting principles (GAAP) enforced by the Financial Accounting Standards Board (FASB), could set up a special purpose entity (SPE) whose activities when positive could enhance the parent company's balance sheet but when negative could be kept separate. (This was how Enron got into trouble.) . . . The IFRS, which many European companies abide by, look at the 'intent' behind the action and would most likely rule an SPE's activity is part and parcel of the parent company . . . . However, without explicit rules in place, some say intent-based accounting opens the door for corporations to commit more fraud, not less. As

The Financial Times has put it, the reporting standards 'are big on principles and low on prescription.'"[4]

Devising one global accounting standard is "a prize which would be magnificent," according to *Accountancy Age*. The online journal goes further, saying: "While FASB and the IASB appear to be moving together on accounting principles, the fundamental question is the attitude of the SEC and especially its new chairman Christopher Cox. While the U.S. may presently be the biggest capital market, it sees competition not only from Europe but also from Japan and China. In that case, the U.S. may be prepared to accept standards that at first glance appear to give less investor protection."

SEC Chairman Cox, in his first speech as chairman, made it clear that U.S. governance regulations are the best in the world and he had no intention of changing them. Cox's hard line will put further pressure on the EU to strengthen its own regulations. According to Nicholas Neveling, reporting in *Accountancy Age*, August 9, 2005: "The EU is in the process of implementing its eighth directive on corporate governance. The new law is due to come into effect later this year and likely to introduce stricter regulations, similar to those prescribed in Sarbanes-Oxley."[5]

According to Kostigen, EU members are having a tough time in adopting the new IFRS standards, asking for more guidance. "But this isn't stopping the IASB from rolling out the new accounting standards to more countries. (The IASB announced that by next year, 100 countries would expect or permit IFRS to be used.)"[6]

The difficulty of converting from various national GAAPs to IFRS will vary from country to country and from industry to industry. Many national GAAPs are based on different principles. Adding to the problem is that many national GAAPs are not going to go away anytime soon, so enterprises will have to maintain two sets of books. While few U.S. companies will be directly affected in 2005, they will have to consider what their balance sheets would look like after convergence, and those with international subsidiaries need to comply now. That means that U.S. chief financial officers (CFOs) will have to disclose information in Europe that they do not disclose in the United States.

The impact on Asia will be more dramatic. Many Asian enterprises are closely held, family controlled, and naturally hesitant to change. Western notions of good governance with independent directors are not normally accepted. Many American joint ventures in Asia are not publicly held. As they decide to go public, a major change in corporate governance will be required.

The move toward a global GAAP will affect internal controls. Most local GAAPs are not as robust as the new IFRS. Though the U.S. GAAP and the IFRS have many differences, their core framework and guidance is basically the same. They will promote robust internal controls. The convergence of the U.S. GAAP and IFRS will create a more level playing field for investors as they seek to compare the financial performance of companies no matter where they are located throughout the globe. Merger and acquisition activities will benefit with the ability to compare company performances no matter where they are located. A global GAAP will help companies compare their financial performance, including internal controls, against competitors throughout the world.

According to PricewaterhouseCoopers (PWC), the biggest changes in adopting the IFRS are expected to be in accounting for financial instruments, deferred taxation, business combinations, and employee benefits.[7]

EXTENSIBLE BUSINESS REPORTING LANGUAGE (XBRL)

There is even a movement toward an Extensible Markup Language (XML) standard to promote a global GAAP. The Extensible Business Reporting Language (XBRL) is an attempt to create an internet-based global reporting language. XBRL would permit investors, analysts, and regulators to review and evaluate financial data more easily and efficiently. Because it is an XML standard, tagged data can be automatically searched and analyzed, greatly reducing the chance of errors. Users will need to learn XML-based data tagging concepts and related XML software tools. XBRL gives the promise to enhance the risk and internal controls analysis required in a Committee of Sponsoring Organizations (COSO) framework.[8]

The spotty history of efforts to create industry-specific and process-specific XML standards would suggest that this will be a difficult and long-term effort. The problems have been based more on the inability to standardize business processes than any technical issues.

The SEC is supporting the adoption of XBRL and has released a proposed rule, "XBRL Voluntary Financial Reporting Program on the EDGAR System,"[9] accompanied by a "concept release" entitled "Enhancing Commission Filings Through the Use of Tagged Data."[10] The comment periods for the proposed rule and the concept release ended in November 2004, and the SEC is evaluating comment letters and the proposed rule.

Exhibit 13.1 is a graphical representation of the framework for preparing financial statements in accordance with IAS using XBRL.[11]

The following are text links to the taxonomies used in Exhibit 13.1:

- PFS: www.xbrl.org/taxonomy/int/fr/ias/ci/pfs/2002-11-15/
- EDAP: www.xbrl.org/taxonomy/int/fr/ias/ci/edap/2002-11-15/
- GCD: www.xbrl.org/Taxonomy/int/br/common/gcd/2002-10-15/
- AR: www.xbrl.org/taxonomy/int/br/rpt/ar/2002-10-15/

The following is a summary of taxonomy status:

- PFS Recommendation
- EDAP Public Working Draft
- GCD Public Working Draft
- AR Public Working Draft[12]

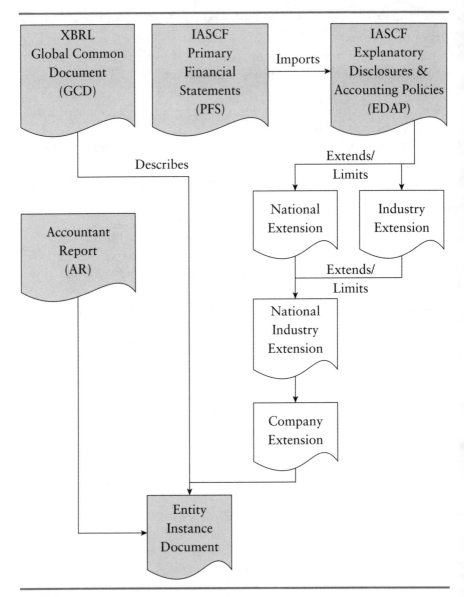

EXHIBIT 13.1 IRS XBRL Framework

Source: Copyright © 2002 XBRL International. IASC Foundation and XBRL International, "International Accounting Standards Expressed in XBRL for Electronic Financial Reporting," http://www.xbrl.org/taxonomy/int/fr/ias/.

ENDNOTES

1. This section references the International Accounting Standards Board, "International Financial Reporting Standards (IFRS)," adopted April 2001, www.iasb.org/standards/index.asp.
2. BearingPoint White Paper, "IFRS Conversion and Finance Transformation with the Rapid Accounting Conversion Methodology (RAC)," 2003.
3. BearingPoint White Paper, "IFRS Conversion and Finance Transformation with the Rapid Accounting Conversion Methodology (RAC)," 2003.
4. Thomas Kostigen, "Accounting Match: U.S. vs. the World," *MarketWatch*, October 13, 2005.
5. Nicholas Neveling, "Cox's Tough Approach May Influence Europe," *Accountancy Age*, Aug. 9, 2005.
6. Thomas Kostigen, "Accounting Match: U.S. vs. the World," *MarketWatch*, October 13, 2005.
7. PriceWaterhouseCoopers White Paper, "Similarities and Differences: A Comparison of IFRS and US GAAP," October 2004.
8. XBRL home web page: www.xbrl.org.
9. www.sec.gov/rules/proposed/33-8496.htm.
10. www.sec.gov/ rules/concept/33-8497.htm.
11. IASC Foundation and XBRL International, "International Accounting Standards Expressed in XBRL for Electronic Financial Reporting," www.xbrl.org/taxonomy/int/fr/ias/.
12. IASC Foundation (www.iascf.com/), and XBRL International (www.xbrl.org/Home/).

CHAPTER 14

Compliance and Internal Controls Impact on Outsourcing[1]

The trend to outsource key business and technical processes will create challenges in regulatory compliance and improving internal controls. There is no Securities and Exchange Commission (SEC), Organization for Economic Cooperation and Development (OECD), or European Union (EU) definition of what constitutes outsourcing, but most agree that it is an activity transferred to a third party that would otherwise be administered and processed internally. Outsourcing to a third-party service provider does not remove the responsibility to certify the viability of the outsourced process. In determining if an outsourced process needs to be audited, the following questions should be asked:

- Does the outsourced process have an impact on your financials?
- Is there evidence that the service provider has conducted the needed risk assessments?
- Is there evidence that the service provider has in place effective internal controls?
- Is there a means to monitor changes to their internal controls that affect your financials?

There are two primary options to certify the outsourced process:

1. Certify the process using your internal or external auditors. It may make sense to audit a service provider if you have substantial

control over its outsourced processes. In these cases, the audit may be looked at as an extension of your normal audit procedures. Put such audit provisions in your contractual agreements with this type of service provider.

2. Rely on the audits provided by the service provider using a Statement of Auditing Standards No. 70 (SAS 70) conducted by its auditor. Auditing certain types of service provider may be impractical in situations where it has many customers seeking various data regarding its internal control.

The SAS 70 has been embraced domestically and internationally as an acceptable auditing standard. SOX Section 404 accepts SAS 70, which was developed by the American Institute of Certified Public Accountants (AICPA). An SAS 70 audit typically addresses critical metrics such as completeness, accuracy, and timeliness of internal control processes and activities. Leading service providers will come to see an SAS 70 as a competitive advantage to demonstrate the quality of their internal controls.

There are two types of SAS 70 audit reports:

1. Type I covers internal controls for a specific point in time.
2. Type II covers a minimum period of six months.

Potential issues with the use of SAS 70 include:

- Is there a timing discrepancy between SAS 70 report and year-end financial reporting?
- The six-month period required for Type II testing could frustrate the meeting of compliance deadlines.
- Conducting quarterly audits avoids the deadline issues with Type II SAS 70 reports, but adds additional audit costs.
- A service provider with the same auditor as its customer could present a conflict of interest. In such situations, the SEC still permits the customer to rely on the SAS 70 Type II from the service provider. However, if the user organization were to engage its audit firm to prepare the SAS 70 Type II report on the service provider, it would be unable to rely on it for purposes of assessing internal control over financial reporting.

In July 2004, the AICPA stated that an SAS 70 was only required when an outsourced activity was part of a company's information system. An SAS 70 is not required for service providers who are performing transactions authorized by the client, such as check account transaction processing by a bank or the execution of securities transactions by a broker. You must mutually agree with your service providers as to what constitutes an outsourced activity, that an SAS 70 will be required, and the nature and timing of the SAS 70.[2]

ENDNOTES

1. This section extensively references and quotes the SAS 70 web site, www.SAS70.com.
2. *In Our Opinion*, The Newsletter of the AICPA Audit and Attest Standards Group, 20:3 Summer 2004.

CHAPTER 15

Civil and Criminal Penalties for Noncompliance

U.S. PENALTIES

The attitudes toward white-collar crime have fundamentally changed. Before the major scandals of the 1990s, white-collar criminals were typically given probation or shorter jail times in minimum security facilities that many equated to country clubs. The fact that most white-collar criminals are white males invited charges of racism. Society seemed to be more fearful of ethnic minorities committing individual blue-collar and violent crimes than of white males who caused financial ruin to several million small investors and thousands of employees.

The massive financial losses from infamous scandals changed this notion, hopefully forever. Many of the victims lost their long-term jobs and life savings. The financial hurt was so great, that the overwhelming sentiment became to prosecute white-collar criminals to the fullest extent possible. Prosecutors have been quick to see the changing political winds and see vigorous prosecutions as a great way to advance their political careers and agendas.

Those who think that the prosecution of corporate wrongdoers is only a passing fad need only read the almost nonstop press coverage of indictments, prosecutions, and convictions. During the press conference announcing the indictment of Kenneth Lay, former CEO of Enron, speakers from the Securities and Exchange Commission (SEC), Justice Department, and the Internal Revenue Service (IRS) delighted in assuring the investment community that no one was above the law. Mr. Lay is facing over 175 years in prison and, by his own account, billions of dollars in litigation. His trial is scheduled to begin in early 2006.

Curt Anderson, in an *Associated Press*, July 13, 2004, article, "Corporate Fraud Convictions Mounting," reported that "Although juries have yet to speak in many cases, Justice Department officials and legal experts say the high-profile crackdown coupled with new laws making chief executive officers personally liable for malfeasance have had a significant deterrent effect. 'Before Enron, it was a rare occurrence when a CEO of any good-sized corporation was prosecuted criminally,' said Robert Mintz, a former federal prosecutor who now oversees securities litigation at a New Jersey law firm. 'I do think these corporate prosecutions have forever changed the corporate landscape.' The task force has prosecuted more than 700 people and obtained more than 300 convictions or guilty pleas, according to the most recent figures available from the Justice Department. A handful of acquittals and mistrials have resulted, and more than 300 investigations still are under way."[1]

A summary of some of the more infamous scandals and resulting prosecutions, include:

- **WorldCom:** In June 2005, a U.S. Federal Judge announced a settlement in which investors will receive over $6 billion in settlements. The massive accounting fraud settlement will go to over 800,000 investors who held stocks or bonds in the telecommunications company around the time of its collapse in 2002. The judge noted that the settlements were "of historic proportions. Given the risks that would have been inherent in proceeding with the trial and any appeals, the settlement amount that will be allocated to the Securities Act claims is more than reasonable." The payouts will be funded by the long list of defendants in the case including investment banks, audit firms, and former directors of WorldCom. The largest part of the payout will come from Citigroup ($2.58 billion) and JP Morgan Chase ($2.0 billion). These and other firms underwrote or traded in WorldCom and are charged with inadequate due diligence in detecting the massive fraud. Plaintiff attorneys had reached settlement deals independently with defendants over the last year but needed the judge's approval to begin collecting payments. WorldCom executives are charged with making billions of dollars in financial statement adjustments to mislead investors. WorldCom's former CEO Bernard Ebbers was convicted in 2005 of fraud and sentenced to 25 years in prison. As part of the settlement, Ebbers will give up many of his personal assets.[2]

- **Tyco:** In September 2005, Former CEO Dennis Kozlowski was sentenced to eight and one-third years to 25 years in prison for stealing hundreds of millions of dollars from the company. Former CFO, Mark Swartz, was also convicted and received the same sentence. Both men are eligible for parole in eight years and four months. Both must pay a total of $134 million in restitution. Each received fines as follows: Kozlowski $70 million and Swartz $35 million.[3]

- **Adelphia:** In June 2005, John Rigas was sentenced to 15 years in prison for his role in looting the cable giant Adelphia Communications Corp. The scandal drove Adelphia into bankruptcy. Timothy Rigas, John's son, was also convicted of bank fraud, securities fraud, and conspiracy, and received a 20-year prison sentence.[4]

- **HealthSouth:** In March 2005, Richard Scrushy, the founder and former CEO of HealthSouth Corp., was acquitted of all charges related to a $2.7 billion earnings overstatement. Scrushy was the first CEO charged under SOX—accused of corporate fraud. Prosecutors developed their case from confessions of Scrushy's CFO and other company executives. Scrushy, in turn, blamed his subordinates for the fraud—including all five of his former CFOs. Indeed, former HealthSouth CFO Bill Owens was sentenced to five years in prison and two years of supervised probation for his role. Since 2003, 15 former HealthSouth executives have pleaded guilty. Scrushy stepped down from HealthSouth's board in December 2005 and asked the firm to pay his $25 million legal fees.[5]

- **Time Warner:** In March 2005, the SEC announced a settlement with Time Warner Inc., the world's largest media company. Time Warner agreed to pay $300 million to settle federal fraud charges for overstating its number of Internet subscribers and its online advertising revenues. As part of the settlement, the company will also restate its financial results from 2000 to 2002, reducing its revenues by $500 million.[6]

■ **Fannie Mae:** In March 2005, Fannie Mae, the largest U.S. buyer of home mortgages, previously accused by regulators of manipulating earnings, disclosed that it will miss its filing deadlines for 2004 and may have to report an additional loss of $2.4 billion. Fannie Mae also acknowledged the discovery of falsified signatures raising the possibility of criminal activity by company employees. The SEC has ordered Fannie Mae to restate its earnings back to 2001—an $8.4 billion correction, erasing nearly one-third of the company's profit since 2001. These events will bring the total potential loss from the restatements to over $10 billion.[7]

Such prosecutions are an excellent way for attorneys general and other officials to advance their political careers as well. Eliot Spitzer, New York's attorney general, is the most notable example, and Oklahoma's attorney general has handed down felony fraud indictments against WorldCom executives as well as senior and middle managers, down five levels in the organization. This has ominous overtones in signaling that lower-level managers will not be exempt from felony prosecution for various jurisdictions. Each WorldCom defendant faces up to 10 years in prison and may face similar actions from other states who feel their pension funds were severely hurt.

CFO.com provides a presentation by Crowe, Chizek, and Company of the criminal penalties for various violations, shown in Exhibit 15.1.

SOX provides protection for whistleblowers within an organization. Stephen Taub, in the June 10, 2004, edition of CFO.com, notes that over 80% of the 228 claims filed as of April have been dismissed. Two of the most frequently cited reasons for the dismissals are that the retaliation claimed occurred before the act became effective and that the claims must be filed no later than 90 days from the date of the retaliation. However, this is early in the process. The main point is that employees will probably not ignore clear violations in the future. Even though C-level executives are typically targeted by the SEC, lower-level managers are not exempt from civil litigation, state, and federal prosecutions.[8] The Scrushy acquittal and convictions of several lower level financial executives also sends a chilling message that CEOs are going to continue to build their defenses by blaming financial subordinates. This is bound to encourage lower level managers to blow the whistle rather than remain silent.

EXHIBIT 15.1   Criminal Penalties for Financial Fraud

Action	Punishment	Reference
"Knowingly" altering, destroying, or falsifying documents in an effort to impede, obstruct, or influence an investigation	Fines up to $15 million and/or imprisonment up to 20 years	Title VIII, Sec. 802
Securities fraud	Fines and/or imprisonment up to 25 years	Title VIIII, Sec. 807
Mail and wire fraud	Imprisonment up to 20 years	Title IX, Sec. 903
"Willfully" certifying financial reports that do not meet regulatory requirements	Fines up to $5 million and/or imprisonment up to 20 years	Title IX, Sec. 906
Violating SEC regulations	May be ineligible to hold a director or officer level position at any publicly traded company	Title XI, Sec. 1105

Source: CFO Roundtable: Section 404—Eve of Implementation, February 12, 2004.

Paul Mickly, writing in the April 8, 2005, issue of the *Washington Business Journal,* "Private cos. not off the hook for Sarbanes-Oxley," notes that the whistleblower protection of SOX applies to private companies as well as public companies and that nearly half of U.S. states are considering smaller versions of SOX that will expand whistleblower protection.[9] SOX creates civil and criminal penalties for retaliation against whistleblowers. The civil provision has produced a wave of litigation, with more than 300 charges filed since July 2002.

In some respects, SOX's civil whistleblower provisions are narrowly tailored: It protects only people who were employed by or otherwise working for publicly traded companies. Significantly, an administrative law judge has ruled that the civil provision applies to employees of private companies that are subsidiaries of publicly held companies, and the civil remedy applies to "contractors and subcontractors" of publicly traded companies, regardless of whether the contractors and subcontractors are themselves publicly traded. (Alleged reprisal against employees of Arthur Andersen, a subcontractor to Enron, helped spur enactment of Sarbanes-Oxley.)

The parallel criminal provision sweeps far more broadly: "Whoever knowingly, with the intent to retaliate, takes any action harmful to any person, including interference with the lawful employment or livelihood of any person, for providing to a law enforcement officer any truthful information relating to the commission or possible commission of any federal offense, shall be fined under this title [$250,000] or imprisoned for not more than 10 years, or both." The provision may apply to any person in any sector of the economy, whether associated with a public company or a private one.[10]

Corporate officials might, at first blush, conclude this statute is unlikely to affect their personnel decisions because, historically, criminal enforcement of such a provision is relatively uncommon. But the reach of the law is so broad and the opportunity for ambitious prosecutors to make a name for themselves so clear that one dare not ignore the potential for criminal liability. And in some jurisdictions, private civil claims may be fashioned under the theory of "wrongful discharge" in violation of public policy.

The potential for mischief is great. Employees anticipating that they will suffer adverse action in their employment can effectively preempt the process by reporting some element of truthful information about any matter governed by federal law and effectively be insulated because of the company's apprehension over the prospect of criminal sanctions or possibly wrongful discharge litigation.

The SEC has provided a limited safe harbor from public and private claims because of the requirement to file 8-K forms in only four days. Some of the safe harbor items include:

- "Item 1.01 Entry into a Material Definitive Agreement
- Item 1.02 Termination of a Material Definitive Agreement
- Item 2.03 Creation of a Direct Financial Obligation or an Obligation under an Off-Balance Sheet Arrangement of a Registrant
- Item 2.04 Triggering Events that Accelerate or Increase a Direct Financial Obligation under an Off-Balance Sheet Arrangement
- Item 2.05 Costs Associated with Exit or Disposal Activities"

To quote the SEC's final ruling: "The safe harbor only applies to a failure to file a report on Form 8-K. Thus, material misstatements or omissions in a Form 8-K will continue to be subject to Section 10(b) and Rule 10b-5 liability."[11]

Compliance Week reports that SOX whistleblower provisions are creating conflicts with local privacy protection laws. Many companies are running into conflicts between SOX and the European Union's (EU's) Data Protection Act of 1998 and legislation in France and Germany. There are concerns that data required to support SOX Section 404 and SOX whistleblower provisions will expose individuals in areas of the world in which individual freedoms are not guaranteed.[12]

Beyond SOX and SEC regulations, other U.S. regulations impose severe penalties:

- **Health Insurance Portability and Accountability Act (HIPAA)—** HIPPA imposes severe penalties for the wrongful disclosure of individual health information with fines up to $50,000 and one year in prison. If the offense is committed under false pretenses, the fines can reach $100,000 and five years in prison. If the "offense is committed with intent to sell, transfer, or use individually identifiable health information for commercial advantage, personal gain, or malicious harm," the fines can reach $250,000 and 10 years in prison.[13]

- **Gramm-Leach-Bliley Act of 1999 (GLBA)**—"Violations are processed via civil actions with the U.S. Attorney General and include the following: the financial institution shall be subject to a civil penalty of not more than $100,000 for each such violation" and "the officers and directors of the financial institution shall be subject to, and shall be personally liable for, a civil penalty of not more than $10,000 for each such violation."[14]

EU AND OECD PENALTIES

The EU has been slow to address corruption and fraud, which is ironic given that its mission, since its inception in the 1950s, has been to safeguard competition and ensure open and free markets. Reasons for the slowness include the perception that corruption has not been viewed as a major problem by many member states, that it has been difficult to tackle, and that high-level political corruption has made it difficult to combat in some countries.[15]

The EU's powers were widened significantly in the 1980s with the Single Act and the Maastricht Treaty, and the EU used this power to address fraud and corruption because they were seen as damaging international trade and were contrary to the EU's spending of vast sums of money for purposes of external assistance and development.

All EU Member States participated actively in anticorruption discussions in the OECD since the late 1980s. The 40-nation Council of Europe has adopted a comprehensive program against corruption and drafted a detailed criminal law convention in its governmental committee. The results of these activities are the following conventions:

The OECD Convention on Combating Bribery of Foreign Public Officials in International Business Transactions

It has been ratified by all the major European countries, Argentina, Australia, Brazil, Canada, Chile, Japan, Korea, Mexico, and the United States. It went into effect in January 1999 and requires signatory countries to pass implementing legislation making it a crime to "offer, promise, or give any undue pecuniary advantage, whether directly or through intermediaries, to any foreign public official . . . in order to obtain or retain business or other improper advantage in the conduct of international business." Provisions include bribery in government procurement, environmental issues, tax payments, regulatory matters, and judicial proceedings. The definition of "foreign official" is broad and includes those who control procurement in areas such as energy, transportation, and telecommunications, as well as legislative and judicial officials, officials of international organizations, and government-controlled enterprises. The convention requires "proportionate and dissuasive" criminal penalties, and provides for mutual legal assistance.[16]

Council of Europe Criminal Law Convention

Broader in scope in its approach to bribery and corruption than the OECD Convention, the Criminal Law Convention opened for signature in 1999. The convention aims to harmonize national laws on corruption; it criminalizes practices such as domestic and international bribery, influence trading, and money laundering of illegal proceeds. The convention applies to the private sector in addition to civil servants, judges, and members of Parliament. The Council of Europe represents 44 European states. The Group of States against Corruption (GRECO) will monitor compliance with this Convention.[17]

European Union (EU) Convention on Corruption

The EU Convention on Corruption, adopted in May 1997, provides for prosecution of corruption involving officials of the EU or member states of the EU. Bribes paid outside the EU are considered criminal under this convention, which requires member states to take "measures necessary to ensure that the acts in question are punishable by effective, proportionate and dissuasive penal sanctions, including, in serious cases, penalties involving loss of freedom and providing for extradition." The EU has formed the European Anti-Fraud Office (OLAF) to investigate fraud, corruption, and other illegal activity affecting EU financial interests.[18]

The number of notorious scandals has been smaller in Europe than in the United States and the prosecutions are in their early phases, but they demonstrate the interdependencies among the United States and EU businesses, banks, and independent auditors. The two most famous EU scandals are Parmalat and Ahold:

Parmalat

In a *Bonds News* report, "Parmalat keeps US bankruptcy shield, judge says," the Italian dairy giant, Parmalat, "filed for bankruptcy in December 2003 after collapsing under about 14 billion euros ($18.1 billion) of debt. . . . Enrico Bondi, Parmalat's administrator and now its chief executive, has sued about 50 banks over the collapse, including Citigroup and Bank of America Corp., for $10 billion each and has also sued former auditors Grant Thornton and Deloitte & Touche. A New Jersey state appeals court rejected Citigroup's attempt to throw out its lawsuit. Citigroup, the world's largest bank, which says it lost more than 500 million euros ($648 million) from Parmalat's fraud, has sued Bondi, accusing him of fraud and negligent misrepresentation in his capacity as Parmalat's representative.[19]

Ahold

Ahold is the third largest food distributor in the world. At the time that it broke into the headlines, Ahold represented the largest scandal in Europe's history. The stock lost two thirds of its value when the scandal broke. Ironically, the scandal stemmed from accounting irregularities from a U.S. subsidiary, US Foodservice, which overstated its income by more than $880 million between 2001 and 2002. US Foodservice appears to have booked vendor allowances as income before they were received. In some cases, they were never received. Dutch and U.S. regulators have ongoing investigations and several U.S. law firms have filed suits claiming Ahold misled investors. Ahold now faces debts of around 12.5 billion euros.[20]

ENDNOTES

1. Curt Anderson, "Corporate Fraud Convictions Mounting," *Associated Press,* July 13, 2004.
2. "Judge Orders $6.1B Returned to Investors in WorldCom Case," NewsMax.com Wires, Sept. 21, 2005.
3. "Ex Tyco Execs Get Prison Terms," NewsMax.com, September 19, 2005.
4. "Adelphia Head, Son Sentenced in Fraud Case," NewsMax.com Wires, June 21, 2005.
5. "Time Warner to Pay $300M to Settle Charges," NewsMax.com Wires, March 21, 2005.
6. "Time Warner to Pay $300M to Settle Charges," NewsMax.com Wires, March 21, 2005.
7. "Fannie Mae Regulators Find Falsified Signatures," NewsMax. com Wires, March 18, 2005.
8. www.CFO.com.
9. Paul Mickly, "Private Cos. Not Off the Hook for Sarbanes-Oxley," *Washington Business Journal,* April 8, 2005.
10. Section 806 of the SOX, 18 U.S.C. 1514A.
11. SEC Final Rule, Additional Form 8-K Disclosure Requirements, and Acceleration of Filing Date, 17 CFR PARTS 228, 229, 230, 239, 240 and 249, RELEASE NOS. 33-8400; 34-49424; File No. S7-22-02, RIN 3235-AI47.
12. Stephen Taub, "Multinational Corporations Find SOX Is Conflicting With Local Laws," *Compliance Week,* Sept. 2005.
13. Public Law 104-191, Aug. 21, 1996, Health Insurance Portability and Accountability Act of 1996, Public Law 104-191, 104th Congress.
14. Gramm-Leach-Bliley Act, 15 USC, Subchapter I, Sec. 6801-6809, Disclosure of Nonpublic Personal Information.
15. Stephen Grey, "Tackling fraud and mismanagement in the European Union," Centre for European Reform.
16. OECD Convention on Combating Bribery of Foreign Public Officials in International Business Transactions, November 21 1997.

17. Council of Europe, Criminal Law Convention on Corruption, CETS No.: 173, Opening for Signature Entry into Force, Strasbourg, January 27, 1999.

18. Commission of the European Communities, Com(2003) 317 Final, Communication from the Commission to the Council, the European Parliament and the European Economic and Social Committee on a Comprehensive EU Policy Against Corruption, Brussels, May 28, 2003.

19. Jonathan Stempel, "Parmalat Keeps US Bankruptcy Shield, Judge Says," *Bonds News,* May 5, 2005.

20. *The Economist,* "A Dutch Crown Jewel Tarnished," Feb. 28, 2003.

CHAPTER 16

Business Penalties for Noncompliance: A Material Weakness

Marie Leone, in CFO.com, describes that a material weakness is considered more severe than a "control deficiency" or a "significant deficiency" by the Public Company Accounting Oversight Board (PCOAB) and creates "a more than remote" chance that a material misstatement will not be prevented or detected" in a company's financial statements. Disclosure of a material weakness often leads to short-term share price volatility, attracts scrutiny from regulators, and even invites shareholder lawsuits.[1] Though companies have long been required to disclose control weaknesses, the annual testing demanded by SOX Section 404 leaves executives with little opportunity to plead ignorance and makes disclosures more likely.[2]

Between November 2004 and March 2006, more than 500 companies have disclosed a control weakness in Securities and Exchange Commission (SEC) filings, of which over half were material weaknesses, according to research by Lehigh University accounting professor Parveen Gupta. The numbers seem to be rising: In a separate analysis, *Compliance Week* concluded that, during October 2004, 63 companies reported a material weakness in an SEC filing, compared with 20 such disclosures in February 2004.[3]

What's more, analysts from Moody's Investors Service expect that many companies will report material weaknesses during the upcoming annual report season. Moody's adds that some of those disclosures could lead to credit rating reviews and perhaps downgrades, which raises the cost of capital for the affected companies.

Moody's officials, however, are quick to quiet panicky speculation. "We've heard stories about investors and credit agencies overreacting to material-weakness charges," says vice president and senior analyst Michael Doss. Though the ratings firm anticipates problems during the first year of compliance with Section 404, Doss says that Moody's divides material weaknesses into two degrees of severity and only the more severe cases will be in deep trouble.

Category A material weaknesses, according to Moody's, are control problems with specific transaction-level processes such as tax accrual, bad debt reserves, and impairment charges. These require attention, but Doss maintains that external auditors can effectively audit around them and deliver an unqualified opinion of the financial statements.

Auditors, however, cannot circumvent the rarer Category B material weaknesses. These offenses can derail an organization, stresses Doss, because they represent company-level control problems such as ineffective control environments, audit committees, and financial reporting processes, encompassing everything from a lax code of conduct, to feeble fraud prevention guidelines, to poor attempts at assigning executive responsibility.[4]

A company that reports a material weakness may feel the effect on its share price, says Paisley Consulting executive Tim Leech, a former head of forensic accounting for Coopers & Lybrand Consulting. Leech, who is working with Gupta on an upcoming study of material weakness disclosures, thinks the professor's final numbers will reveal a percentage decrease in the share price averaging in the low single digits.

Leech warns, however, of additional negative effects if investors assume that the disclosure is proof that management was concealing material information rather than fumbling through an accounting mistake. In such a case, he adds, a disclosure could affect directors' and officers' insurance, making coverage more restrictive and more costly.[5]

What about the timing of a material weakness disclosure? Finance executives must strike a delicate balance, says Mary Ann Jorgenson, an attorney with law firm Squire Sanders. Balanced against the disclosure imperative, says Jorgenson, are many shifting factors. For instance, releasing premature findings that require further adjustments could expose a company to fresh charges from shareholder plaintiffs with each correction.[6]

On the brighter side, none of the experts Marie Leone of CFO.com spoke to believes that the effects of Section 404 pose a long-term issue, except, of course, in the case of material weaknesses that are themselves severe enough to bring down a company.[7]

Stephen Taub, in CFO.com, highlighted the costs of poor internal controls as evidenced by the filing of a material weakness under SOX. According to an analysis conducted by the Netherlands-based research firm A.R.C. Morgan:

- Nearly two thirds of CFOs resigned or were forced out within three months.
- Over 85% of the material weaknesses were discovered by external auditors.
- Less than 15% of material weaknesses were discovered by management or consultants as part of their compliance projects.
- Over half of the internal control weaknesses were related to fraud.
- More than 65% of the filers that disclosed material weaknesses subsequently restated their earnings, "causing significant shareholder impact."
- Auditor fees typically grew by 150% when a material weakness was uncovered compared with between 30% and 50% percent for companies without a material weakness.[8]

The bigger cost is a loss of investor confidence. In the emerging global market, investors will reward companies with strong compliance results and punish those with poor compliance results. Ironically, investors seem to have given companies the benefit of doubt in resolving material weaknesses. In spite of predictions about a major negative impact on share prices, most companies have not been seriously impacted by material weaknesses. It appears that investors will tolerate material weaknesses as long as a company can show that it is making good faith efforts and showing progress.

A major factor in investors' patience is the admission by the SEC that many material weaknesses and restatements have stemmed from overly complex accounting rules. Another factor is that the first two years of complying with U.S. SOX has compelled a major cleanup in accounting practices. The resulting material weaknesses have not typically exposed fraud or major errors, or given investors reason to invest elsewhere.

ENDNOTES

1. Marie Leone, "Where a Material Weakness Really Matters," CFO.com, Nov. 18, 2004.
2. Alix Nyberg Stuart, "Raising Red Flags," CFO.com, Sept. 1, 2004.
3. Marie Leone, "Where a Material Weakness Really Matters," CFO.com, Nov. 18, 2004.
4. Marie Leone, "Where a Material Weakness Really Matters," CFO.com, Nov. 18, 2004.
5. Tim Leach, "Regulatory Revolution Risks Civil War," *Algo Research Quarterly Magazine*, 5:2, Summer 2002.
6. Marie Leone, "Where Material Weaknesses Really Matter," CFO.com, November 18, 2004.
7. Marie Leone, "Where Material Weaknesses Really Matter," CFO.com, November 18, 2004.
8. Stephen Taub, "How a Material Weakness Can Cost You," CFO.com, November 19, 2004.

CHAPTER 17

Revenue Recognition Requirements: U.S. SAB 101 and 104

According to the Committee of Sponsoring Organizations (COSO), half of all corporate fraud relates to revenue issues.[1] Revenue recognition has been one of the largest causes of material weaknesses and financial restatements since the enactment of the Sarbanes-Oxley Act of 2002 (SOX). Recent rulings and guidance by various regulatory agencies do not appear to have helped much.

The Securities and Exchange Commission (SEC) issued Staff Accounting Bulletin (SAB) 101 in 1999[2] and SAB 104 in 2003[3] to provide guidance to auditors and public companies on recognizing, presenting, and disclosing revenue in financial statements. SABs 101 and 104 spell out the criteria for revenue recognition based on existing accounting rules, which say that companies should not recognize revenue until it is realized or realizable and earned.

Specifically, SABs 101 and 104 argue that transactions must meet the following criteria before revenue is recognized:

- There is persuasive evidence of an arrangement.
- Delivery has occurred or services have been rendered.
- The seller's price to the buyer is fixed or determinable.
- Collectability is reasonably assured.

The following are SEC examples and criteria of Revenue Recognition:

Persuasive Evidence of an Arrangement: SAB 104 Example

"*Facts:* Company A has product available to ship to customers prior to the end of its current fiscal quarter. Customer Beta places an order for the product, and Company A delivers the product prior to the end of its current fiscal quarter. Company A's normal and customary business practice for this class of customer is to enter into a written sales agreement that requires the signatures of the authorized representatives of the Company and its customer to be binding. Company A prepares a written sales agreement, and its authorized representative signs the agreement before the end of the quarter. However, Customer Beta does not sign the agreement because Customer Beta is awaiting the requisite approval by its legal department. Customer Beta's purchasing department has orally agreed to the sale and stated that it is highly likely that the contract will be approved the first week of Company A's next fiscal quarter.

Question: May Company A recognize the revenue in the current fiscal quarter for the sale of the product to Customer Beta when (1) the product is delivered by the end of its current fiscal quarter and (2) the final written sales agreement is executed by Customer Beta's authorized representative within a few days after the end of the current fiscal quarter?

Interpretive Response: No. Generally the staff believes that, in view of Company A's business practice of requiring a written sales agreement for this class of customer, persuasive evidence of an arrangement would require a final agreement that has been executed by the properly authorized personnel of the customer. In the staff's view, Customer Beta's execution of the sales agreement after the end of the quarter causes the transaction to be considered a transaction of the subsequent period. Further, if an arrangement is subject to subsequent approval (e.g., by the management committee or board of directors) or execution of another agreement, revenue recognition would be inappropriate until that subsequent approval or agreement is complete. Customary business practices and processes for documenting sales transactions vary among companies and industries."[4]

Delivery Has Occurred or Services Have Been Rendered: SAB 104 Example

"Facts: Company A receives purchase orders for products it manufactures. At the end of its fiscal quarters, customers may not yet be ready to take delivery of the products for various reasons. These reasons may include, but are not limited to, a lack of available space for inventory, having more than sufficient inventory in their distribution channel or delays in customers' production schedules.

Question: May Company A recognize revenue for the sale of its products once it has completed manufacturing if it segregates the inventory of the products in its own warehouse from its own products? May Company A recognize revenue for the sale if it ships the products to a third-party warehouse but (1) Company A retains title to the product and (2) payment by the customer is dependent upon ultimate delivery to a customer-specified site?

Interpretative Response: Generally, no. The staff believes that delivery generally is not considered to have occurred unless the customer has taken title and assumed the risks and rewards of ownership of the products specified in the customer's purchase order or sales agreement. Typically this occurs when a product is delivered to the customer's delivery site (if the terms of the sale are FOB destination) or when a product is shipped to the customer (if the terms are FOB shipping point)."

Delivery Has Occurred or Services Have Been Rendered: SAB 104 Criteria

"1. The risks of ownership must have passed to the buyer;
2. The customer must have made a fixed commitment to purchase the goods, preferably in written documentation;
3. The buyer, not the seller, must request that the transaction be on a bill and hold basis. The buyer must have a substantial business purpose for ordering the goods on a bill and hold basis;
4. There must be a fixed schedule for delivery of the goods. The date for delivery must be reasonable and must be consistent with the buyer's business purpose (e.g., storage periods are customary in the industry);
5. The seller must not have retained any specific performance obligations such that the earning process is not complete;

6. *The ordered goods must have been segregated from the seller's inventory and not be subject to being used to fill other orders; and*
7. *The equipment [product] must be complete and ready for shipment."*

Seller's Price to the Buyer Is Fixed or Determinable: SAB 104 Example

"Facts: Company M is a discount retailer. It generates revenue from annual membership fees it charges customers to shop at its stores and from the sale of products at a discount price to those customers. The membership arrangements with retail customers require the customer to pay the entire membership fee (e.g., $35) at the outset of the arrangement. However, the customer has the unilateral right to cancel the arrangement at any time during its term and receive a full refund of the initial fee. Based on historical data collected over time for a large number of homogeneous transactions, Company M estimates that approximately 40% of the customers will request a refund before the end of the membership contract term. Company M's data for the past five years indicates that significant variations between actual and estimated cancellations have not occurred, and Company M does not expect significant variations to occur in the foreseeable future.

Question: May Company M recognize in earnings the revenue for the membership fees and accrue the costs to provide membership services at the outset of the arrangement?

Interpretive Response: No. In the staff's view, it would be inappropriate for Company M to recognize the membership fees as earned revenue upon billing or receipt of the initial fee with a corresponding accrual for estimated costs to provide the membership services. This conclusion is based on Company M's remaining and unfulfilled contractual obligation to perform services (i.e., make available and offer products for sale at a discounted price) throughout the membership period. Therefore, the earnings process, irrespective of whether a cancellation clause exists, is not complete. In addition, the ability of the member to receive a full refund of the membership fee up to the last day of the membership term raises an uncertainty as to whether the fee is fixed or determinable at any point before the end of the term. Generally, the staff believes that a sales price is not fixed or determinable when a customer has the unilateral right to terminate or cancel the contract and receive a cash refund. A sales price or fee that is variable until the occurrence of *future events (other than product returns that are within the scope of Statement 48) generally is not fixed or determinable until the future event occurs. The revenue from such transactions should not be recognized in earnings until the sales price or fee becomes fixed or determinable. Moreover, revenue should not be recognized in earnings by assessing the probability that significant but unfulfilled terms of a contract will be fulfilled at some point in the future. Accordingly, the revenue from such transactions should not be recognized in earnings prior to the refund privileges expiring. The amounts received from customers or subscribers (i.e., the $35 fee mentioned above) should be credited to a monetary liability account such as customers' refundable fees."*

Nontraditional Business Models and Revenue Recognition: SAB 101

"For companies that do not employ traditional business models, such as e-commerce companies and companies with a large percentage of Internet transactions, however, SAB 101 provides additional guidance on these revenue recognition issues:

- *Timing of approval for sales agreements*
- *"Side" arrangements to the master contract*
- *Consignment/financing arrangements*
- *Criteria for delivery (bill and hold sale)*
- *Layaway programs*
- *Nonrefundable, up-front fees*
- *Cancellation or termination provisions*
- *Membership fees/services*
- *Contingent rental income*
- *Right of return"*

DISCLOSURE REQUIREMENTS

According to SABs 101 and 104, "companies should disclose changes in estimated product returns in financial statements if material and MD&A should note the following:

- A favorable or unfavorable material effect on revenue
- The relationship between revenue and costs of revenue

- Analysis of reasons and factors for an increase or decrease in revenue
- A gain or loss from the sale of an asset(s)"

Accounting Principles Board (APB) Opinion No. 2 states that "Transactions the SEC staff specifically has said companies should disclose or discuss because they may contain problem areas are:

- Product shipments at the end of a reporting period that significantly reduce customer backlog and might be expected to result in fewer shipments and lower revenue in the next period.
- Extended payment terms that will result in a longer collection period for accounts receivable (regardless of whether the revenue has been recognized) and slower cash inflows from operations, and the effect on liquidity and capital resources. (The fair value of trade receivables should be disclosed in the footnotes to the financial statements when it does not approximate the carrying amount.)
- Changing trends in shipments into, and sales from, a sales channel or separate customer class that could be expected to significantly affect future sales or returns.
- More sales to a different class of customer, such as a reseller distribution channel that has a lower gross profit margin than existing sales principally made to end users. Also, increasing service revenue that has a higher profit margin than product sales.
- Seasonal trends or variations in sales.
- A gain or loss from the sale of an asset(s)."[5]

AICPA Example of Hi-tech Manufacturing[6]

Indirect vs. Direct Selling:

"Some high-tech manufacturers sell their products directly to end-users, typically with standard rights of return. Direct consumer sales (and small dollar sales to other end users) usually have relatively standard terms and conditions.

Other manufacturers use a direct sales approach combined with a network of value-added resellers (VARs) and distributors to sell their products to end users. Sales made through distributors, as well as significant single sales (in terms of size to the seller or purchaser), often can have unique, nonstandard terms. It is common for the manufacturer to provide incentives or sales concessions to their VARs and distributors that go beyond the rights of return granted to end users. Many of the incentives and concessions granted to distributors raise revenue recognition issues. The most common of sales concessions include:

- *Price protection agreements*
- *Guaranteed margin agreements*
- *Stock balancing arrangements*
- *Sales subject to sale to the end user*
- *Extended payment terms*
- *Issuance of equity or other equity instruments to customers"*[7]

Bill and Hold Sales:

"It is not uncommon for high-technology companies to enter into bill and hold transactions. In a bill and hold transaction, a customer agrees to purchase the goods but the seller retains physical possession until the customer requests shipment to designated locations. Normally, such an arrangement does not qualify as a sale because delivery has not occurred. Under certain conditions, however, when a buyer has made an absolute purchase commitment and has assumed the risks and rewards of the purchased product but is unable to accept delivery because of a compelling business reason, bill and hold sales may qualify for revenue recognition."

The Move toward Total-Solution Selling and Bundled Sales:

"Many companies in the high-technology manufacturing sector sell standardized products. For example, manufacturers of electronic components, semiconductors, and to a large degree, computer peripherals, are engaged primarily in the design, manufacture, and sale of a product. The product is shipped to a customer, who takes immediate title and bears all the responsibility for installation.

However, other companies (most notably computer manufacturers) are moving toward providing their customers with a total solution, in response to customer need for outsourcing Information Technology (IT) functions and a desire to work with vendors that provide one-stop shopping.

This trend leads to companies migrating from shipping hardware to the customer site and having the customer be responsible for completing the implementation, to the company selling a total solution, which requires installation, customization, and any other services necessary to make the product functional. The customer may not accept the solution until functionality is achieved.

Some entities may not have the resources to provide total solutions but nevertheless may bundle their products together with other products or services. For example, this strategy may be undertaken as a way to increase sales or differentiate the company from its competitors. The bundling of installation or other services with product sales (whether or not these are part of a total solution) can complicate the revenue recognition process, as described in paragraph 3.27."

International Sales:

"Technology manufacturing companies may make sales in non-U.S. legal jurisdictions. The laws in these jurisdictions relating to product sales can vary significantly from U.S. laws. For example, some countries may prohibit the billing for goods until delivery occurs or may have rules regarding transfer of title (for example, title may not transfer until delivery or receipt of payment) that may be significantly different from U.S. rules."[8]

AICPA Example of Software Sales[9]

"Sometimes a company's software resides on its own (or a third party's) hardware and the customer accesses and uses the software as needed over the Internet or on a dedicated line (called 'hosting'). With this type of arrangement, the customer does not necessarily take possession of the software. Depending on the complexity of the software, the arrangement may also include additional services and updates or enhancements. Usually, companies pay an initial fee, followed by additional periodic payments over the life of the arrangement.

Essentially, the arrangements this issue addresses involve two rights:

1. To use the software
2. To store software on the vendor's or third party's hardware.

Arrangements that do not allow customers to take possession of the software at any time during the hosting period without significant penalty (so they can run the software on their own or a third party's hardware) are considered service contracts and fall outside the scope of both this issue and SOP 97-2.

Consensus: The EITF has concluded revenue should be allocated to the software element and hosting element based on vendor-specific evidence of fair value. Revenue should be recognized on the software element when the delivery has occurred and on the hosting element when services are performed."[10]

AICPA Example of Internet Sales[11]

"Many companies sell goods or services over the Internet without stocking the inventory themselves. Instead, they employ independent warehouses to store merchandise and ship to the customer upon request. These companies may also offer services provided by an Internet service provider. Companies choose one of two ways to report revenue. The revenue is recognized:

- At the gross amount charged. The cost of goods sold reflects the cost of the goods or services sold to the customer plus the company's cost of executing the transaction.
- At the net amount (reflecting only the commission or net profit). Then the cost of goods sold reflects only the company's cost of executing the transaction.

Under either method, net income or gross profit is the same. However, companies wishing to maximize revenues to maintain executive compensation or enhance stock price prefer reporting revenue at the gross amount.

Consensus: If the company performs as an agent or broker without assuming the risks and rewards of ownership of the goods, it should report sales on a net basis. The EITF prepared a list of factors or indicators that companies should review in deciding whether to report at gross or net. The task force noted that none of these indicators was presumptive or determinative and that companies should consider the relative strength of each indicator. The EITF Abstract for this issue also includes several examples of the applications of these indicators that should be useful in practice."

Revenue Recognition Questionnaire[12]

"The following questionnaire may be helpful in determining revenue recognition requirements:

Define the business processes that require revenue to be deferred.

When and how is the revenue deferred?
Do you have any criteria (e.g., value) based on which you defer revenue or is it always deferred?
When and how is the revenue recognized? For example, which events trigger revenue to be recognized?
Do you have partial recognition of revenue?
Do you have time based or event based revenue recognition?
Do you defer cost of goods sold and warranty? If yes, how do you recognize them?
Do you review revenue recognition issues for inter-company transactions? If yes, please explain.
What is the revenue recognition process for the returns process?
Do you bill your customers on a specific billing frequency? How do you defer and recognize this revenue?
Is there any section of SAB104 that is applicable to your business? If yes, which one (e.g. sell through) and please explain?"

ENDNOTES

1. COSO, "Fraudulent Financial Reporting: 1987–1997, An Analysis of U.S. Public Companies," March 1999.
2. SEC, 17 CFR Part 211, Staff Accounting Bulletin No. 101, Revenue Recognition in Financial Statements, 1999.
3. SEC, 17 CFR Part 211, Staff Accounting Bulletin No. 104, Revenue Recognition in Financial Statements, 2003.
4. SEC, 17 CFR Part 211, Staff Accounting Bulletin No. 104, Revenue Recognition in Financial Statements, 2003.
5. APB Opinion, No. 2 December 1962, Accounting for the Investment Credit.
6. AICPA Audit Guide, Chapter 3, 2001.
7. AICPA Audit Guide, Chapter 3, 2001.
8. AICPA Audit Guide, Chapter 3, 2001.
9. AICPA Audit Guide, Chapter 3, 2001.
10. AICPA Audit Guide, Chapter 3, 2001.
11. AICPA Audit Guide, Chapter 3, 2001.
12. AICPA Audit Guide, Chapter 3, 2001.

CHAPTER 18

Data Retention Requirements

INTRODUCTION

Data should be archived for a variety of business and regulatory reasons. This means both electronic and physical control of data. A first and primary reason to retain data is the survival of the organization. Electronic data are so critical that data retention must include regular backups with rapid and cost-effective access, plus disaster recovery programs to cover the loss of entire facilities caused by natural and man-made disasters.

A second reason is to provide the necessary data to feed a growing number of business intelligence softwares to develop metrics, and benchmarks upon which to make tactical and strategic decisions. As compliance softwares grow, they will be able to use historical data to improve detective and preventative controls.

A third reason is to comply with regulatory requirements. Data retention requirements vary by country and regulatory agency, but typically range from three years to permanent retention. In the United States, federal and state regulations typically require:

- Business records: 7 years to permanent
- Contracts: 7 years to permanent
- Employee records: 3 years
- Payroll records: 3 to 7 years[1]

SOX SECTION 802

SOX Section 802 requires accountants who audit or review an organization's financial statements to retain certain records relevant to that audit or review. These records include work papers and other documents that form the basis of the audit or review, and memoranda, correspondence, communications, other documents, and records (including electronic records), which are created, sent, or received in connection with the audit or review, and contain conclusions, opinions, analyses, or financial data related to the audit or review. To coordinate with forthcoming auditing standards concerning the retention of audit documentation, the rule requires that these records be retained for seven years after the auditor concludes the audit or review of the financial statements rather than the proposed period of five years from the end of the fiscal period in which an audit or review was concluded. As proposed, the rule addresses the retention of records related to the audits and reviews of not only an organization's financial statements but also the financial statements of registered investment companies. Penalties for violating document requirements include fines up to $5 million and or up to 20 years in jail.[2]

In her article, "Data Retention Regulations: Keeping It Legal," Elizabeth Clark provides an overview of the data retention requirements imposed by the Securities and Exchange Commission (SEC). Clark notes that the SEC's Code of Federal Regulations (CFR) 17a-3 and 17a-4 targets members of the financial services industry. "This rule indicates the type of records that brokers and dealers are required to create, how long they must be stored, and under what media requirements . . . . Depending on the type of record involved, retention periods vary from three years to six or more, and records must be easily accessible for two years."[3]

Clark explains the SEC requirement that records be stored on a nonrewritable, nonerasable medium. "In the past, this basically meant WORM technologies such as optical media, or so-called WORM tape approaches. In 2004, the SEC modified this requirement by announcing that it would accept "WORM-like magnetic-disk storage systems. Some of these products are based on inexpensive Advanced Technology Attachment (ATA) disks that can be used for on-line or near-line storage . . . . Under SEC 17a-3 and 17a-4, the records must also be time-stamped, and copies must be stored in separate locations. In essence, the authenticity, accuracy, and accessibility of these records must be ensured."

HIPAA

The Health Insurance Portability and Accountability Act of 1996 (HIPAA) requires the physical control of paper documents and the control of electronic documents. Clark's 2004 article also provides an overview of the data retention requirements imposed by the HIPAA. The HIPAA "requires that members of the health care industry retain patient information for six years, as well as ensure the confidentiality of these records. Violations can result in fines of up to $250,000 and imprisonment for up to ten years . . . . HIPAA doesn't specify the type of storage media required, but the implications of retaining an increasing number of electronic documents, such as patient files and x-ray images, are substantial."

Clark describes the three levels of data retention that most organizations will want to consider in their data retention protocols:

1. Data that's frequently accessed or that needs to be produced quickly should be stored on line. (On-line storage typically refers to disk-based systems that are available at all times, usually Fibre Channel or SCSI arrays.)
2. Data that's less frequently accessed, or that you're less likely to have to produce quickly, can be stored on near-line media, such as optical systems or tape libraries.
3. Finally, data that's rarely accessed can be stored off line on archived tapes.[4]

Though these are all U.S.-based regulations, they will serve as a model for data retention regulations elsewhere. The threat of litigation may impose a larger requirement. Organizations subject to litigation are going to want to demonstrate that critical data are accessible in a timely and efficient basis.

EUROPEAN UNION

The European Union has struggled with data retention issues for years. Complicating the adoption of regulations are conflicting requirements to fight international terrorism and protect personal privacy. A wide variety of European organizations have consistently opposed the adoption of data retention and surveillance regulations. In July 2002 the EU enacted the Directive on Privacy and Electronic Communications (Directive 2002/58/EC) that permits each member state to adopt laws authorizing data retention. The 2002 Directive reverses the 1997 Telecommunications Privacy Directive by permitting EU member countries to compel telecommunication companies and Internet service providers to store and retain subscribers' communications data. The data retention provision of the new directive was designed to protect personal privacy, but the ability to require ISPs and telecommunications companies to store all data about all of their subscribers invites charges of privacy invasion.[5]

ENDNOTES

1. Mark Lewis, "The Guidelines of Data Retention," SearchStorage .com Site Editor, July 29, 2003.
2. SEC Final Rule: Retention of Records Relevant to Audits and Reviews, 17 CFR Part 210 [Release Nos. 33-8180; 34-47241; IC-25911; FR-66; File No. S7-46-02], RIN 3235-AI74.
3. Elizabeth Clark, "Retention Regulations: Keeping It Legal," *Network Magazine*, March 3, 2004.
4. Elizabeth Clark, "Retention Regulations: Keeping It Legal," *Network Magazine*, March 3, 2004.
5. Directive 2002/58/Ec of the European Parliament and of the Council Concerning the Processing of Personal Data and the Protection of Privacy in the Electronic Communications Sector (Directive on Privacy and Electronic Communications).

CHAPTER 19

Compliance and Internal Control Software

Eric Laursen, writing in CFO.com, referenced a survey by CFO Research services of 180 finance executives showing that automating compliance is a high priority for over three quarters of respondents. The same survey showed that about half of the respondents would "prefer to leverage automated controls with their ERP systems rather than streamline their manual controls, while the margin jumps to 56 percent for respondents who consider automation of compliance and controls to be a top-priority item over the next 12 months." Laursen noted that most executives surveyed see automation as a critical component in making compliance sustainable while seeing compliance as a catalyst for automation.[1]

There have been many evaluations of what has been called Sarbanes-Oxley software. They typically discuss the software tools that facilitate the internal and external auditor process. Unfortunately, this is only one part, albeit an important one, of the compliance process. These reviews do a disservice in failing to point out that the audit tools will support almost all compliance requirements based on a Committee of Sponsoring Organizations (COSO) framework for the management of risk. A second group of software automates the enforcement application and database controls levels with detection, prevention, and monitoring capabilities. Finally, a third group of software supports improved internal controls by improving business processes.

The selection and deployment of any software to support the compliance process will be guided by auditor requirements that these solutions must be in place for a reasonable amount of time in running an organization. While there is no hard and fast rule, 90 days is probably a good general guideline if the software has a significant impact on internal controls. It could be argued that software that adds monitoring and other "nice-to-have" capabilities may not need to be in place for as much time. To relate this to organizations with a calendar year-end, this would mean compliance software should be in place by the end of September. If an organization wants its internal auditors to review the viability of the software before the external auditors arrive, this date could be earlier to meet a year-end requirement.

AUDITOR SUPPORT SOFTWARE

The large majority of organizations are not using software solutions to support the audit process and, instead, rely on MS Office software tools often combined with document management software. These typically include MS Office tools to perform the following processes:

- Questionnaires (Word)
- Narratives (Word)
- Process Flows (Visio)
- Control Matrixes (Excel)
- Testing (Excel or Word)
- Remediation Reports (Excel or Word)

Peter Loftus, reporting in the April 25, 2005, issue of the *Dow Jones Newswires*, asked, "Can technology help companies comply with Sarbanes-Oxley? Here's a look at what helps," and noted AMR Research's estimate that companies will spend over $1.7 billion in 2005 on compliance technology. This works out to about $500,000 in compliance software on average for larger companies. Initially the software will help automate the audit process and will typically be based on a COSO framework, which includes defining business processes, the relative risks associated with each process, the controls required to mitigate the risks, the testing to validate that controls are effective, and the remediation required when controls are found to be ineffective.[2]

The larger Enterprise Resource Planning (ERP) systems have developed their own auditor support software. Point solutions provide the same functionality. These tools will evolve to include detective and preventative controls, automated testing, graphical dashboards, and electronic workflows.

AUTOMATED INTERNAL CONTROL ENFORCEMENT SOFTWARE[3]

Many software solutions are emerging to help to automate the enforcement of internal control to improve corporate governance and compliance. These software solutions can be generalized as providing detection, prevention, and monitoring/visualization with dashboards. There are solutions that provide after-the fact detection only, but this may be inadequate in providing adequate internal controls.

There are three elements to good security management that support efforts to improve internal control. We will use the analogy of a burglar alarm to demonstrate them:

1. **Prevention** is the strong lock on the door.
2. **Detection** is the alarm system which is triggered upon attempted entry and may include monitors to record the activities of the intruder.
3. **Monitoring/Visualization** is the means to identify actual intrusions versus numerous false alarms using dashboards.

Software providers focus on each of the three elements. Some providers offer detection and prevention capabilities. The leaders are moving to offer all three, which are essential in a robust compliance software solution. What follows are the basic elements for each of the three types:

1. Prevention:
   - Automate key data changes within business applications.
   - Secure master-level data, such as customers, suppliers, and items.
   - Ensure data integrity, that data are entered accurately to prevent reporting issues and downstream control problems.
   - Enforce tolerance limits on the number fields to which a user has access.

- Enforce approvals within key process flows and updates, such as application setups, credit limits, and signing limits.
- Enforce segregation of duties (SOD) down to the function and user level.
- Provide change control and system monitoring.
- Prevent assignment of responsibility and function conflicts.
- Prevent unauthorized updates to sensitive setup or transactional data.
- Restrict access to pick lists, pull-down menus, and lists of values by user or responsibility.
- Provide alerts if a violation is attempted as to its time, origin, and nature.

2. Detection:
- Monitor existing responsibility and function conflicts.
- Monitor key data changes within business applications.
- Monitor failed transactions or stuck interface transactions.
- Monitor changes in process controls.
- Report on responsibility and function conflicts.
- Report on control violations, e.g., segregation of duty conflicts.
- Provide a comprehensive audit history at the field level for key data changes, e.g., setups, master data, transactions.

3. Monitoring/Visualization:
- Provide a visual and global dashboard which captures all relevant internal controls.
- Create alerts for the dashboard when out-of-tolerance situations occur such as past due dates, violations of security protocols, and potential material events.
- Provide hierarchical functionality which summarizes alerts at an executive level and permits drill-down navigation for more details as to the origin and nature of the alert.
- Provide alternatives to the popular red light/green light alerts to support users who are visually impaired.[4]

Leading software providers have combined prevention and detection capabilities. Obviously, a strong lock that prevents entry is the most essential element, followed by a means to detect break-ins. In larger organizations with thousands of users creating several thousand transactions on a daily basis, there is a need to feed all these outputs into a user-friendly compliance dashboard which summarizes data and provides concise and visual alerts when problems arise. This type of monitoring is known as a "visualization" solution or "dashboard" and is seen as an essential element by the best compliance solutions.

Interestingly, many of these solutions rely on popular red light/green light graphics as part of their dashboards to alert users to out of tolerance situations, but are sensitive to users who are visually impaired. Section 508 of the U.S. Rehabilitation Act is voluntary at this stage and calls for text backups to graphics. As an example, the text "Green," "Good," and "Pass" would appear in a green field. Another example is to avoid the use of flashing lights within certain frequency ranges due to the danger of causing epileptic seizures.

Fortunately, a number of compliance solutions became available in the last year to help organizations with these compliance efforts. While many solutions fill specific needs, combining solutions is often an effective way to mitigate control issues and prevents the risk of material weakness within an organization.

ADDITIONAL SOFTWARE TO SUPPORT COMPLIANCE

There are a wide variety of software offerings that will enhance compliance in a variety of ways, but have in common their ability to automate and standardize a manual process and provide an electronic audit trail.

Document Management

These tools can provide users with a secure means of communications and can document sharing including access and revision controls and also user groups who are notified when documents are accessed and/or revised.

Event Management

These tools can provide key players with customized workflow notifications and document sharing in a secure environment with clear audit trails. They may support audit controls including the means to document that a process has been certified by each process owner as possessing adequate internal controls. This includes the dates and results of the last audit.

Contract Management

Contract management tools automate the creation and maintenance of contractual agreements, including leasing agreements. This includes publishing and controlling standardized terms and conditions. The controls can include electronic approval workflows for any changes in sales discounts, which have proven to be a major concern in many organizations. A best practice would be to control all agreements with such a tool including electronic approval workflows.

Supplier and Customer Collaboration Portals

Many ERP systems support collaboration portals to transmit, review, accept, or reject sales and purchase orders electronically with time outs and exception flagging. Such a system assures a consistent and efficient process with an audit trail. Leading portals support various levels of technological sophistication depending on the sophistication and volume of transactions. At their simplest, they support a web-based means for users to key in data. At their most complex, they support machine-to-machine communications using EXtensible Markup Language (XML) or Electronic Data Interface (EDI) protocols. A best practice would be to move all purchasing and customer communications over a collaboration portal, which would provide an audit trail.

Product Lifecycle Management (PLM)

PLM tools are emerging to ease the inventory and development pains for product introduction and end-of-life. This can include revision controls, user groups, and workflows for engineering documents and engineering change orders. A best practice would be to use PLM tools to reduce the risk of slow moving and obsolete inventory.

Supplier and Customer Relationship Management

These solutions are known by many names. They can automate and standardize static and dynamic data processes and transactions by using configurable workflows, advanced reporting, and alerts when out-of-tolerance situations occur.

Data Storage and Retention Programs

These tools assure data integrity while enforcing data retention rules. Data can be retained for a defined period. Some newer products even contain a hold button to suspend policy enforcement during periods of regulatory action or civil action enforcement retaining all data if an official investigation or civil litigation is threatened.

Radio Frequency Identification (RFID)

RFID chips provide the ability to track individual assets through the supply chain process while providing more extensive product information than possible with 12-digit bar coding standards that they replace. Effective July 1, 2004, the Patriot Act no longer permitted international shipments to arrive ahead of shipping manifests and packing lists. The same rules are bound to be extended to domestic shipments. RFID adoption has been aggressively promoted by Wal-Mart, the world's largest retailer. RFID chips are passive and low cost and will demonstrate an auditable electronic process that also reduces the cost of inventory control.

Advanced Business Intelligence and Reporting Tools

Advanced business intelligence and reporting tools can provide critical data in a timely manner to support both repetitive activities as well as critical activities, which may rise to the threshold of material events. Many of these solutions include customizable desktop dashboards, providing a snapshot of key performance indicators by overlaying many other programs. Such dashboards will need to include analytical alert software that monitors data such as customer payments, sales, and inventory, and that alerts if a large account is seriously past due. This process will need to feed information up the chain of command to support a chief financial officer (CFO) filing an 8-K form within four working days. These tools overlap detective compliance tools in that they require powerful analytic engines to evaluate data.

SOFTWARE AND TECHNOLOGY BEST PRACTICES TO SUPPORT COMPLIANCE

The following are suggested technology best practices to support compliance:

- **Consolidate ERP and Financial Systems:** A best practice does not require an organization to select the most sophisticated or expensive tier-one ERP/financial solution, but a best practice would replace disparate ERP/financial systems with one organization/enterprise-wide solution in which business processes are standardized and well documented with all users trained in their use. This will facilitate the consolidation of period-end financial reporting—one of the most significant causes of material weaknesses and significant deficiencies.
- **One ERP and Financial Instance:** After consolidating ERP systems, a best practice would be to consolidate various instances into one global instance of the ERP system. The one global instance would be based on the best business practices the organization has developed.

ENDNOTES

1. Eric Laursen, "Automation and Sarbanes-Oxley Compliance," CFO.com, October 18, 2005.
2. Peter Loftus, "Can Technology Help Companies Comply with Sarbanes-Oxley?" *Dow Jones Newswires,* April 25, 2005.
3. Parts of this section copied with permission from the publisher, "The Security Management Triple Play: Prevention, Detection, and Visualization for SOX Compliance," by Anthony Tarantino, *Cutter IT Journal,* 15:4, 6; March 2005.
4. Visit the U.S. Government's Voluntary Accessibility Program site: www.section508.gov/.

CHAPTER 20

Auditing Internal Controls

INTRODUCTION[1]

This section is *not* intended to present best practices in auditing internal control. It is intended to present examples of internal audit practices that are in common use as of this writing. This is a critical distinction, because what passed as acceptable practices a few years ago have become considered highly suspect. The first year of the U.S. Sarbanes-Oxley Act of 2002 (SOX) witnessed an almost panic response to improve audit practices. As the dust is settling, the Public Company Accounting Oversight Board (PCAOB) and the Securities and Exchange Commission (SEC) are reevaluating audit practices with the realization that what is needed is a prioritized risk approach tailored to individual organizations. In short, a cookie-cutter checklist will not work.

The changes in year-one to year-two SOX Section 404 audit practices reinforced the EU and UK contention that SOX was an emotional and expensive overreaction to U.S.-based corruption problems. The "Big Four" audit firms enjoyed a doubling of audit fees from 2003 to 2004.[2] It is highly unlikely that organizations doubled the quality of their internal controls through this process. The second and third years of SOX will undoubtedly see organizations improving internal control with business process improvements and automating audit processes. Consequently, organizations will demand and receive rollbacks in audit fees.

Before the wave of global compliance initiatives, an internal audit was often understaffed, underfunded, and looked upon as a necessary evil. The external audit was often relegated to green staffers who did minimal testing and evaluations. The U.S. scandals of the last few years and the resulting legislation have changed all that. The framework and processes have not changed much but have become more exacting and thorough.

Typically, the auditing of internal controls begins by applying five general classes of assertions as part of the methodology for performing internal control audits. These audit assumptions are the means to collect adequate evidence to support financial statement items and are identified in the Statement of Accountant Standards (SAS) 31, Evidential Matter, which was created in August 1980. The five general classes of assertions can be classified as follows: Existence, Completeness, Valuation, Rights and Obligations, and Presentation and Disclosure.

Existence

SAS 31 states, "Assertions about existence or occurrence deal with whether assets or liabilities of the entity exist at a given date and whether recorded transactions have occurred during a given period." The auditor's process will typically look like this:

- An auditor should start by looking at the books and general ledger (G/L) for evidence that a transaction has occurred in that the accounting system has captured the transaction by recording it.
- The auditor should test for existence outside of the books for that which has been recorded.
- The auditor should extend the search beyond finding supporting debits and credits in a book of original entry to include persuasive evidence of the existence of applicable tangible or intangible assets or liabilities.
- The auditor's testing process may involve substantive testing with an outside third party, such as confirmation of receivables with the organization or person to whom the confirmation has been sent. Another typical test would be the confirmation of cash account balances.

Completeness

SAS 31 states, "Assertions about completeness deal with whether all transactions and accounts that should be presented in the financial statements are so included." The auditor's process will typically look something like this:

- The auditor should find adequate and competent evidence that transactions that should be recorded have been recorded. This does not mean that all transactions for a given process are tested, but that the concept of materiality has been applied so a sufficient number of transactions have been recorded.
- Testing to support completeness originates with externally generated documentation that transactions have been tested. Examples of completeness include the presence of a tangible asset in a retail company's physical possession as evidence the asset has been properly acquired. Another example would include a supplier's invoice and a corresponding receiving document and report for stockroom personnel as evidence that the proper transactions had occurred.

Valuation

SAS 31 states that "assertions about valuation or allocation deal with whether asset, liability, revenue, and expense components have been included in the financial statements at appropriate amounts." Auditors can use Generally Accepted Accounting Principles (GAAP) to help determine the measure or to disclose transactions and balances. An example would include using the aging current accounts receivable to determine if the allowance account is adequate.

Rights and Obligations

SAS 31 states that "assertions about rights and obligations deal with whether assets are the rights of the entity and liabilities are the obligations of the entity at a given date." The use of off-balance sheet (OBS) financing under GAAP to keep accounts off of financial statements while retaining the use of the asset was a major cause of the Enron scandal. Under off-statement financing, organizations have received the use of an item without measuring or disclosing the transaction in their statements. Special purpose entities (SPEs) can be used to support off-financial-statement items. An example would be a build-to-order lease transaction in which the SPE lessor retains title to a leased asset but relinquishes all control and risk to the lessee, which in turn assumes the risks of ownership. Section 401a of SOX tightened the controls over OBS financing and obligations.

Presentation and Disclosure

SAS 31 states that "assertions about presentation and disclosure deal with whether particular components of the financial statements are properly classified, described, and disclosed." Account balances must be properly and adequately measured, described, and disclosed. Examples would include trade receivables such as a loan to an employee or a loan to a third party. These are all receivables and should be measured at their net realizable value. The presentation of each of these must capture their unique and individual characteristics. Another example is inventory accounts, in which proper disclosure includes presenting the method of inventory valuation, the stage of completion if a part of a manufacturing process, and any financial arrangements involving the pledging of the assets.

Exhibit 20.1 presents a high-level overview of one approach to the auditing process.

The audit process will typically include the following elements, but not necessarily in this order:

- High-level interviews and questionnaires for key stakeholders and process owners
- Flowcharts to present a simple graphical view of processes and controls
- Process narratives that describe processes and controls
- Risk and control matrixes that describe the risks and controls for business processes that impact financial reporting

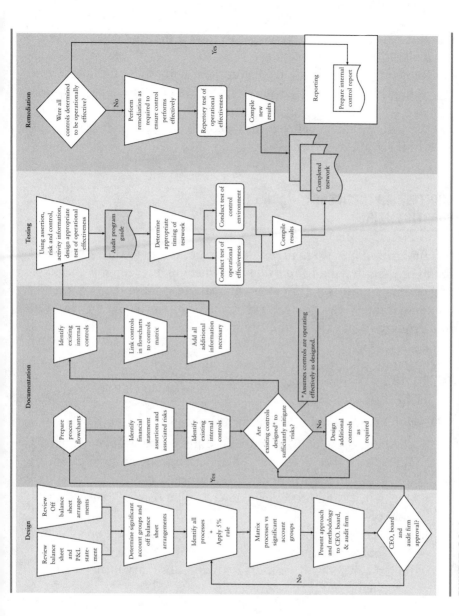

EXHIBIT 20.1 Auditing Internal Controls Overview

- Test plans that detail the tests to validate that the described controls exist and are effective
- Remediation feedback from auditors with their findings from testing and recommendations to improve controls

We will use the procure-to-pay process to provide examples for each of these audit elements.

AUDITING METHODOLOGY: SAMPLE P2P QUESTIONNAIRE

A standardized questionnaire is always a good way to start. At a minimum, it saves having to reinvent the wheel by providing a checklist and permits auditors without a great deal of business acumen to conduct initial interviews and surveys. Exhibit 20.2 provides an example of a procure-to-pay (P2P) questionnaire.

EXHIBIT 20.2 Sample P2P Questionnaire

Develop and Maintain Procurement Policies:

1. Are purchasing policies and procedures formally documented?
2. Who is responsible for documenting, maintaining, and updating purchasing policies and procedures?
3. Are policies and procedures updated on a regular basis? If so, how often?
4. Have copies of the purchasing policies and procedures been distributed to appropriate personnel or is there a copy maintained in a centralized location (e.g., subsidiary intranet site) for all employees to reference?
5. How are changes to the policies and procedures communicated to the appropriate personnel?

Purchase Merchandise and Services:

1. What is the structure of the purchasing department?
2. Are purchase orders utilized for *all* purchases? If not, what are the exceptions?

---

3. Can purchases be made without a PO? If so, what types of purchases? What procedures are in place for purchases made without a PO? Have these procedures been formally documented and communicated to all employees?

4. Are the purchase orders created manually, computer generated, or both? If computerized, what software is being used to generate purchase orders?

5. Who has system access to the PO module? Who determines who can access the PO module? Do those persons with access to create, modify, and delete POs have responsibilities involving supplier invoice processing and payments?

6. How long is the PO data retained in the software system?

7. If manual POs are used, where are they stored and who has access to them? What controls are in place to ensure that they are properly and promptly approved?

8. Are reorder points established in the system? If not, what is the process buyers use to determine when to reorder inventory? Who, if anyone, reviews POs for inventory?

9. Who approves POs, and what are the authority limits established for each individual who creates POs?

10. Are authorized approval limits documented?

11. How are PO approvals documented?

12. Are POs prenumbered or sequentially numbered? If so, is this process manual or automatic? If the process is manual, is there a log of POs maintained? If automated, does the system allow a duplicate PO number to be entered?

13. When a PO is created, does the price of the items being purchased automatically appear when the item number is entered or must it be entered manually? If the price is connected to the item number, can the price be overridden? If so, is there an edit report of price changes available to management, and who is reviewing it?

14. How are POs transmitted to vendors?

15. Are Blanket POs used? If so, who approves and monitors them?

16. Is an Open PO Report generated and reviewed? If so, who reviews it and how frequently is it reviewed? What is a reasonable period of time for POs to be outstanding? Who is

(continued)

EXHIBIT 20.2 Sample P2P Questionnaire *(continued)*

responsible for investigating open POs that have been outstanding beyond this reasonable period?

17. Can individuals related to the invoice processing and payment functions create, modify, or cancel POs?

18. Who authorizes the purchase of services? Are there documented approval limits for authorizing services? Who maintains and updates these limits?

19. Does the system require the following fields be completed when entering a PO in the system: supplier name/code, order type, order date, item number, quantity, and location number?

Manage Supplier Contracts:

1. Does the company have contracts (International, National, or Local) with suppliers? Who is responsible for negotiating these contracts?

2. Who maintains copies of supplier contracts, and where are they kept? Is there a listing maintained (in Excel or Access) of supplier contracts (International, National, or Local) and the related terms and expiration dates?

3. How does the information from supplier contracts get entered into the master files (vendor, item, etc.) in the software system to ensure that all purchases are made in accordance with the contract terms?

4. Who ensures that the contract terms in the system agree to those in the supplier contract?

5. Who has authority to approve supplier contracts?

6. How are the contract changes and modifications processed/recorded? By whom?

Receive Merchandise and Services:

1. Are policies and procedures for receiving formally documented?

2. Are these policies and procedures updated on a regular basis? If so, how often are they updated and who is responsible for maintaining and updating them?

3. Have copies of the receiving policies and procedures been distributed to appropriate personnel or is there a copy maintained in a centralized location (general policy manual or subsidiary intranet site) for all employees to reference?
4. How are changes to the policies and procedures communicated to the appropriate personnel?
5. Who receives merchandise? Are these individuals the same individuals who assume custody of the merchandise?
6. Explain the receiving process. Are receivers (proof-of-delivery documentation) used? If so, are they prenumbered or sequentially numbered by the system? What other document(s) does the receiving department use to verify items and quantities being received? Is there a line-by-line comparison from the PO or blank receiving report to the packing slip? How do they document quantities received and or quantity variances? If using a receiving report (system generated), is it a blind receiving report?
7. Is the merchandise inspected for damage prior to being accepted? If the merchandise is damaged, is it accepted or sent back to the supplier immediately? Are the procedures for receiving or denying damaged goods documented?
8. What system is used for tracking the receipt of merchandise? Is this system interfaced with the general ledger? If so, how often is the general ledger updated to reflect new information entered? If not, how does the information from this system get recorded in the general ledger, and who is responsible for the transfer of the information, and how frequently is the transfer performed?
9. Who has access to the system?
10. Is the system password protected?
11. Who enters the receipt of merchandise into the Oracle system? Please specify what information is entered.
12. When are the receipts entered into the system?
13. Can merchandise/goods be received without a valid PO?
14. Is a receiving log maintained? What is recorded on it, and who is responsible for it?

(continued)

EXHIBIT 20.2   Sample P2P Questionnaire *(continued)*

15. Who is responsible for creating and processing credit memos? Is system access restricted to these individuals? Where do these individuals get the information necessary to create and process credit memos?
16. Can individuals who order and receive goods create or process credit memos?
17. Who is responsible for shipping returns to vendors?
18. Is a Returned Goods Authorization obtained from the supplier prior to shipping of returns?
19. How are returns to suppliers tracked, and who is responsible for this process?
20. How does the company ensure credit is received for returned goods, and who is responsible for this?
21. What are the month-end procedures in the receiving department to ensure proper month-end cut-off? Are these procedures documented? Have the employees in receiving received a copy of these procedures or are the procedures located in a centralized place where employees have access to them? How are changes in the procedures communicated to the employees?
22. Is an accrual made for outstanding POs for which the ownership of goods is transferred prior to delivery? Who is responsible for the accrual, and what are the sources of the information necessary to calculate and record the accrual?
23. Who is responsible for receiving customer returns? Is approval required from authorized personnel to accept customer returns? If so, who must approve the returns?
24. How is the information regarding customer returns transmitted to the Accounting Dept.? Who in the Accounting Dept. is responsible for processing the customer credit? Explain the process for recording the return and customer credit in the Accounting Dept. What source documents are used and retained, and where are they maintained?
25. Who analyzes gross margin reports? Specify what the reviewer is analyzing, and how this information is communicated to management personnel.

Process Accounts Payable

1. Are receivers prenumbered by the (PO) system?
2. Are unmatched receivers and/or supplier invoices investigated timely and accrued appropriately? Are invoices without POs reviewed and approved? Is the approval noted on the invoice? How do you ensure that these invoices are properly coded?
3. What policies and procedures are in place to ensure that all invoices are approved?
4. What are the policies and procedures surrounding the recording of merchandise received, not invoiced? What measures are in place to ensure that this entry captures all goods received by period end?
5. Does your software have a "payment hold" function? If so, who has access to use it? Who reviews and ensures that invoices placed on payment hold are promptly resolved? Who reviews the "Payment Hold" report? How often is the "Payment Hold" report reviewed?
6. If accruals are necessary, what procedures are utilized to ensure that the amount is correct and that all liabilities are recorded in the proper period? Who is responsible to calculate and book these accruals? Who reviews and approves these accruals?
7. Do you use a recurring payment function in your software system? If so, how does it function? What policies and procedures do you utilize to ensure that the proper controls are in place to utilize this function? If your system does not accommodate recurring payments, or if you choose not to use it, how do you process recurring payments such as rents and utilities (i.e., does someone check a list to ensure that all supplier invoices have been received, or vouchers entered if no invoice is received, in the proper period)?
8. Does the PO system determine the general ledger account coding of a supplier's invoice based on the transaction type utilized when entering the PO? If so, please briefly explain how this function works. Who sets up the general ledger codes in use? Who has access to the setup function?

(continued)

EXHIBIT 20.2   Sample P2P Questionnaire *(continued)*

9. Does the software system prohibit posting or accepting a purchase order number more than once? Do Accounts Payable clerks check that all supplier invoices and related POs have the proper authorization based on the dollar amount of the invoice?

Process Disbursements:

1. Is a 3-way match of the receiver, PO, and invoice completed? How is it completed, and who completes it? What computer programs are involved in the 3-way match? If a computer-based 3-way match is available and not used, please explain why. If a 3-way match is not performed, explain the process for ensuring that payments are made only for valid purchases received.
2. Who is responsible for processing invoices for payments? Can individuals in the purchasing function process payments?
3. How are supplier invoices and other related source documents cancelled after they have been processed for payment?
4. Who is responsible for resolving matching problems (quantity and dollar variances) between supplier invoices, receivers, and POs? How are matching problems solved? What procedures are in place to ensure that variances are resolved prior to payment?
5. Does the Accounts Payable Department have tolerance limits for differences in quantity and/or price when paying invoices? What are the specified tolerance limits, who sets these limits, who approves them, and how are often are they reviewed?
6. How are invoices for services authorized for payment, and what supporting documentation is required?
7. Is the system configured to prevent duplicate payments of supplier invoices? Does an error message appear if the same invoice is processed for payment more than once? Can the message be overridden or bypassed? If so, is an override report available to management personnel? If so, is it being reviewed and is there physical evidence of this review?

8. How are partial vendor's invoices processed to ensure that the subsequent invoices do not exceed the PO amount? Is a listing of payments, along with supporting documentation, reviewed and approved by management personnel prior to checks being cut? Who is reviewing the list and does this person sign-off on the list to show evidence of approval?

9. Does the company make payments via EFT? Specify the payments made via EFT. Who has the authority to authorize these payments? Is there a documented list of individuals authorized to make these payments? Is a call-back required from the bank for EFT payments?

10. How often are checks cut? Who runs the checks? Who is the back-up?

11. What computer program is used to run the checks?

12. Are the checks prenumbered or are they sequentially numbered by the system?

13. Is the system configured to prevent the same check number from being used twice?

14. If the printer becomes jammed while printing checks, how is the damaged check voided? Are all "VOID" checks voided in the same manner? What are the differences?

15. Where are voided checks stored? Is access to them properly restricted? Who has access to them?

16. Is a check log maintained? Who maintains it?

17. Where is the check stock kept? Is it properly secured? Who has access to it?

18. Who has signature authority for signing the checks?

19. Do the individuals with signature authority have signature stamps? Where are they kept? Is access to these signature stamps properly restricted?

20. Are signature plates used when printing the checks? Where are they kept? Is access to the signature plates properly restricted? Once the checks are printed, are they reviewed and approved by appropriate personnel as evidenced by a signature?

21. Are manual checks ever issued? What are the circumstances under which manual checks would be issued? Who has the authority to issue a manual check? Are manual checks

(continued)

EXHIBIT 20.2 Sample P2P Questionnaire *(continued)*

computer generated or is there separate check stock for manual checks? If separate check stock is used, where are the manual checks kept and is access to them restricted? Who has access to them?

22. Who has signature authority for manual checks?

23. Is the Accounts Payable module interfaced with the general ledger? If so, is the general ledger update automatically performed at specified times by the system or does it require human intervention, and how often is the general ledger updated? If there is no interface of the Accounts Payable module with the general ledger, how does the information from this module get recorded in the general ledger, who is responsible for the transfer of the information, and how frequently is the transfer performed?

24. Is a reconciliation of the Accounts Payable subledger/module to the general ledger performed? Who does the reconciliation, and what is the frequency of the reconciliation? Who reviews the reconciliation, and does this individual sign-off on the reconciliation?

25. Are supplier statements reconciled to supplier accounts in the Accounts Payable subledger? Who does this reconciliation? Who investigates and resolves differences?

26. Who reviews an Accounts Payable Aging Report? What is the frequency of this review? Is there evidence of this review (i.e., a signature)? How are older items investigated and resolved? Under what circumstances is a request made for a check from a supplier for a debit balance?

27. Who is responsible for matching credit memos to corresponding invoices to ensure that the proper credit or adjustment is received?

28. What are the month-end procedures in the accounts payable department to ensure the recording of liabilities in the appropriate accounting period? Are these procedures documented? Have the employees in the accounts payable department

received a copy of these procedures or are the procedures located in a centralized place where employees have access to them? How are changes in the procedures communicated to the employees?

29. Are the bank accounts reconciled on a regular basis? Who performs the reconciliation? Is this person independent of the payables processing function? How often is the reconciliation performed? Who reviews the reconciliation, and does this person sign-off as evidence of review on the reconciliation?

Maintain Supplier Master File:

1. Is a standard form used to request changes to the supplier master file? If so, are these forms prenumbered?
2. What supporting documentation must accompany requests for changes to the supplier master file?
3. Who is responsible for the supplier master file? Is this person independent of the payables processing function? Is system access to the supplier master file restricted to this person? If not, who else has access?
4. Is an edit report of changes to the supplier master file generated and reviewed by appropriate management personnel?
5. Is a periodic review of the supplier master file performed? How often is the review performed? Who is responsible for the review? What evidence exists to verify that the review has been performed?
6. Are supplier master files ever deleted or inactivated? Under what circumstances would supplier master files be deleted or inactivated?
7. Does the supplier master maintenance process include a sort by name to identify redundant suppliers (i.e., the same supplier is listed multiple times under slightly different names)?
8. Does the supplier master system provide the means to capture a parent/child hierarchical relationship (e.g., several Home Depot stores supply a company's many facilities throughout the country, but the total spend with Home Depot Corporation is not captured)?

AUDITING METHODOLOGY: SAMPLE P2P FLOWCHARTS

Exhibits 20.3–20.5 contain very high-level flowcharts for the P2P process. The "PO" symbols indicate controls referenced in the control narrative and control matrix. It may be advisable to begin a graphic exercise on a whiteboard in which key stakeholders, business owners, and process users describe how their processes flow. After

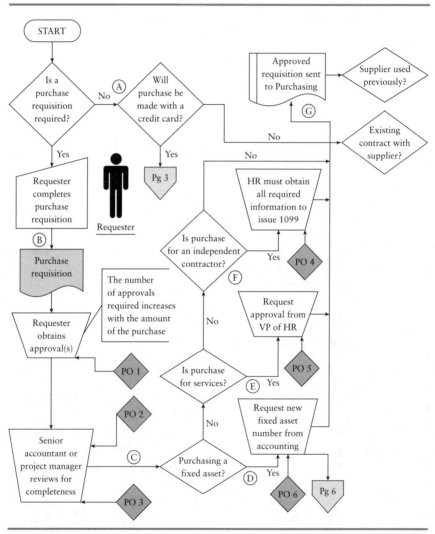

EXHIBITS 20.3   Purchase Request Flowchart

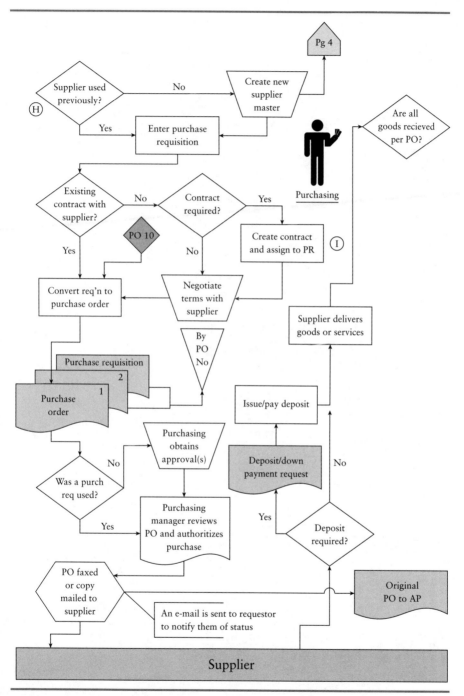

EXHIBITS 20.4 Purchase Order Flowchart

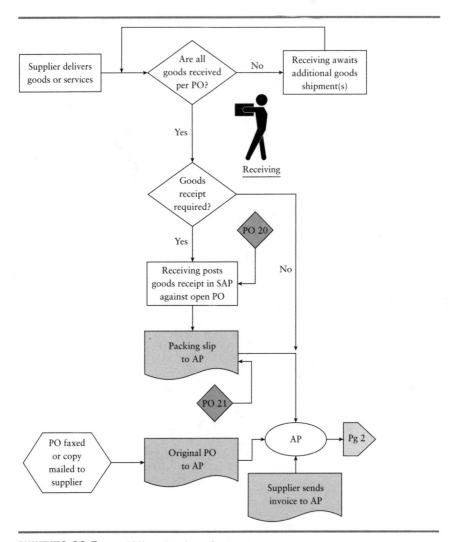

EXHIBITS 20.5 Fulfillment Flowchart

a few iterations, the whiteboard can be converted to flowcharting software. Some of the more sophisticated document management tools create a flowchart from a process narrative. Generally speaking, everyone loves cartoon and graphical images to tell a story. It is easier to spot omissions or mistakes in a process using a simple flowchart than it is in a narrative.

AUDITING METHODOLOGY: SAMPLE CASE STUDY

The following sample case study is from a mid-size manufacturing company not using an Internet procurement system, electronic catalogs, or electronic approval workflows, so it is not very sophisticated but is a good example of how to describe each process step.

INTRODUCTION

The company procures materials and services required by the company for ordinary and necessary business purposes only. The majority of purchases go through an approved purchase requisition to a purchase order (PO), but all purchases are made following management's authorization. Some smaller purchases may be executed with a purchasing card.

Disbursements are controlled and access to assets is safeguarded. Supplier invoices are posted against related POs or are approved by the receiving manager before authorization for payment. Accounts payable (AP) creates a voucher for review with each printed check. The check signer(s) review each purchase for reasonableness and agreement (between voucher and check amount). A preapproved signature authority levels policy determines who may or must sign each disbursement.

Procurement at the company includes reimbursements for travel expenses and fixed asset purchases. It also includes any required disbursements for taxes, regulatory fees, royalties, and so on. Disbursements for such items where no materials or services are received require similar authorization and appropriate supporting documentation, which may not include a supplier's invoice.

Process Owner(s): Requestor, Line Manager, Purchasing Manager, Controller, Shipping and Receiving Clerk, AP Clerk, Cash Accountant, GL Accountant

GL Accounts Affected:

GL No.	Account Description	GL No.	Account Description
.			

Applications involved: Enterprise Resource Planning (ERP) system, Spreadsheet

Reports used in this process: Purchase Requisition, PO, Wire or check request form, and AP Aging

Assessed risk level: High

Significance: Significant

Purchase Requests:

All procurement is governed by the company's procurement policy and begins with identification of goods or services needed for the business. Purchases greater than $500 require the requestor to complete a purchase requisition (PO1). Even purchase cardholders who make some purchases directly are required to use a requisition for amounts greater than five hundred dollars. In these cases, the cardholder gets authorization from the appropriate level of management before executing the Purchase. Employees can access the online purchase requisition, fill it in (including their cost center), and circulate it to the appropriate managers for approval. The company has a signature authority levels policy specifying the approval levels required for purchases. One approval that is needed for every purchase is that of the controller (PO3). Some purchases require special attention such as the purchase of assets or procuring the services of a consultant. In addition to the normal approvals, consultants must be preapproved by the vice president (VP) of human resources (HR) (PO5).

One specialized subset of purchases is for fixed assets. These must be routed through accounting to get a new fixed asset ID number (PO4). The ERP system has a separate subledger for fixed assets and purchases of assets must be recorded here. The fixed asset accountant reviews the requisition for a description of the new asset and creates a new Asset Master Record in the ERP system using the correct asset class. The selection of the correct asset class determines the asset depreciation period, so all assets in the same class have the same depreciation life. At the end of each month, the Fixed Asset accountant prepares a report of all fixed asset deletions and additions as well as a complete detailed list of all fixed assets. These lists are reviewed by the Accounting Manager (PO34).

Materials to build prototypes are another subset of purchases. The Materials Director in Manufacturing Operations handles all such purchases. Some of the time, she receives a completed Purchase Requisition, but more often, she receives a Bill of Materials that specifies particular parts needed by engineering. The authorized Bill of Materials fulfills the requirement for management authorization.

Purchase Orders (POs):

The requestor is responsible for obtaining all required approvals, and dropping off the completed Purchase Requisition with the Supply Chain Manager. If a supplier is specified, the Supply Chain Manager checks in the ERP system to see if the supplier has been used previously. If not, she must create a new supplier master record. If no supplier is specified, the Supply Chain Manager will identify an appropriate supplier. In some cases, the supplier requires a contract. If so, the Supply Chain Manager negotiates a contract with the supplier and assigns the Purchase Request to the new contract.

Next, the Supply Chain Manager or Materials Manager uses the ERP system to create a Purchase Order (PO7) that is then printed and signed by the Supply Chain Manager or Materials Manager. When a PO is created in the ERP system, it always includes the related cost center and the appropriate GL account to debit when the invoice is received. This information is automatically transferred at the time the AP clerk posts the invoice against the PO. If the PO was created without a related Purchase Requisition, the Supply Chain Manager must obtain the appropriate management approvals before sending the PO to the Supplier. In some limited circumstances, a blanket PO is created with a specified maximum and a limited duration (e.g., the company makes multiple routine purchases of telecom equipment covered by a blanket PO). For POs related to prototype materials, the Materials Manager obtains signatures directly on the PO for purchases exceeding $10,000.

The Supply Chain Manager or Materials Manager has an option when creating the PO to require or not require goods receipt. Generally, if the PO is for tangible goods, she will require goods receipt; if the PO is for services, she will not require goods receipt.

The original PO is sent to AP; generally one copy is sent to the supplier (via mail, e-mail, or fax), and the Supply Chain Manager or Materials Manager files a copy with the approved Purchase Requisition. POs are not sent to the supplier if the Purchase will be executed using a Purchase Card.

Purchase Cards:

The company's Controller manages the Purchase Card program. She is authorized to direct the Purchase Card Company to issue cards (PO9) and the card company establishes the corporate limit for all combined Purchasing cards (PO10). Therefore, the number of cardholders is limited, each cardholder has a specific spending limit, and the total exposure on all Purchasing cards is limited. The cardholders are trained (PO11) on the proper use of their Purchasing cards and the limits for the card's use. The training includes how to maintain a log of all purchases and how to complete a monthly reconciliation (PO12). Once the cardholders have been properly trained and they have received their Purchasing card from the bank, the Supply Chain Manager may request them to use their company credit card to execute a purchase. The PO then serves as backup for the cardholder's monthly reconciliation.

The cardholder completes a monthly reconciliation and forwards this to accounts payable. The AP accountants reconcile these to a separate statement received directly from the card company (PO13) and ensure that a receipt properly supports each Purchase on the corporate statement. They ensure all purchases the cardholder made were for ordinary and necessary business purposes. In some rare cases, the cardholder may have used the company's Purchasing card to make a Purchase for personal reasons. The AP accountant notifies the cardholder and ensures that the cardholder reimburses the company for the proper amount (PO14).

Vouchers with a PO:

For POs created with goods receipt required, the AP accountant is able to post the supplier's invoice against the open PO only after the goods received transaction is completed (PO17). The ERP system performs three-way matching internally (PO, goods received, and the invoice-PO20), and the newly posted AP becomes open for selection on an upcoming check run. As mentioned above, the correct cost center and GL account are transferred from the PO created earlier.

Vouchers without a PO:

In some cases, a supplier's invoice arrives without a corresponding PO (e.g., the utility bill, legal invoices, tax statements), or the PO was created without goods receipt required (e.g., for contractor services). In those cases, the AP accountant determines the appropriate cost center and GL account then obtains authorization for payment to the Supplier by the appropriate company manager directly on the invoice. If such approval is not obtained before posting the invoice, the AP accountant places a "block" on the payment until the manager approves the invoice (PO18). The invoice from American Express also arrives without a corresponding PO. For this invoice, the AP accountant collects the monthly reconciliations from each purchasing cardholder with original receipts attached. These reconciliations provide authorization for payment allocations. See Exhibit 20.6.

AUDITING METHODOLOGY: SAMPLE P2P TESTING

Testing has the goal of validating the design and effectiveness of internal controls in the P2P process as it relates to financial reporting. The following areas will be reviewed: documentation and communication of policies and procedures:

- Applicable expertise of employees involved in initiating, authorizing, recording, and overall reporting
- Process review for purchase requests, purchase orders, purchase cards, fulfillment, receiving, vouchers, disbursements, and reconciliations
- System integrity (system access and overall accuracy and completeness of inputs and outputs)
- Review and follow up by management
- Existence of proper segregation of duties

EXHIBIT 20.6 Auditing Methodology—Sample P2P Control Matrix

Control No	Financial Statement Assertions	Objectives	Risks	Controls in Place	Controls			
					Manual or Automated	Preventive or Detective	Key or Secondary	Fraud or Asset Safeguard
PO 1	Occurrence	Transactions are executed in accordance with mgtmt.'s authorization	The company could be obligated to pay for something not properly authorized	Every purchase requires a requester to complete a Purchase Requisition except for purchases made with corporate credit cards.	Manual	Preventive	S	Fraud
PO 2				In order to ensure the required approvals have been obtained, the Accounting Manager reviews each PR for appropriate approvals during the PR to PO conversion process.	Manual	Preventive	S	Asset Safeguard
PO 3				The company's purchasing procedures and forms documentation are available online at http\\xxxx.xxxx.com. Approved PRs for hardware, software, and facilities related supplies are routed through the Sr. Accountant for PO generation.	Automated	Preventive	S	Fraud
PO 5				Access to the ERP system's purchasing function is limited to buyers and purchasing management only.	Manual	Preventive	S	
PO 6				The Accounting Manager or the Supply Chain Manager uses the ERP system to create a Purchase Order. A copy is e-mailed or faxed to the original requester for review and order initiation.	Automated	Preventive	S	Asset Safeguard

Policies and Procedures

The following policies and procedures apply:

- Obtain the following documents from company management:
  - Process narrative(s)
  - Process flowchart(s)
  - Policy
  - Internal control matrix
- Review process narratives and flowcharts to verify the following:
  - Such documentation is complete and appropriate.
  - Controls are identified and documented regarding process narrative.
- Verify the accuracy and completeness of process narratives and flowcharts by performing system walkthrough documenting any exceptions and appropriate follow-up action with staff.
- Review internal controls matrix for the following:
  - Controls identified throughout process narrative are contained in the matrix.
  - High-level design effectiveness (i.e., controls entirely missing or controls not properly designed).
  - Ensure the designed control objective appropriately addresses the related risks from a financial reporting perspective.
  - Review with management any control design weaknesses identified.

Purchase Requests and Purchase Orders

The following apply:

- Obtain a listing of all POs initiated during the year, randomly select 45 POs (perform 2/3 of testing for Q1/Q2 and the remaining 1/3 in Q3/Q4), and perform the following:
  - Obtain the PO and the related purchase requisition or bill of materials.
  - Agree the detail on the PO to the requisition or bill of materials, if applicable.

- Note evidence that approvals have been obtained from appropriate levels of management in accordance with Appendix 1 to the Procurement Policy (on the requisition, bill of materials, or PO).
- If the PO relates to the services of a consultant, ensure approval was obtained from the VP of HR.
- Note evidence of G/L account code assignment on the requisition and ensure reasonableness.
- Note evidence of review by the Controller if amount is greater than $500 (either on requisition, bill of materials, or PO).
- Determine whether the PO was created with Goods Receipt required.

■ Obtain copy of the fiscal 2004 annual budget. Inquire of the Budget Analyst as to the process involved in creating this budget. Specifically inquire about the budgeting process for purchases and how the budget amounts are determined. Examine supporting documentation where available.

■ Randomly select six months (perform 2/3 of testing for Q1/Q2 and the remaining 1/3 in Q3/Q4) and perform the following:

- Obtain the PO Creation Review report prepared by the Assistant Controller.
- Note evidence of review by the Assistant Controller.

Purchasing Cards

The following apply:

■ Obtain confirmation from credit card company that the Controller is the only individual authorized to issue new purchase cards.

■ Obtain all purchase card applications processed during the fiscal year and note evidence of approval by the Assistant Treasurer.

■ Ask the Controller as to the process involved in managing the purchase card program. Specifically, inquire as to the process followed to ensure that spending limits are appropriate at the individual cardholder level. Review a monthly American Express statement to establish the current corporate spending limit.

■ Randomly select four purchase cardholders and ask them what training they received on the use of purchase cards. Ensure the comments from these individuals are consistent with the internal control documentation.

- Randomly select six months (perform 2/3 of testing for Q1/Q2 and the remaining 1/3 in Q3/Q4) and perform the following:
  - Obtain all reconciliations prepared by purchase cardholders.
  - Ensure reconciliations are complete, and that the combined reconciliations agree to the overall credit card company statement received directly by AP.
  - Agree the receipts to the credit card company statement.
  - Note evidence of review by AP, and discuss any reconciling items.
- Inquire of AP as to the process involved in ensuring that the Company is properly reimbursed for any personal purchases made with a purchase card.

Information Technology (IT)

The following apply:

- Obtain a listing from the IT department that details the individuals with access to the Fixed Asset functions within the Fixed Asset module of the ERP system. Ask if these individuals have restricted/unrestricted access to functions within the module. If there is restricted access, determine which individuals have the ability to create Fixed Asset records. Ensure that individuals with access to the Fixed Asset functions are appropriate and that no issues exist regarding the segregation of duties.
- Obtain a listing from the IT department that details the individuals with access to the purchasing functions within the supply chain module of the ERP system. Ask if these individuals have restricted/unrestricted access to functions within the module. If there is restricted access, determine which individuals have the ability to create purchase orders. Ensure that individuals with access to the purchasing functions are appropriate and that no issues exist regarding the segregation of duties.
- Obtain a listing from the IT department that details individuals with access to supplier master files in the ERP system. Ensure that individuals with access to the master files are appropriate and that no issues exist regarding the segregation of duties.

- Verify that the ERP system produces a warning when posting an invoice against an open PO where the goods receipt has not yet been performed.
- Obtain a listing from the IT department that details the individuals with access to the cash disbursement functions within the FI module of SAP. Ensure that individuals with access to the cash disbursement functions are appropriate and that no issues exist regarding the segregation of duties (SOD).

Segregation of Duties (SOD)

The following apply:

- Based on levels of involvement, review client process/control matrix in order to ensure proper SOD with the following categories:
  - Initiation
  - Authorization
  - Recording
  - Processing
  - Reporting
  - Custody of assets

Summary of Findings

The following apply:

- Prepare a summary of design weaknesses, specifically noting the following:
  - Missing controls
  - Missing control objectives
  - Incompatible duties
  - Inappropriate mix of control attributes
- Prepare summary of operational effectiveness weaknesses for controls identified and tested.
- Obtain management response for all deviations noted and corrective action to be taken as a result of such deviations.

- Assess each weakness identified, both design and operational, and consider whether such deviations rise to the level of significant or material.

AUDITING METHODOLOGY: SAMPLE P2P REMEDIATION MATRIX

An auditor's remediation form may look something like Exhibit 20.7.

The control activities that an auditor will be looking for will typically include but not be limited to the following:

- PO entry data are compared to source documents by individuals who are independent of the PO entry process.
- POs are batched and batch input is balanced; out-of-balance batches are corrected promptly.
- Purchase order data is edited and validated; identified errors are corrected promptly.
- Invoices, credit notes, and other adjustments related to AP are batched and batch input data are balanced; out-of-balance batches are corrected promptly.
- Goods returned notes are matched to credit notes, and differences are investigated promptly.
- Purchase requisitioning, purchasing, inventory management, and AP functions are performed by an integrated application system.
- The G/L is automatically updated for receipt and disbursement transactions.
- Bank statements are reconciled to the G/L regularly.
- Disbursements at, before, or after the end of an accounting period are scrutinized to ensure complete and consistent recording in the appropriate accounting period.
- Recorded changes to the supplier master file are compared to authorized source documents to ensure they were inputted accurately.
- Significant changes to the supplier master file are approved by management.
- Supplier master file data are periodically reviewed by management for accuracy and ongoing pertinence.

EXHIBIT 20.7 Sample Remediation Form

Auditor's Control Objective No.	Control Objective Required to Be Met	Company's Control No.	Company's Control Activities	Auditor's Comments	Company's Control Activities	Company's Comments	Company's Comment Date	Auditor's Control Activity No.	Auditor's Control Activity No.
1	All valid changes to the supplier master file are input and processed.	None documented	None documented	How does the Company ensure that all necessary changes to the supplier master file are input and processed?	1-May-05			1.a	Requests to change supplier master file data are logged; the log is reviewed to ensure that all requested changes are processed timely.
		None documented	None documented	How does the Company ensure the compeleteness and the validity of changes made to the supplier master file?	2-May-05			1.b	Supplier master file data is periodically reviewed by management for accuracy and ongoing pertinence.
		None documented	None documented		3-May-05			1.c	Requests to change supplier masterfile data are submitted on prenumbered forms; the numerical sequence of such forms is accounted for to ensure that all requested changes are processed timely.

176

- Requests to change supplier master file data are logged; the log is reviewed to ensure all requested changes are processed in a timely manner.
- Requests to change supplier master file data are submitted on prenumbered forms; the numerical sequence of such forms is accounted for to ensure all requested changes are processed in a timely manner.
- Supplier master file data are edited and validated; identified errors are corrected promptly.
- Suppliers that have not been used for a significant period of time are reviewed and marked for deletion by the application, if appropriate.

ENDNOTES

1. This section references and extensively quotes Statement of Accountant Standards (SAS) 31—Evidential Matter, August 1980.
2. Deborah Solomon, "At What Price?" *Wall Street Journal*, October 17, 2005.

CHAPTER 21

Best Practices in Internal Controls: Enterprise Risk Management[1]

The graphic in Exhibit 21.1 is from the Committee of Sponsoring Organizations' (COSO's) executive introduction to and overview of the new Enterprise Risk Management (ERM) process. It was published in September 2004 and represents a modernization of the 25-year-old COSO Framework. The four objectives categories—strategic, operations, reporting, and compliance—are represented by the vertical columns, the eight components by horizontal rows, and an entity's units by the third dimension. The goal is to provide the flexibility to attack an organization's ERM from a global or entity level down through its divisions or locations, and down to its subsidiaries. ERM takes nothing away from the internal control in COSO I, and it builds on COSO I to provide a more comprehensive and strategic framework while taking event management into consideration.

ERM's graphic looks like a Rubik's Cube and the Executive Overview to ERM explains "enterprise risk management is not strictly a serial process, where one component affects only the next. It is a multidirectional, iterative process in which almost any component can and does influence another." See Exhibit 21.1.

COSO's ERM—Integrated Framework Executive Summary—states that "Enterprise risk management enables management to effectively deal with uncertainty and associated risk and opportunity, enhancing the capacity to build value . . . . Value is maximized when

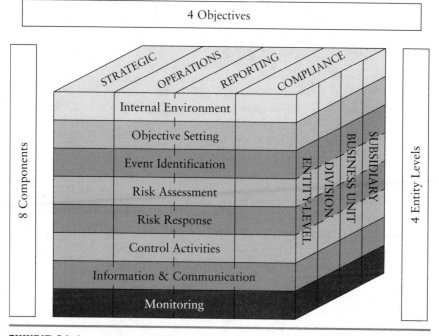

EXHIBIT 21.1   COSO ERM Graphic

management sets strategy and objectives to strike an optimal balance between growth and return goals and related risks, and efficiently and effectively deploys resources in pursuit of the entity's objectives."

The Executive Summary summarizes ERM's scope as follows:

- "Aligning risk appetite and strategy—Management considers the entity's risk appetite in evaluating strategic alternatives, setting related objectives, and developing mechanisms to manage related risks.
- Enhancing risk response decisions—Enterprise risk management provides the rigor to identify and select among alternative risk responses—risk avoidance, reduction, sharing, and acceptance.
- Reducing operational surprises and losses—Entities gain enhanced capability to identify potential events and establish responses, reducing surprises and associated costs or losses.
- Identifying and managing multiple and cross-enterprise risks— Every enterprise faces a myriad of risks affecting different parts of the organization, and enterprise risk management facilitates

effective response to the interrelated impacts, and integrated responses to multiple risks.

- Seizing opportunities—By considering a full range of potential events, management is positioned to identify and proactively realize opportunities.
- Improving deployment of capital—Obtaining robust risk information allows management to effectively assess overall capital needs and enhance capital allocation."

COSO defines ERM as follows: "Enterprise risk management is a process, effected by an entity's board of directors, management and other personnel, applied in strategy setting and across the enterprise, designed to identify potential events that may affect the entity, and manage risk to be within its risk appetite, to provide reasonable assurance regarding the achievement of entity objectives." The definition includes the following assumptions that ERM is:

- "A process, ongoing and flowing through an entity
- Effected by people at every level of an organization
- Applied in strategy setting
- Applied across the enterprise, at every level and unit, and includes taking an entity level portfolio view of risk
- Designed to identify potential events that, if they occur, will affect the entity and to manage risk within its risk appetite
- Able to provide reasonable assurance to an entity's management and board of directors
- Geared to achievement of objectives in one or more separate but overlapping categories"

EVENTS—RISKS AND OPPORTUNITIES

ERM adds the concept of event management to COSO I. This is a very important change in that COSO I's internal controls work best for repetitive tasks and processes. One-off special events can cause grief to controls designed for day-to-day and repetitive processes. ERM's overview explains it this way: "Events can have negative impact, positive impact, or both. Events with a negative impact represent risks, which can prevent value creation or erode existing value.

Events with positive impact may offset negative impacts or represent opportunities. Opportunities are the possibility that an event will occur and positively affect the achievement of objectives, supporting value creation or preservation. Management channels opportunities back to its strategy or objective-setting processes, formulating plans to seize the opportunities."

Examples of events that can stress controls include major disruptions in operations caused by natural disasters, upgrades or changes in financial software, and mergers and acquisitions. For example, a business merger can require the combining of two or more disparate ERP systems, each with its own charts of accounts naming conventions, units of measures, and numbering systems for master level data (item master, customer master, supplier master, etc.). When the disparate systems are dumped together there is a much greater possibility that errors will occur—redundant master level data with no cross-references to the duplicates.

ACHIEVEMENT OF OBJECTIVES

The ERM overview states:

> *Within the context of an entity's established mission or vision, management establishes strategic objectives, selects strategy, and sets aligned objectives cascading through the enterprise. This enterprise risk management framework is geared to achieving an entity's objectives, set forth in four categories:*
>
> 1. *Strategic – high-level goals, aligned with and supporting its mission*
> 2. *Operations – effective and efficient use of its resources*
> 3. *Reporting – reliability of reporting*
> 4. *Compliance – compliance with applicable laws and regulations.*

The addition of a component approach to risk management with ERM is critical. There are distinct and but overlapping requirements to attack risk at a strategic versus tactical level. The ERM overview notes that:

this categorization of entity objectives allows a focus on separate aspects of enterprise risk management. These distinct but overlapping categories—a particular objective can fall into more than one category—address different entity needs and may be the direct responsibility of different executives. This categorization also allows distinctions between what can be expected from each category of objectives. Another category, safeguarding of resources, used by some entities, also is described . . . . Because objectives relating to reliability of reporting and compliance with laws and regulations are within the entity's control, enterprise risk management can be expected to provide reasonable assurance of achieving those objectives. Achievement of strategic objectives and operations objectives, however, is subject to external events not always within the entity's control; accordingly, for these objectives, enterprise risk management can provide reasonable assurance that management, and the board in its oversight role, are made aware, in a timely manner, of the extent to which the entity is moving toward achievement of the objectives.

COMPONENTS OF ENTERPRISE RISK MANAGEMENT

ERM is made up of eight interrelated components. The eight components are based on an organization's management approach and processes. The components are as follows:

1. **Internal Environment:** This encompasses the tone of an organization, especially the tone at the top of an organization, and establishes the basis for how risk is managed including risk management philosophy, risk appetite, integrity and ethical values, and the environment in which they operate. This is new to ERM and not part of COSO I.

2. **Objective Setting:** Identifying and prioritizing objectives is an essential step that must be completed before addressing potential events affecting the achievement of objectives. ERM has a goal of ensuring that management has in place a process to set objectives and that the chosen objectives support and align with the entity's mission and are consistent with its risk appetite.

Contrary to the traditional view, internal audit should be chartered to meet a company's objectives. Their role in risk management is a means to meeting a company's objectives. This is new to ERM and not part of COSO I.

3. **Event Identification:** Internal and external events affecting achievement of an entity's objectives must be identified, distinguishing between risks and opportunities. Opportunities are channeled back to management's strategy or objective-setting processes. This is new to ERM and not part of COSO I.

4. **Risk Assessment:** Risks are analyzed, considering their likelihood and their impact, as a basis for determining how risks should be managed. Risks are assessed on an inherent and a residual basis. Inherent risk management, sometimes called gross or absolute risks, assesses the consequence and likelihood of a risk occurring before any controls are taken into account. Residual risk management, sometimes called net or controlled risks, assesses the consequence and likelihood of a risk occurring after any controls are taken into account. This is part of COSO.

5. **Risk Response:** Management selects risk responses—avoiding, accepting, reducing, or sharing risk—developing a set of actions to align risks with the entity's risk tolerances and risk appetite. An important part of risk response is evaluating the cost versus benefits of the various risk management alternatives. This is part of COSO I.

6. **Control Activities:** Policies and procedures are established and implemented to help ensure the risk responses are effectively carried out. This is part of COSO I.

7. **Information and Communication:** Relevant information is identified, captured, and communicated in a form and timeframe that enable people to carry out their responsibilities. Effective communication also occurs in a broader sense, flowing down, across, and up the entity. This is part of COSO I, but will be greatly expanded in ERM.

8. **Monitoring:** The entirety of enterprise risk management is monitored and modifications made as necessary. Monitoring is accomplished through ongoing management activities, separate evaluations, or both. This is part of COSO I, but the monitoring required for ERM will be greatly expanded over COSO I.

ENDNOTE

1. This chapter references and extensively quotes COSO's Executive Summary, "Enterprise Risk Management—Integrated Framework," September 2004. Copyright © 2004 by the Committee of Sponsoring Organizations of the Treadway Commission. Reproduced with permission from the AICPA acting as authorized copyright administrator for COSO.

CHAPTER 22

Best Practices in Internal Controls: IT Risk Management & SDLC (NIST 800-30)[1]

The National Institute of Standards and Technology (NIST) has statutory responsibilities under the Computer Security Act of 1987 and the Information Technology Management Reform Act of 1996 to provide information technology (IT) guidelines for U.S. federal agencies. NIST's Special Publication 800-30 (Risk Management Guide for Information Technology Systems, July 2002) provides IT risk management recommendations which can be viewed as a best practice in improving internal controls for any IT organization. What follows are excerpts from the introduction.

Risk Management and IT

Every organization has a mission. In this digital era, as organizations use automated information technology (IT) systems to process their information for better support of their missions, risk management plays a critical role in protecting an organization's information assets, and therefore its mission, from IT-related risk.

An effective risk management process is an important component of a successful IT security program. The principal goal of an organization's risk management process should be to protect the organization and its ability to perform their mission, not just its IT assets. Therefore, the risk management process should not be treated primarily as a technical function carried out by the IT experts who operate and manage the IT system, but as an essential management function of the organization.

Three Processes in Risk Management:

1. *Risk assessment, which includes identification and evaluation of risks and risk impacts, and recommendations of risk-reducing measures*
2. *Risk mitigation, which refers to prioritizing, implementing, and maintaining the appropriate risk-reducing measures recommended from the risk assessment process*
3. *Evaluation and assessment, which includes continual evaluation process and keys for implementing a successful risk management program.*

Risk management is the process that allows IT managers to balance the operational and economic costs of protective measures and achieve gains in mission capability by protecting the IT systems and data that support their organizations' missions. This process is not unique to the IT environment; indeed it pervades decision-making in all areas of our daily lives . . . . The head of an organizational unit must ensure that the organization has the capabilities needed to accomplish its mission. These mission owners must determine the security capabilities that their IT systems must have to provide the desired level of mission support in the face of real world threats. Most organizations have tight budgets for IT security; therefore, IT security spending must be reviewed as thoroughly as other management decisions. A well-structured risk management methodology, when used effectively, can help management identify appropriate controls for providing the mission-essential security capabilities.

System Development Life Cycle (SDLC) in Risk Management:

Minimizing negative impact on an organization and need for sound basis in decision making are the fundamental reasons organizations implement a risk management process for their IT systems. Effective risk management must be totally integrated into the System Development Life Cycle (SDLC). An IT system's SDLC has five phases: initiation, development or acquisition, implementation, operation or maintenance, and disposal. In some cases, an IT system may occupy several of these phases at the same time. However, the risk management methodology is the same regardless of the SDLC phase for which the assessment is being conducted. Risk management is an iterative process that can be performed during each major phase of the SDLC.

See Exhibit 22.1.

The following are key roles in IT risk management:

- **Senior Management.** Senior management, under the standard of due care and ultimate responsibility for mission accomplishment, must ensure that the necessary resources are effectively applied to develop the capabilities needed to accomplish the mission. They must also assess and incorporate results of the risk assessment activity into the decision making process. An effective risk management program that assesses and mitigates IT-related mission risks requires the support and involvement of senior management.
- **Chief Information Officer (CIO).** The CIO is responsible for the agency's IT planning, budgeting, and performance including its information security components. Decisions made in these areas should be based on an effective risk management program.
- **System and Information Owners.** The system and information owners are responsible for ensuring that proper controls are in place to address integrity, confidentiality, and availability of the IT systems and data they own. Typically the system and information owners are responsible for changes to their IT systems. Thus, they usually have to approve and sign off on changes to their IT systems (e.g., system enhancement, major changes to the software and hardware). The system and information owners must therefore understand their role in the risk management process and fully support this process.
- **Business and Functional Managers.** The managers responsible for business operations and IT procurement process must take an active role in the risk management process. These managers are the individuals with the authority and responsibility for making the trade-off decisions essential to mission accomplishment. Their involvement in the risk management process enables the achievement of proper security for the IT systems, which, if managed properly, will provide mission effectiveness with a minimal expenditure of resources.

EXHIBIT 22.1 System Development Life Cycle Phases

SDLC Phases	Phase Characteristics	Support from Risk Management Activities
Phase 1 Initiation	The need for an IT system is expressed and the purpose and scope of the IT system is documented	Identified risks are used to support the development of the system requirements, including security requirements, and a security concept of operations (strategy)
Phase 2 Development or Acquisition	The IT system is designed, purchased, programmed, developed, or otherwise constructed	The risks identified during this phase can be used to support the security analyses of the IT system that may lead to architecture and design tradeoffs during system development
Phase 3 Implementation	The system security features should be configured, enabled, tested, and verified	The risk management process supports the assessment of the system implementation against its requirements and within its modeled operational environment. Decisions regarding risks identified must be made prior to system operation
Phase 4 Operation and Maintenance	The system performs its functions. Typically the system is being modified on an ongoing basis through the addition of hardware and software and by changes to organizational processes, policies, and procedures	Risk management activities are performed for periodic system reauthorization (or re-accreditation) or whenever major changes are made to an IT system in its operational, production environment (e.g., new system interfaces)
Phase 5 Disposal	This phase may involve the disposition of information, hardware, and software. Activities may include moving, archiving, discarding, or destroying information and sanitizing the hardware and software	Risk management activities are performed for system components that will be disposed of or replaced to ensure that the hardware and software are properly disposed of, that residual data are appropriately handled, and that system migration is conducted in a secure and systematic manner

Source: The National Institute of Standards and Technology (NIST), Special Publication 800-30, "Risk Management Guide for Information Technology Systems, July 2002.

- **ISSO.** Information System Security Officers (ISSOs) are responsible for their organizations' security programs, including risk management. Therefore, they play a leading role in introducing an appropriate, structured methodology to help identify, evaluate, and minimize risks to the IT systems that support their organizations' missions. ISSOs also act as major consultants in support of senior management to ensure that this activity takes place on an ongoing basis.

- **IT Security Practitioners.** IT security practitioners (e.g., network, system, application, and database administrators; computer specialists; security analysts; security consultants) are responsible for proper implementation of security requirements in their IT systems. As changes occur in the existing IT system environment (e.g., expansion in network connectivity, changes to the existing infrastructure and organizational policies, introduction of new technologies), the IT security practitioners must support or use the risk management process to identify and assess new potential risks and implement new security controls as needed to safeguard their IT systems.

- **Security Awareness Trainers** (Security/Subject Matter Professionals). The organization's personnel are the users of the IT systems. Use of the IT systems and data according to an organization's policies, guidelines, and rules of behavior is critical to mitigating risk and protecting the organization's IT resources. To minimize risk to the IT systems, it is essential that system and application users be provided with security awareness training. Therefore, the IT security trainers or security/subject matter professionals must understand the risk management process so that they can develop appropriate training materials and incorporate risk assessment into training programs to educate the end users."

ENDNOTE

1. This chapter references and extensively quotes The National Institute of Standards and Technology (NIST), Special Publication 800-30, "Risk Management Guide for Information Technology Systems, July 2002.

CHAPTER 23

Best Practices in Internal Controls: Mapping COBIT to COSO I, COSO II, & PCAOB

Control Objectives for Information and Related Technology (COBIT) is growing in its global acceptance with the European Union (EU) approving it as one of three acceptable standards. COBIT is a comprehensive framework for managing risk and control of information technology (IT), comprising four domains, 34 IT processes, and 318 detailed control objectives. A best practice is to map IT controls, such as COBIT, to the appropriate Committee of Sponsoring Organizations (COSO), COSO II (Enterprise Risk Management), and Public Company Accounting Oversight Board (PCAOB) components. Many of COBIT's IT processes have relationships with more than one COSO component. This should not be surprising considering the nature of general IT controls which form the basis for reliable information systems. According to COBIT: "This multiple relationship attribute further demonstrates why IT controls are the basis for all others and are essential for a reliable internal control program."

Exhibit 23.1 shows a matrix that maps COBIT to COSO I, COSO II, and PCAOB.

EXHIBIT 23.1   Mapping COBIT to COSO I, COSO II, and PCAOB Matrix

	COBIT Area			COSO I Component					COSO II (ERM) Component			PCAOB IT General Control Heading			
Number	Company Level	Activity Level	Description	Control Environment	Risk Assessment	Control Activities 1	Info & Communication	Monitoring	Internal Environment	Objective Setting	Event Identification	Program Development	Program Changes	Computer Operations	Access to Programs & Data
			Plan and Organize (IT Environment)												
1	X		IT strategic planning	X	X		X	X							
2	X		Information architecture			X	X								
3			Determine technological direction						X	X					
4	X		IT organization and relationships	X			X								
5			Manage the IT investment						X	X					
6	X		Communication of management aims and direction						X	X					
7	X		Management of human resources	X			X								
8	X		Compliance with external requirements												
9	X		Assessment of risks		X										
10			Manage projects												
11	X		Management of quality	X		X	X	X							

(continued)

EXHIBIT 23.1   Mapping COBIT to COSO I, COSO II, and PCAOB Matrix *(Continued)*

No.			Description													
			Acquire and Implement (Program Development and Program Change)													
12			Identify automated solutions													
13		X	Aquire or develop application software			X							X	X	X	X
14		X	Acquire technology infrastructure			X							X	X	X	X
15		X	Develop and maintain policies and procedures			X	X		X	X			X	X	X	X
16		X	Install and test application software and technology Infrastructure			X							X	X	X	X
17		X	Manage changes			X					X	X	X				X
			Deliver and Support (Computer Operations and Access to Programs and Data)													
18		X	Define and manage service levels	X		X		X				X	X	X	X	X
19		X	Manage third-party services	X	X	X		X					X	X	X	X
20	X		Manage performance and capacity			X		X								
21			Ensure continuous service													
22		X	Ensure systems security			X	X	X						X	X	
23			Identify and allocate costs													
24		X	Educate and train users	X			X									

25			Assist and advise customers												
26		X	Manage the configuration			X	X							X	X
27		X	Manage problems and incidents			X	X	X		X			X		
28		X	Manage data			X	X							X	X
29	X		Manage facilities	X											
30		X	Manage operations			X	X							X	X
Monitor and Evaluate (IT Environment)															
31	X		Monitoring				X	X							
32	X		Adequacy of internal controls					X	X						
33	X		Independent assurance	X				X							
34	X		Internal audit					X	X						

Source: COBIT.

CHAPTER 24

Best Practices in Internal Controls: COBIT IT Control Objectives

Exhibits 24.1, 24.2, and 24.3 are samples of COBIT IT control objectives, including sample controls and sample control tests.

EXHIBIT 24.1　Manage Third-Party Services Guidance

Manage Third-party Services–Control Guidance	
Control Objective—Controls provide reasonable assurance that third-party services are secure, accurate, and available, support processing integrity, and are defined appropriately in performance contracts. **Rationale**—Managing third-party services includes the use of outsourced service providers to support financial applications and related systems. Deficiencies in this area could significantly impact financial reporting and disclosure of an entity. For instance, insufficient controls over processing accuracy by a third-party service provider may result in inaccurate financial results.	
Illustrative Controls	**Illustrative Tests of Controls**
A designated individual is responsible for regular monitoring and reporting on the achievement of the third-party service level performance criteria.	Determine if the management of third-party services has been assigned to appropriate individuals.

Selection of vendors for outsourced services is performed in accordance with the organization's vendor management policy.	Obtain the organization's vendor management policy and discuss with those responsible for third-party service management if they follow such standards. Obtain and test evidence that the selection of vendors for outsourced services is performed in accordance with the organization's vendor management policy.
IT management determines that, before selection, potential third parties are properly qualified through an assessment of their capability to deliver the required service and a review of their financial viability.	Obtain the criteria and business case used for selection of third-party service providers. Assess whether these criteria include a consideration of the third party's financial stability, skill, and knowledge of the systems under management, and controls over security, availability, and processing integrity.
Third-party service contracts address the risks, security controls, and procedures for information systems and networks in the contract between the parties.	Select a sample of third-party service contracts and determine if they include controls to support security, availability, and processing integrity in accordance with the company's policies and procedures.
Procedures exist and are followed to ensure that a formal contract is defined and agreed for all third-party services before work is initiated, including definition of internal control requirements and acceptance of the organization's policies and procedures.	Review a sample of contracts and determine whether: • There is a definition of services to be performed. • The responsibilities for the controls over financial reporting systems have been adequately defined. • The third party has accepted compliance with the organization's policies and procedures, e.g., security policies and procedures. • The contracts were reviewed and signed by appropriate parties before work commenced. • The controls over financial reporting systems and subsystems described in the contract agree with those required by the organization. Review gaps, if any, and consider further analysis to determine the impact on financial reporting.
A regular review of security, availability, and processing integrity is performed for service-level agreements and related contracts with third-party service providers.	Inquire whether third-party service providers perform independent reviews of security, availability, and processing integrity, e.g., service auditor report. Obtain a sample of the most recent review and determine if there are any control deficiencies that would impact financial reporting.

EXHIBIT 24.2   Ensure Systems Security Control Guidance

Ensure Systems Security–Control Guidance	
Control Objective—Controls provide reasonable assurance that financial reporting systems and subsystems are appropriately secured to prevent unauthorized use, disclosure, modification, damage, or loss of data. **Rationale**—Managing systems security includes both physical and logical controls that prevent unauthorized access. These controls typically support authorization, authentication, nonrepudiation, data classification, and security monitoring. Deficiencies in this area could significantly impact financial reporting. For instance, insufficient controls over transaction authorization may result in inaccurate financial reporting	
Illustrative Controls	**Illustrative Tests of Controls**
An information security policy exists and has been approved by an appropriate level of executive management.	Obtain a copy of the organization's security policy and evaluate the effectiveness. Points to be taken into consideration include: • Is there an overall statement of the importance of security to the organization? • Have specific policy objectives been defined? • Have employee and contractor security responsibilities been addressed? • Has the policy been approved by an appropriate level of senior management to demonstrate management's commitment to security? • Is there a process to communicate the policy to all levels of management and employees?
A framework of security standards has been developed that supports the objectives of the security policy.	Obtain a copy of the security standards. Determine whether the standards framework effectively meets the objectives of the security policy. Consider whether the following topics, which are often addressed by security standards, have been appropriately covered: • Security organization • Asset classification and control • Personnel security • Software security policy • Physical and environmental security • Workstation security • Computing environment management • Network environment management • System access control • Business continuity planning • Compliance • System development and maintenance Determine if there are processes in place to communicate and maintain these standards.

An IT security plan exists that is aligned with overall IT strategic plans.	Obtain a copy of security plans or strategies for financial reporting systems and subsystems and assess their adequacy in relation to the overall company plan.
The IT security plan is updated to reflect changes in the IT environment as well as security requirements of specific systems.	Confirm that the security plan reflects the unique security requirements of financial reporting systems and subsystems.
Procedures exist and are followed to authenticate all users to the system to support the validity of transactions.	Assess the authentication mechanisms used to validate user credentials for financial reporting systems and validate that user sessions time-out after a predetermined period of time.
Procedures exist and are followed to maintain the effectiveness of authentication and access mechanisms (e.g., regular password changes).	Review security practices to confirm that authentication controls (passwords, IDs, two-factor, etc.) are used appropriately and are subject to common confidentiality requirements (IDs and passwords not shared, alphanumeric passwords used, etc.).
Procedures exist and are followed to ensure timely action relating to requesting, establishing, issuing, suspending, and closing user accounts.	Confirm that procedures exist for the registration, change, and deletion of users from financial reporting systems and subsystems on a timely basis and the procedures are followed. Validate that attempts to gain unauthorized access to financial reporting systems and subsystems are logged and are followed up on a timely basis. Select a sample of new users and determine if management approved their access and the access granted agrees with the access privileges that were approved. Select a sample of terminated employees and determine if their access has been removed, and was done in a timely manner. Select a sample of current users and review their access for appropriateness based upon their job functions.
A control process exists and is followed to periodically review and confirm access rights.	Inquire whether access controls are reviewed for financial reporting systems and subsystems on a periodic basis by management. Assess the adequacy of how exceptions are reexamined, and if the follow-up occurs in a timely manner.

(continues)

EXHIBIT 24.2   Ensure Systems Security Control Guidance (*Continued*)

Where appropriate, controls exist to ensure that neither party can deny transactions and controls are implemented to provide nonrepudiation of origin or receipt, proof of submission, and receipt of transactions.	Determine how the organization establishes accountability for transaction initiation and approval. Test the use of accountability controls by observing a user attempting to enter an unauthorized transaction. Obtain a sample of transactions, and identify evidence of the accountability or origination of each.
Where network connectivity is used, appropriate controls, including firewalls, intrusion detection, and vulnerability assessments, exist and are used to prevent unauthorized access.	Determine the sufficiency and appropriateness of perimeter security controls including firewalls and intrusion detection systems. Inquire whether management has performed an independent assessment of controls within the past year (e.g., ethical hacking, social engineering). Obtain a copy of this assessment and review the results, including the appropriateness of follow-up on identified weaknesses. Determine if antivirus systems are used to protect the integrity and security of financial reporting systems and subsystems. When appropriate, determine if encryption techniques are used to support the confidentiality of financial information sent from one system to another.
IT security administration monitors and logs security activity, and identified security violations are reported to senior management.	Inquire whether a security office exists to monitor for security vulnerabilities and related threat events. Assess the nature and extent of such events over the past year and discuss with management how they have responded with controls to prevent unauthorized access or manipulation of financial systems and subsystems.
Controls relating to appropriate segregation of duties over requesting and granting access to systems and data exist and are followed.	Review the process to request and grant access to systems and data and confirm that the same person does not perform these functions.
Access to facilities is restricted to authorized personnel and requires appropriate identification and authentication.	Obtain polices and procedures as they relate to facility security, key and card reader access—and determine if those procedures account for proper identification and authentication. Observe the in and out traffic to the organization's facilities to establish that proper access is controlled. Select a sample of users and determine if their access is appropriate based upon their job responsibilities.

EXHIBIT 24.3 Manage the Configuration Control Guidance

Ensure Systems Security–Control Guidance	
Control Objective—Provide reasonable assurance that all IT components, as they relate to security, processing, and availability, are well protected, would prevent any unauthorized changes, and assist in the verification and recording of the current configuration. **Rationale**—Configuration management ensures that security, availability, and processing integrity controls are set up in the system and maintained through its lifecycle. Insufficient configuration controls can lead to security and availability exposures that may permit unauthorized access to systems and data and impact financial reporting.	
Illustrative Controls	**Illustrative Tests of Controls**
Only authorized software is permitted for use by employees using company IT assets.	Determine if procedures are in place to detect and prevent the use of unauthorized software. Obtain and review the company policy as it relates to software use to see that this is clearly articulated. Consider reviewing a sample of applications and computers to determine if they are in conformance with organization policy.
System infrastructure, including firewalls, routers, switches, network operating systems, servers and other related devices, is properly configured to prevent unauthorized access.	Determine if the organization's policies require the documentation of the current configuration, as well as the security configuration settings to be implemented. Review a sample of servers, firewalls, routers, etc., to consider if they have been configured in accordance with the organization's policy.
Application software and data storage systems are properly configured to provision access based on the individual's demonstrated need to view, add, change, or delete data.	Conduct an evaluation of the frequency and timeliness of management's review of configuration records. Assess whether management has documented the configuration management procedures. Review a sample of configuration changes, additions, or deletions, to consider if they have been properly approved based on a demonstrated need.
IT management has established procedures across the organization to protect information systems and technology from computer viruses.	Review the organization's procedures to detect computer viruses. Verify that the organization has installed and is using virus software on its networks and personal computers.
Periodic testing and assessment is performed to confirm that the software and network infrastructure is appropriately configured.	Review the software and network infrastructure to establish that it has been appropriately configured and maintained, according to the organization's documented process.

CHAPTER 25

Best Practices in Compliance and Internal Controls: ASX 10 Principles[1]

The Australian Stock Exchange (ASX) Corporate Governance Council created 10 principles to good governance, including best practices for each. Listed below is a summary of the principles and best practices to achieve them.

PRINCIPLE 1: LAY SOLID FOUNDATIONS FOR MANAGEMENT AND OVERSIGHT

"Recognize and publish the respective roles and responsibilities of board and management." The company's framework should be designed to:

- Enable the board to provide strategic guidance for the company and effective oversight of management.
- Clarify the respective roles and responsibilities of board members and senior executives in order to facilitate board and management accountability to both the company and its shareholders.
- Ensure a balance of authority so that no single individual has unfettered powers.

Recommendation 1.1: Formalize and disclose the functions reserved to the board and those delegated to management[2]

Role of the board and management It is suggested that the board adopt a formal statement of matters reserved to it or a formal board charter that details the functions and responsibilities of the board. Another alternative is a formal statement of authority delegated to management. The nature of matters reserved to the board and delegated to management will necessarily depend on the size, complexity, and ownership structure of the company, and will be influenced by its tradition and corporate culture, and by the skills of directors and managers. Disclosing the division of responsibility assists those affected by corporate decisions to better understand the respective accountabilities and contributions of board and management of the particular company. That understanding can be further enhanced if the disclosure includes an explanation of the balance of responsibility among the chairperson, the lead independent director (if any), and the chief executive officer (or equivalent).

The division of responsibility may vary with the evolution of the company. Regular review of the balance of responsibilities may be appropriate to ensure that the division of functions remains appropriate to the needs of the company.

Responsibilities of the board Usually the board would be responsible for

- Having oversight of the company, including its control and accountability systems
- Appointing and removing the chief executive officer (or equivalent)
- Ratifying the appointment and, where appropriate, the removal of the chief financial officer (or equivalent) and the company secretary
- Inputting into and final approval of management's development of corporate strategy and performance objectives
- Reviewing and ratifying systems of risk management and internal compliance and control, codes of conduct, and legal compliance
- Monitoring senior management's performance and implementation of strategy, and ensuring appropriate resources are available

- Approving and monitoring the progress of major capital expenditure, capital management, and acquisitions and divestitures
- Approving and monitoring financial and other reporting

Allocation of individual responsibilities   It is appropriate that directors clearly understand corporate expectations of them. To that end, formal letters of appointment for directors setting out the key terms and conditions relative to that appointment are useful.

PRINCIPLE 2: STRUCTURE THE BOARD TO ADD VALUE

Have a board of an effective composition, size, and commitment to discharge its responsibilities and duties adequately. An effective board is one that facilitates the efficient discharge of the duties imposed by law on the directors and adds value in the context of the particular company's circumstances. This requires that the board be structured in such a way that it:

- Has a proper understanding of, and competence to deal with, the current and emerging issues of the business
- Can effectively review and challenge the performance of management and exercise independent judgment

Ultimately, the directors are elected by the shareholders. However, the board and its delegates play an important role in the selection of candidates for shareholder vote.

Recommendation 2.1: A majority of the board should be independent directors

Assessment of independence   An independent director is independent of management and free of any business or other relationship that could materially interfere with—or could reasonably be perceived to materially interfere with—the exercise of their unfettered and independent judgment.

Disclosure of independence   The board should regularly assess the independence of each director in light of interests disclosed by them. So it can do this, each independent director should provide to the board all relevant information. Directors considered by the board to be independent should be identified as such in the corporate governance section of the annual report. The board should state its reasons if it considers a director to be independent notwithstanding the existence of relationships. In this context, the board must consider materiality thresholds from the perspective of the company and its directors, and to disclose these. The tenure of each director is important to an assessment of independence. The board should disclose the period of office of each director in the corporate governance section of the annual report. Where the independent status of a director is lost, this should be immediately disclosed to the market.

Independent decision making   All directors should bring an independent judgment to bear in decision making. To facilitate this, there should be a procedure agreed by the board for directors to take independent professional advice if necessary at the company's expense. Nonexecutive directors should consider the benefits of conferring regularly at scheduled sessions without management present. Their discussions can be facilitated by the chairperson or lead independent director. Family ties and cross-directorships may be relevant in considering interests and relationships that may compromise independence, and should be disclosed by directors to the board.

Recommendation 2.2: The chairperson should be an independent director

Role of chairperson   The chairperson is responsible for leadership of the board, for the efficient organization and conduct of the board's function, and for the briefing of all directors in relation to issues arising at board meetings. The chairperson must facilitate the effective contribution of all directors and promote constructive and respectful relations between board members and between board and management. Where the chairperson is not an independent director, it may be beneficial to consider the appointment of a lead independent director. The chairperson must commit the time necessary to discharge that role effectively. In that context, the number of other positions, and time commitment associated with them, should be taken into account.

Recommendation 2.3: The roles of chairperson and chief executive officer should not be exercised by the same individual

There needs to be a clear division of responsibility at the head of the company. The division of responsibilities between the chairperson and the chief executive officer should be agreed by the board and set out in a statement of position authority. The chief executive officer (CEO) should not go on to become chairperson of the same company.

Recommendation 2.4: The board should establish a nomination committee

Purpose of the nomination committee   Particularly in larger companies, a nomination committee can be a more efficient mechanism for the detailed examination of selection and appointment practices meeting the needs of the company. The existence of a nomination committee should not be seen as implying a fragmentation or diminution of the responsibilities of the board as a whole. It is recognized that for smaller boards, the same efficiencies may not be apparent from a formal committee structure.

Composition of nomination committee   The nomination committee should

- Consist of a minimum of three members, the majority being independent directors

- Be chaired by the chairperson of the board or an independent director

Charter The nomination committee should have a charter that clarifies its role and responsibilities, composition, and structure and membership requirements.

Responsibilities Responsibilities of the committee should include

- Assessment of the necessary and desirable competencies of board members
- Review of board succession plans
- Evaluation of the board's performance
- Recommendations for the appointment and removal of directors

Selection process A formal and transparent procedure for the selection and appointment of new directors to the board helps promote investor understanding and confidence in that process.

Director competencies Corporate performance is enhanced when there is a board with the appropriate competencies to enable it to discharge its mandate effectively. An evaluation of the range of skills, experience, and expertise on the board is, therefore, beneficial before a candidate is recommended for appointment. Such an evaluation enables identification of the particular skills, experience, and expertise that will best complement board effectiveness. The nomination committee should consider developing and implementing a plan for identifying, assessing, and enhancing director competencies. The nomination committee should also consider whether succession plans are in place to maintain an appropriate balance of skills, experience, and expertise on the board.

Composition and commitment The board must be of a size and composition conducive to making decisions expediently, with the benefit of various perspectives and skills, and in the best interests of the company as a whole rather than of individual shareholders or interest groups. The size of the board should be limited to encourage efficient decision making. Individual board members must devote the necessary time to the important tasks entrusted to them. In this context, all directors should consider the number and nature of their directorships and calls on their time from other commitments. In support of their candidature for directorship, nonexecutive directors should provide the nomination committee with details of other commitments and an indication of time involved. Nonexecutive directors should specifically acknowledge to the company prior to appointment or being submitted for election that they will have sufficient time to meet what is expected of them. The nomination committee should regularly review the time required from a nonexecutive director, and whether directors are meeting this. A nonexecutive director should inform the chairperson and the nomination committee before accepting any new appointments.

Election of directors   The guidelines in Attachment A concerning notices of meeting are designed to facilitate better communication with shareholders. They contain guidance about how to frame resolutions for the election of directors. The names of candidates submitted for election as director should be accompanied by the following information to enable shareholders to make an informed decision on their election:

- Biographical details, including competencies and qualifications and information sufficient to enable an assessment of the independence of the candidate
- Details of relationships between
  - The candidate and the company
  - The candidate and directors of the company
- Directorships held
- Particulars of other positions which involve significant time commitments
- The term of office currently served by any directors subject to reelection
- Any other particulars required by law.

Term of directorship   Nonexecutive directors should be appointed for specific terms subject to reelection and to the ASX Listing Rules and ASX Corporations Act provisions concerning removal of a director. Reappointment of directors should not be automatic.

Recommendation 2.5: Provide the information indicated in the guide to reporting on Principle 2

The following material should be included in the corporate governance section of the annual report:

- The skills, experience, and expertise relevant to the position of director held by each director in office at the date of the annual report
- The names of the directors considered by the board to constitute independent directors and the company's materiality thresholds
- A statement as to whether there is a procedure agreed by the board for directors to take independent professional advice at the expense of the company
- The term of office held by each director in office at the date of the annual report
- The names of members of the nomination committee and their attendance at meetings of the committee
- An explanation of any departures from best practice recommendations 2.1, 2.2, 2.3, or 2.5

The following material should be made publicly available, ideally by posting it to the company's web site in a clearly marked corporate governance section:

- A description of the procedure for the selection and appointment of new directors to the board
- The charter of the nomination committee or a summary of the role, rights, responsibilities, and membership requirements for that committee
- The nomination committee's policy for the appointment of directors

Application of Principle 2 in relation to trusts References to "board" and "directors" should be applied as references to the board and directors of the responsible entity of the trust. There may be a technical conflict in implementing the recommendations that the chairperson be an independent director or a lead independent director, where the responsible entity is a wholly owned subsidiary of a fund manager and all the directors are employees of the parent. This should be discussed and clarified in any explanation of departure from the best practice recommendations included in the corporate governance section of the annual report. Refer also to Section 601JA(2) of the ASX Corporations Act, which sets out the criteria for independence of a director of a responsible entity.

PRINCIPLE 3: PROMOTE ETHICAL AND RESPONSIBLE DECISION MAKING

Actively promote ethical and responsible decision making. The company should

- Clarify the standards of ethical behavior required of company directors and key executives (i.e., officers and employees who have the opportunity to materially influence the integrity, strategy, and operation of the business and its financial performance) and encourage the observance of those standards.
- Publish its position concerning the issue of board and employee trading in company securities and in associated products which operate to limit the economic risk of those securities.

Recommendation 3.1: Establish a code of conduct

Establish a code of conduct to guide the directors, the CEO (or equivalent), the chief financial officer (CFO) (or equivalent), and any other key executives as to 3.1.1 (the practices necessary to maintain confidence in the company's integrity) and 3.1.2 (the responsibility and accountability of individuals for reporting and investigating reports of unethical practices).

Good corporate governance ultimately requires people of integrity. Personal integrity cannot be regulated. However, investor confidence can be enhanced if the company articulates the practices by which it intends directors and key executives to abide. Each company should determine its own policies designed to influence appropriate behavior by directors and key executives. A code of conduct is an effective way to guide the behavior of directors and key executives and demonstrate the commitment of the company to ethical practices. Adopting a separate code for directors and key executives is unnecessary. Principle 10 recommends corporate codes of conduct. Depending on the nature and size of the company's operations, the code of conduct for directors and key executives may stand alone or be part of the corporate code of conduct recommended in Principle 10.

Recommendation 3.2: Disclose the policy concerning trading in company securities by directors, officers, and employees

Public confidence in the company can be eroded if there is insufficient understanding about the company's policies governing trading by "potential insiders." The law prohibits insider trading, and the ASX Corporations Act and the ASX Listing Rules require disclosure of any trading undertaken by directors or their related entities in the company's securities. In the interests of investor confidence, companies should consider complementing these requirements with a formal policy governing trading practices. For the purpose of this policy, a "potential insider" is a person likely to possess inside information and includes the directors, the CEO (or equivalent), the CFO (or equivalent), staff members who are involved in material transactions concerning the company, and any other member of staff who is likely to be in the possession of inside information. "Inside information" is information concerning the company's financial position, strategy, or operations, which, if made public, would be likely to have a material impact on the price of the company's securities.

PRINCIPLE 4: SAFEGUARD INTEGRITY IN FINANCIAL REPORTING

Have a structure to independently verify and safeguard the integrity of the company's financial reporting. This requires the company to put in place a structure of review and authorization designed to ensure the truthful and factual presentation of the company's financial position. For example, the structure would include

- Review and consideration of the accounts by the audit committee
- A process to ensure the independence and competence of the company's external auditors

Such a structure does not diminish the ultimate responsibility of the board to ensure the integrity of the company's financial reporting.

Recommendation 4.1

Require the CEO (or equivalent) and the CFO (or equivalent) to state in writing to the board that the company's financial reports present a true and fair view, in all material respects, of the company's financial condition and operational results and are in accordance with relevant accounting standards.

Interaction with ASX Corporations Act   The requirement to make this statement encourages management accountability and provides an underpinning for the statements required by the directors under the ASX Corporations Act in relation to the company's financial reports.

Recommendation 4.2: The board should establish an audit committee

Purpose of the audit committee   Particularly for larger companies, an audit committee can be a more efficient mechanism than the full board for focusing the company on particular issues relevant to verifying and safeguarding the integrity of the company's financial reporting. The existence of an audit committee should not be seen as implying a fragmentation or diminution of the responsibilities of the board as a whole. It is recognized that for smaller boards, the same efficiencies may not be apparent from a formal committee structure.

Importance of the audit committee   The existence of an independent audit committee is recognized internationally as an important feature of good corporate governance. If there is no audit committee, it is particularly important that the company disclose how its alternative approach assures the integrity of the financial statements of the company and the independence of the external auditor, and why an audit committee is not considered appropriate.

Recommendation 4.3

Structure the audit committee so it consists of

- Only nonexecutive directors
- A majority of independent directors
- An independent chairperson, who is not chairperson of the board
- At least three members

The audit committee should be of sufficient size, independence, and technical expertise to discharge its mandate effectively.

Importance of independence   The ability of the audit committee to exercise independent judgment is vital. International best practice is moving toward an audit committee comprised of only independent directors. The ASX Corporate Governance Council encourages companies to move toward such a composition within the next three years and will be monitoring audit committee composition and international developments in this area.

Technical expertise   The audit committee should include members who are all financially literate (i.e., are able to read and understand financial statements); have at least one member who has financial expertise (i.e., is a qualified accountant or other financial professional with experience of financial and accounting matters); and contain some members who have an understanding of the industry in which the entity operates.

Recommendation 4.4: The audit committee should have a formal charter[4]

Charter   The charter should set out the audit committee's role and responsibilities, composition, structure, and membership requirements. The audit committee should be given the necessary power and resources to meet its charter. This will include rights of access to management and to auditors (external and internal) without management present and rights to seek explanations and additional information.

Responsibilities   The audit committee should review the integrity of the company's financial reporting and oversee the independence of the external auditors.

Meetings   The audit committee should meet often enough to undertake its role effectively. The audit committee should keep minutes of its meetings and these should ordinarily be included in the papers for the next full board meeting after each audit committee meeting.

Reporting   The audit committee should report to the board. The report should contain all matters relevant to the committee's role and responsibilities, including

- Assessment of whether external reporting is consistent with committee members' information and knowledge and is adequate for shareholder needs
- Assessment of the management processes supporting external reporting
- Procedures for the selection and appointment of the external auditor and for the rotation of external audit engagement partners
- Recommendations for the appointment or removal of an auditor,
- Assessment of the performance and independence of the external auditors and whether the audit committee is satisfied that independence of this function has been maintained having regard to the provision of non-audit services
- Assessment of the performance and objectivity of the internal audit function
- The results of its review of risk management and internal compliance and control systems

Principle 7 provides further guidance on this matter.

Recommendation 4.5: Provide the information indicated in the guide to reporting on Principle 4

Guide to reporting on Principle 4   The following material should be included in the corporate governance section of the annual report:

- Details of the names and qualifications of those appointed to the audit committee or, where an audit committee has not been formed, those who fulfill the functions of an audit committee
- The number of meetings of the audit committee and the names of the attendees
- Explanation of any departures from best practice recommendations 4.1, 4.2, 4.3, 4.4, or 4.5

The following material should be made publicly available, ideally by posting it to the company's web site in a clearly marked corporate governance section:

- The audit committee charter
- Information on procedures for the selection and appointment of the external auditor, and for the rotation of external audit engagement partners

PRINCIPLE 5: MAKE TIMELY AND BALANCED DISCLOSURE

Promote timely and balanced disclosure of all material matters concerning the company. This means that the company must put in place mechanisms designed to ensure compliance with the ASX Listing Rules requirements so

- All investors have equal and timely access to material information concerning the company—including its financial situation, performance, ownership, and governance.
- Company announcements are factual and presented in a clear and balanced way.

"Balance" requires disclosure of positive and negative information.

Recommendation 5.1

Establish written policies and procedures designed to ensure compliance with ASX Listing Rules disclosure requirements and to ensure accountability at a senior management level for that compliance.

There should be vetting and authorization processes designed to ensure that company announcements

- Are made in a timely manner
- Are factual
- Do not omit material information
- Are expressed in a clear, objective manner that allows investors to assess the impact of the information when making investment decisions

Recommendation 5.2: Provide the information indicated in the guide to reporting on Principle 5

The following material should be included in the corporate governance section of the annual report: an explanation of any departures from best practice recommendation 5.1 or 5.2.

The following material should be made publicly available, ideally by posting it to the company's web site in a clearly marked corporate governance section: a summary of the policies and procedures designed to guide compliance with ASX Listing Rules disclosure requirements.

PRINCIPLE 6: RESPECT THE RIGHTS OF SHAREHOLDERS

Respect the rights of shareholders and facilitate the effective exercise of those rights. This means that a company should empower its shareholders by

- Communicating effectively with them
- Giving them ready access to balanced and understandable information about the company and corporate proposals
- Making it easy for them to participate in general meetings

Recommendation 6.1

Design and disclose a communications strategy to promote effective communication with shareholders and encourage effective participation at general meetings. Publishing the company's policy on shareholder communication will help investors to access the information.

Electronic communication   Companies should consider how best to take advantage wherever practicable of new technologies that provide

- Greater opportunities for more effective communications with shareholders
- Improved access for shareholders unable to be physically present at meetings

Meetings   Consider how to use general meetings effectively to communicate with shareholders and allow reasonable opportunity for informed shareholder participation.

The ASX Corporate Governance Council was asked to develop guidelines for improving shareholder participation through the design and content of notices and through the conduct of the meeting itself.

Communication with beneficial owners   Companies may wish to consider allowing beneficial owners to choose to receive shareholder materials directly, for example, by electronic means.

Web site   Companies are encouraged, but not required, to maintain a company web site and to communicate with shareholders via electronic methods. If the company does not have a web site, it must make relevant information available to shareholders by other means;

for example, a company may provide the information on request by e-mail, facsimile, or post.

Recommendation 6.2

Request the external auditor to attend the annual general meeting and be available to answer shareholder questions about the conduct of the audit and the preparation and content of the auditor's report.

PRINCIPLE 7: RECOGNIZE AND MANAGE RISK

Establish a sound system of risk oversight and management and of internal control. This system should be designed to identify, assess, monitor, and manage risk and to inform investors of material changes to the company's risk profile. This structure can enhance the environment for identifying and capitalizing on opportunities to create value.

Recommendation 7.1

The board or appropriate board committee should establish policies on risk oversight and management.

Purpose of the committee   Particularly for larger companies, a committee can be a more efficient mechanism than the full board for focusing the company on risk oversight and management and on internal control. The appropriate board committee may be the audit committee, the risk management committee, or some other relevant committee. The existence of a committee should not be seen as implying a fragmentation or diminution of the responsibilities of the board as a whole. For smaller boards, the same efficiencies may not be apparent from a formal committee structure.

Policies   The policies should clearly describe the roles and respective accountabilities of the board, audit committee (or other appropriate board committee), management, and any internal audit function. They should include the following components: oversight; risk profile; risk management; compliance and control; and assessment of effectiveness.

Oversight of the risk management system   It is part of the board's oversight role to oversee the establishment and implementation of the risk management system and to review at least annually the effectiveness of the company's implementation of that system.

Risk profile   The risk profile should be a description of the material risks facing the company. Material risks include financial and nonfinancial matters. The risk profile should be regularly reviewed and updated.

Risk management and compliance & control   Management should establish and implement a system for identifying, assessing, monitoring, and managing material risk throughout the organization. This system will include the company's internal compliance and control systems.

Assessment of effectiveness   A company will require some means of analyzing the effectiveness of its risk management and internal compliance and control system and of the effectiveness of its implementation. This will generally be undertaken by the internal audit function, but an alternative mechanism may be employed to achieve the same outcome depending on the company's size and complexity and the types of risk encountered.

A company, particularly a substantial company, is encouraged to have an internal audit function.

Internal audit function   The audit committee should recommend to the board the appointment and dismissal of any chief internal audit executive. The internal audit function should be independent of the external auditor. The internal audit function should report to management and should have all necessary access to management and the right to seek information and explanations. The audit committee should oversee the scope of the internal audit and should have access to the internal audit function without the presence of management. To enhance the objectivity and performance of the internal audit function, companies should consider a second reporting line from the internal audit function to the board or relevant committee.

Recommendation 7.2

The CEO (or equivalent) and the CFO (or equivalent) should state to the board in writing that the statement given in accordance with best practice recommendation 4.1 (the integrity of financial statements) is founded on a sound system of risk management and internal compliance and control, which implements the policies adopted by the board, and that the company's risk management and internal compliance and control system is operating efficiently and effectively in all material respects. The integrity of the company's financial reporting depends on the existence of a sound system of risk oversight and management and internal control. The requirement to make this statement encourages management accountability in this area.

Recommendation 7.3: Provide the information indicated in the guide to reporting on Principle 7

Guide to reporting on Principle 7 The following material should be included in the corporate governance section of the annual report: an explanation of any departures from best practice recommendations 7.1, 7.2 or 7.3.

The following material should be made publicly available, ideally by posting it to the company's web site in a clearly marked corporate governance section: a description of the company's risk management policy and internal compliance and control system.

PRINCIPLE 8: ENCOURAGE ENHANCED PERFORMANCE

Fairly review and actively encourage enhanced board and management effectiveness. This means that directors and key executives should be equipped with the knowledge and information they need to discharge their responsibilities effectively, and that individual and collective performance is regularly and fairly reviewed.

Recommendation 8.1: Disclose the process for performance evaluation of the board, its committees and individual directors, and key executives

Performance review The performance of the board and key executives should be reviewed regularly against measurable and qualitative indicators. The nomination committee should take responsibility for evaluating the board's performance.

Facilitating performance by education The company should implement induction procedures designed to allow new board appointees to participate fully and actively in board decision making at the earliest opportunity. New directors cannot be effective until they have a good deal of knowledge about the company and the industry within which it operates. An induction program should be made available that enables directors to gain an understanding of:

- The company's financial, strategic, operational, and risk management position
- Their rights, duties, and responsibilities
- The role of the board committees

The nomination committee should be responsible for ensuring that an effective induction process is in place and should regularly review its effectiveness. Similar induction processes may be desirable for key executives. Directors and key executives should have access to continuing education to update and enhance their skills and knowledge. This should include education concerning key developments in the company and within the industry and environments within which it operates.

Access to information The board should be provided with the information it needs to discharge its responsibilities efficiently. In particular:

- There must be a procedure agreed by the board for directors to take independent professional advice if necessary, at the company's expense.

- All directors must have access to the company secretary.
- The appointment and removal of the company secretary must be a matter for decision by the board as a whole.

Management should supply the board with information in a form, timeframe, and quality that will enable the board to discharge its duties effectively. Directors should be entitled to, and prepared to request, additional information where they consider that the information supplied by management is insufficient to support informed decision making.

Role of the company secretary   The company secretary plays an important role in supporting the effectiveness of the board by monitoring that board policy and procedures are followed and in coordinating the completion and dispatch of board agenda and briefing materials. The company secretary should be accountable to the board, through the chairperson, on all governance matters.

PRINCIPLE 9: REMUNERATE FAIRLY AND RESPONSIBLY

Ensure that the level and composition of remuneration is sufficient and reasonable and that its relationship to corporate and individual performance is defined. This means that companies need to adopt remuneration policies that attract and maintain talented and motivated directors and employees to encourage enhanced company performance. There must be a clear relationship between performance and remuneration, and investors must understand the policy underlying executive remuneration.

Recommendation 9.1: Provide disclosure in relation to the company's remuneration policies to enable investors to understand the costs and benefits of those policies and the link between remuneration paid to directors and key executives and corporate performance

Reporting   Disclosing the remuneration policy is a fundamental requirement for remuneration reporting. The interests of shareholders and the market are best served through a transparent and readily understandable framework for executive compensation and its costs and benefits. Transparency as to the remuneration policy should be complemented by full and effective disclosure, in keeping with the spirit and intent of the ASX Corporations Act and the ASX Listing Rules, of the remuneration paid to directors and senior management.

Annual disclosure   The ASX Corporations Act requires annual disclosure by a listed company of the details of the nature and amount of each element of the fee or salary of

- Each director.
- Each of the five highest paid officers of the company.
  - This includes disclosure in respect of nonmonetary components, such as options.
  - To facilitate consistency and clarity of reporting.
  - Any employee or officer who has the opportunity to materially influence the integrity, strategy, and operation of the business and its financial performance.

"Officer" is defined in Section 6 of the ASX Corporations Act.

Disclosure should focus on the remuneration components related to continuing employment with the company or other companies in the same group. Accordingly, if an executive has been terminated during the year and the termination and other benefits paid classify that executive as one of the five highest paid executives, the relevant disclosure should include the five highest paid executives continuing in employment. Any loans to executives and directors (other than those made on commercial terms) should be included with this disclosure, including the amount and the interest rate. Benefits such as motor vehicles, rent, travel and relocation allowances, and other benefits should be included. Effective disclosure requires valuing the various components and describing the valuation techniques used.

Continuous disclosure   Entering employment agreements with key executives, or obligations under these agreements falling due, may trigger a continuous disclosure obligation under ASX Listing Rule 3.1. Where this is the case, disclosure to the market should include a summary of the main elements and terms of the agreement, including termination entitlements. In considering the appropriate matters for disclosure to the market and fostering a constructive relationship with shareholders, the sensitivities of significant payments to key executives should be considered.

Improving corporate behavior Australia needs a framework for disclosure that will produce sustainable improvements in corporate behavior concerning remuneration practices. The issues associated with the establishment of such a framework are complex. The right framework requires:

- Clarification of the disclosure policy and requirements of the ASX Corporations Act relative to matters such as the value of stock options and disclosure of accruals of termination and other payments
- Complementary Australian Accounting Standards Board (AASB) standards, including finalization of the proposed AASB standard on director, executive, and related-party disclosures
- A careful balance in the amount and type of disclosure, so its outcome is relevant information to investors and not simply enhanced market conditions for increasing levels of individual remuneration to the detriment of shareholders

The enhanced framework for determining, reviewing, and reporting on remuneration of directors and executives outlined in this document is a significant step in improving the information available to investors and influencing corporate behavior. However, the ASX Corporate Governance Council has agreed as a matter of priority to examine the need for additional disclosure, including for a wider range of executives. The ASX Corporate Governance Council encourages companies to restore investor confidence by adopting disclosure practices designed to enhance awareness of key aspects of the remuneration framework and its link to performance.

Eliminating surprise Shareholder concern about executive payments is often exacerbated by a lack of information concerning core entitlements when they are agreed. This can be alleviated if, for example, the nature of the termination entitlements of the CEO (or equivalent) is disclosed to the market at the time it is agreed as well as at the time the actual payment is settled.

Recommendation 9.2: The board should establish a remuneration committee

Purpose of the remuneration committee Particularly for larger companies, a remuneration committee can be a more efficient mechanism than the full board for focusing the company on appropriate remuneration policies that are designed to meet the needs of the company and to enhance corporate and individual performance. The existence of a remuneration committee should not be seen as implying a fragmentation or diminution of the responsibilities of the board as a whole. For smaller boards, the same efficiencies may not be apparent from a formal committee structure.

Composition of remuneration committee The remuneration committee should

- Consist of a minimum of three members, the majority being independent directors.
- Be chaired by an independent director.

Charter The remuneration committee should have a formal charter that defines its role and responsibilities, composition, structure, and membership requirements.

Responsibilities The responsibilities of the remuneration committee should include a review of and recommendation to the board on:

- Executive remuneration and incentive policies
- The remuneration packages of senior management
- The company's recruitment, retention, and termination policies
- Procedures for senior management
- Incentive schemes
- Superannuation arrangements
- The remuneration framework for directors

Remuneration policies The company should design its remuneration policy so it motivates directors and management to pursue the long-term growth and success of the company within an appropriate control framework, and so it demonstrates a clear relationship between key executive performance and remuneration. The remuneration framework for directors is often addressed by the nomination committee rather than the remuneration committee. The remuneration committee may seek input from individuals on remuneration policies, but individuals should not be directly involved in deciding their remuneration. The remuneration committee should ensure that the board, management, and the remuneration committee are provided with sufficient information to ensure informed decision making. Executive remuneration packages should involve a balance between fixed and incentive pay, reflecting short-term and long-term performance objectives appropriate to the company's circumstances and goals. A proportion of executive directors' remuneration should be structured in a manner designed to link rewards to corporate and individual performance.

Recommendation 9.3: Distinguish the structure of non-executive directors' remuneration from that of executives

Where schemes for retirement benefits for nonexecutive directors are in place, their existence and terms should be clearly disclosed in the corporate governance section of the annual report, including the provision accrued each year together with the total amount accrued to date. The relevant amount should be disclosed as a component of each participating director's remuneration.

Recommendation 9.4: Ensure that payment of equity-based executive remunerations is made in accordance with thresholds set in plans approved by shareholders

Recommendation 9.5: Provide the information indicated in the guide to reporting on Principle 9

PRINCIPLE 10: RECOGNIZE THE LEGITIMATE INTERESTS OF STAKEHOLDERS[5]

Recognize legal and other obligations to all legitimate stakeholders. Companies have a number of legal and other obligations to nonshareholder stakeholders, such as employees, clients/customers, and the community as a whole. There is growing acceptance of the view that organizations can create value by better managing natural, human, social, and other forms of capital. Increasingly, the performance of companies is being scrutinized from a perspective that recognizes these other forms of capital. That being the case, companies must demonstrate their commitment to appropriate corporate practices.

Recommendation 10.1: Establish and disclose a code of conduct to guide compliance with legal and other obligations to legitimate stakeholders

Most companies are subject to a number of legal requirements that affect the way business is conducted. These include trade practices and fair dealing laws, consumer protection, respect for privacy, employment law, occupational health and safety, equal employment opportunity, superannuation, and environmental and pollution controls. In several areas, directors and officers are held personally responsible for corporate behavior inconsistent with these requirements, and penalties can be severe. Aside from the need to manage risk effectively and support compliance with the company's legal obligations, there is the broader issue of enhancement of corporate reputation. In this context, consultation with the governments and communities in whose territory business is conducted is important. Public or social accountability by corporations is generally based on notions of legitimacy, fairness, and ethics. The board has a responsibility to set the tone and standards of the company and to oversee adherence to these. Company codes of conduct which state the values and policies of the company can assist the board in this task and complement the company's risk management practices.

Corporate code of conduct   Codes of conduct should address matters relevant to the company's compliance with its legal obligations to stakeholders. A code of conduct should enable employees to alert management and the board in good faith to potential misconduct without fear of retribution, and should require recording and investigation of such alerts. The company should have a system for ensuring compliance with its code of conduct and for dealing with complaints. In devising and implementing that system, the laws concerning defamation and privacy need to be considered.

ENDNOTES

1. This chapter extensively quotes the "Code of Conduct for Chief Financial Officers," Group of 100, December 2002. See www.group100.com.au web site.
2. For further guidance, see *A Guide to Directors and Officers Liability Insurance*, 1st edition, June 2001, by C. Smith, N. Milne, and F. Morris. Published by Australian Institute of Company Directors.
3. For further guidance, see "Code of Conduct for Chief Financial Officers," Group of 100, December 2002. www.group100.com.au web site. Further guidance may be found at www.csaust.com and at www.companydirectors.com.au. Also, see ASX Listing Rule 3.19A: Regarding Disclosure by the Company of Directors' Modifiable Interests within Five Business Days.
4. A detailed guide to the responsibilities of the audit committee is provided in *Best Practice Guide—Audit Committees*, Auditing & Assurance Standards Board of the Australian Accounting Research Foundation, Institute of Internal Auditors, Australian Institute of Company Directors, 2nd edition, August 2001. See www.aarf.asn.au web site.

5. For further guidance, see *AS3806-Compliance Programs,* Standards Australia, 1998. See www.standards.com.au, *Draft DR03027 (Project ID: 4303)—Organizational Codes of Conduct,* Standards Australia, 2003. See www.standards.com.au, *Draft DR03028 (Project ID: 4304)—Corporate Social Responsibility,* Standards Australia, 2003. See www.standards.com.au, *Draft DR03029 (Project ID: 4305)—Whistleblowing Systems for Organizations,* Standards Australia, 2003.

CHAPTER 26

Best Practices in Internal Controls: Segregation of Duties (SOD)

INTRODUCTION

Segregation of duties (SOD) has received much greater scrutiny with the internal controls requirements mandated by Section 404 of the Sarbanes Oxley Act of 2002 (SOX). Virtually all protocols to improve internal controls include provisions to enforce SOD. According to Anne Burt at the University of Florida (May 5, 2004), SOD should include the assurance that no individual has the physical and system access to control all phases of a business process or transaction, whether from authorization to custody, and to recordkeeping. When conflicts exist in SOD, organizations can be exposed to significant risks. Auditors are looking for conflicts in SOD in which one individual has access to responsibilities which are inherently in conflict with one another, such as purchasing and accounts payable, purchasing and receiving, general ledger and supply management, etc. The conflicts can be caused by innocent and unintentional errors or by intentional and criminal fraud. Burt warns that no matter the reason, an organization can be held liable if caused by the lack of adequate and auditable process controls.

Internal and external auditors have tested for conflicts in SOD over the years. Most audit firms have created a matrix of conflicting duties where functions, such as Accounts Payable (AP), Accounts Receivable (A/R), and inventory control are at odds.

The evolution of application software has included a trend to expand the responsibilities to super users who can access functions beyond traditional business models. This trend has been accelerated by wave after wave of downsizing organizations to the point that wearing multiple functional hats has become the norm. What follows are examples of conflicts that can occur with super users:

Order Management Super User

An individual may have the ability to release customer orders while creating and maintaining customer master information. This creates the risk that one user could release sales orders to customers who have unacceptable credit and then enter invalid or fraudulent sales orders.

Accounts Receivable Super User

An individual may have the ability to enter A/R receipts, credit memos, and invoices while entering and maintaining customer master information. This creates the risk that one user could create fraudulent or erroneous sales and A/R transactions.

General Ledger (G/L) Super User

An individual may have the ability to maintain G/L setups while entering and posting journals. This creates the risk that one user could modify setup financial configurations, make invalid and unauthorized journal entries, make erroneous consolidation mappings resulting in erroneous financial statement consolidations, and make unauthorized intercompany transactions.

Accounts Payables Super User

An individual may have the ability to enter and approve invoices while entering and maintaining employee master information. This creates the risk that users could commit fraud by setting themselves up as a supplier and then entering and approving fraudulent invoices to their fraudulent supplier.

Purchasing Super User

An individual may have the ability to enter and maintain purchase order (PO) transactions while maintaining supplier master information and entering receiving/inventory transactions. This creates the risk that one user could commit fraud by creating fraudulent suppliers, POs to the fraudulent supplier, and fraudulent receipts against fraudulent POs.

Procure-to-Pay Super User

In organizations with a materials or supply chain management approach an individual may have the ability to access and control inventory, purchasing, receiving, and supplier master information. This creates the risk that one user could commit fraud in many ways. A successful SOD would typically segregate the following functions:

- Inventory control
- Purchasing
- Receiving
- Supplier master

The conventional view of most auditors is that good SOD will reduce the chances of unilateral errors or fraud and will require collusion between or among multiple employees for errors to occur without detection. Though this is true, it is a narrow view that ignores how SOD conflicts can occur beyond the silo of one system or instance of an Enterprise Resource Planning (ERP) or financial system. Best practices will provide controls to prevent SOD violations in the following:

- Over time
- In a shared services environment

- In cases of a three-way conflict
- In hierarchical approvals

Best practices will include the use of e-business tools to automate the detection and prevention of SOD violations which will provide the following:

- Detection (monitoring and reporting)
- Prevention (application and database controls)
- Monitoring and visibility (hierarchical dashboards with alters)

Finally, best practices will include a rationalization, consolidation, and standardization of all roles and responsibilities. Many organizations have created hundreds of roles and responsibilities in a haphazard and ad hoc basis. In many cases, little thought was given to SOD and there was poor or nonexistent management oversight. The best evidence of this is the discovery of several thousand violations of SOD in organization after organization. SOD has been a key area of internal control in the United States and Organization for Economic Cooperation and Development (OECD) Principles for some time. The existence of so many SOD violations demonstrates the disconnect between the audit process and information technology (IT), the lack of enforcement, and the lack of technology tools to discover, monitor, and prevent the violations.

SOD IN A MULTIOPERATIONAL ENVIRONMENT (SHARED SERVICES)

Many larger organizations have multiple operations, which use multiple instances of one or more ERP systems. These ERP instances can be the same version level of the software and there is little standardization across instances. Many of these organizations have created shared services to lower costs and improve efficiencies. AP and purchasing have been frequent candidates for shared services.

A multioperational environment may include the use of a shared services approach. Though shared services presents opportunities to lower costs and improve efficiencies, it creates additional challenges in maintaining good segregation of duties. In our example, a commodity buyer supports various operating units. Each operating unit has it own ERP instance: two Oracle instances and the two ERP system instances. In such an environment, the commodity manager creates corporate-wide agreements, which need to be supported with blanket POs in various organizations.

When one individual has access to multiple ERP instances, the opportunities for violations of SOD increase and are more difficult to discover. Most audit protocols look for violations within an ERP instance. In a shared services environment, it will be essential to look for violations across ERP instances. The difficulty of doing this will be compounded in a heterogeneous IT environment with disparate ERP and financial systems.

In the example in Exhibit 26.1, a commodity manager supports procurement for the entire company. Responsibilities would include contract negotiations and management and then codification of agreements in each operating unit with blanket or contract-type POs. In our example, it could mean access to two separate instances of Oracle and two separate instances of the ERP system. The danger is that the commodity manager could commit fraud by setting up a bogus supplier in one operating unit, by creating bogus POs to be shipped to other operating units, and by creating bogus receiving transactions. None of these would be easy to discover since the violations occur across instances and not within one instance of the ERP system.

Even if there are no shared services, multiple and independent ERP systems complicate compliance and internal control efforts. Best practices to reduce the chance of fraud while improving internal control would include establishing a global standard for user naming

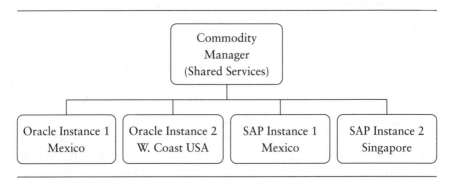

EXHIBIT 26.1   Sample High-Risk Arrangement

conventions, responsibilities, reporting relationships, and conflict matrices. One production ERP instance would be set as the standard after careful review and approval. This would include a global standard for business rules and internal control. The standard ERP instance would then be copied over to all other ERP instances. With this in place, viable prevention and detection would be a more realistic goal.

SOD OVER TIME

SOD needs to be maintained over time. Most efforts to enforce SOD consist of a snapshot at a given point of time. Clever people intent on committing fraud could violate SOD over time by obtaining a specific responsibility to launch events and then quickly end that responsibility. The process would be continued for other specific responsibilities to achieve the desired fraud. An example of creating a bogus supplier, orders, and payments follows:

- Grants himself supplier master responsibility and creates himself as a bogus supplier.
- End dates his supplier master responsibility.
- Grants himself purchasing responsibility and creates a bogus purchase order to his bogus supplier.
- End dates his purchasing responsibility.
- Grants himself receiving responsibility.
- Receives his bogus purchase order.
- End dates his receiving responsibility.
- Invoices the company. The invoice will be paid in that it meets a three-way match.

A best practice to prevent SOD violations over time would include running periodic reports that capture user responsibilities over time, with start and end dates.[1]

THREE-WAY SOD

Though it may take two to tango, in many cases, it takes three to commit fraud. The great majority of SOD efforts have addressed two-way conflicts, but fail to look for a third conflict often required to commit fraud. The bogus supplier is a popular example used in many SOD presentations, but these presentations typically fail to explain that it takes three responsibilities to commit fraud:

1. A corrupt employee, with supplier master access, creates herself or an accomplice as a supplier.
2. The same corrupt employee with purchasing access creates a bogus purchase order to her bogus supplier.
3. The same corrupt employee, with receiving access, creates a bogus receiving transaction to receive her bogus purchase order. Then she issues an invoice and packing list and forwards the documents to her company's AP.

The invoice will be paid in that there is a three-way match (PO, receiving transaction, and invoice), but it took three violations of SOD to commit fraud.

HIERARCHICAL SOD (HSOD)[2]

Hierarchical, or multilevel, approvals refer to a concept whereby authorizations are attached to positions in a hierarchy, rather than to individual users. With hierarchical approvals, you can determine how authorizations are to be passed up and down within an organization. Many organizations have adopted electronic workflows to automate and standardize the approval hierarchy process. SOD will not address the inherent conflicts that occur in many organizations in that the conflicting functions eventually report to the same supervisor or manager. See Exhibit 26.2.

Further complicating the ability to maintain SOD and provide viable checks and balances, consider the same reporting relationship in a global organization in which each functional area is located in different time zones or even different continents, with users speaking different languages. In many of these locations, American-based notions of ethics and corporate governance are not understood or followed. Many of those who handle these transactions may be clerical-level personnel who are conditioned to follow instructions without questioning or evaluating them. Exhibit 26.3 is based on actual global organizations.

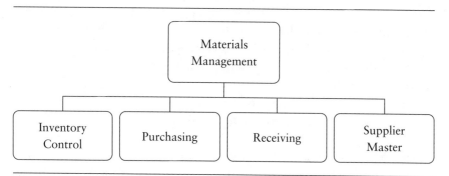

EXHIBIT 26.2   Sample Arrangement Where Segregated Duties Flow to Same Supervisor

In such organizations, supply, materials, or logistics supervisors and managers direct the activities of subordinates who have little reason to suspect potential errors or wrongdoing. Though the existing SOD controls may be able to identify and prevent obvious conflicts that occur at clerical and transactional levels, they do nothing to address the ease with which higher-level supervisors and managers may make mistakes or commit fraud. Just as important, a narrow SOD approach does not address the need for executive-level SOD (i.e., the need for critical business decisions to be reviewed and approved by key stakeholders outside of their area). For instance, supply management decisions regarding long-term planning and forecasts should be reviewed by key stakeholders in finance and sales, and sales forecasts should be approved by key stakeholders in supply management and finance.

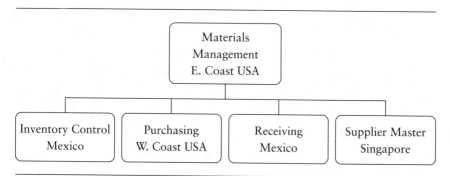

EXHIBIT 26.3   Sample Arrangement for Global Organization

In our example, good business practice would argue that supplier master control should be segregated from all supply chain and procurement responsibilities fairly high up in the hierarchy.

What is needed is an HSOD approach that at a minimum would do the following:

- Identify individual conflicts in segregation of duties.
- Identify the roles and responsibilities of the individuals involved.
- Identify the reporting relationships of the individuals involved.
- Identify HSOD conflicts that occur at higher levels within the organization.
- Help in providing checks and balances for critical planning and forecasting decisions. See Exhibit 26.4.

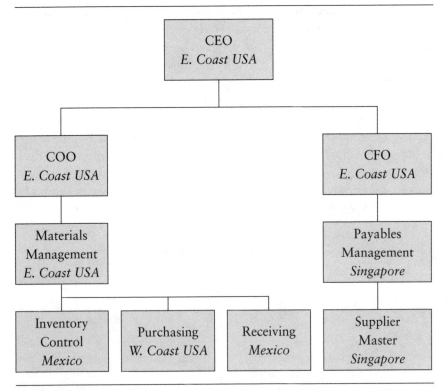

EXHIBIT 26.4   Example of Hierarchical Segregation of Duties (HSOD) Approach

The prevention of errors and wrongdoing is only one aspect of the HSOD process. What follows is a checklist of areas of concern in the procure-to-pay (P2P) process that will benefit from SOD monitoring and prevention processes and tools and from an HSOD approach overall:

- **Auditor Tests—a Snapshot in Time:** Auditor tests, done manually and using software tools, are often only a snapshot in time. Their activities and schedules are typically well understood by company employees. There may be little to prevent internal users from changing responsibilities to pass an audit and then changing them back after the auditors depart. Most organizations lack the sophisticated controls to catch the switch.
- **Planning, Scheduling, and Forecasting Controls:** Ironically, most organizations have developed robust controls for procurement and payments in the P2P process but have typically done less to control the overall master scheduling, planning, and forecasting process. One error or intentional fraud at this level can cascade down into hundreds of mistakes at the execution level within procurement and supply management. This process is complicated by the global and outsourced nature of many organizations. It is difficult to control the process when the players are located in different countries or are the product of multiple mergers and acquisitions. The SOD approach does not address these issues. A robust HSOD solution should include approval workflows that standardize and automate the review and approval of master schedules, forecasts, and plans. Ideally, the process would include a risk assessment around the various planning and forecasting assumptions and decisions.
- **Buyer/Planner Approach:** Many organizations have adopted a buyer/planner (or buyer/scheduler) approach in which the traditional purchasing and planning functions are merged under one individual. The segregation of these functions has provided checks and balances but created inefficiencies and delays. As mentioned above, tight controls are typically in place to control procurement within most organizations, but the controls around the master scheduling, planning, and forecasting processes are typically looser. This is true at a senior level or at a buyer/planner

level. Auditors may lack an understanding of the complexity of this process to develop adequate tests scenarios and audits.

■ **Super Users:** Many IT departments and external system integrators have almost unlimited access as system administrators and super users. During system implementations and upgrades, the intent is to limit these super user accesses to testing environments, but there is often a need to access actual "production" environments. Though SOD may address the more obvious conflicts, HSOD would be needed to see conflicts beyond individual players.

So Why Is This Essential? Examples of SOD and HSOD Fraud

Various surveys have shown that most fraud is committed at executive levels of organizations. This is not to minimize the impact of fraud at lower levels which SOD will help to prevent. What follows is an example of SOD and HSOD fraud. We will suggest that HSOD fraud is a larger risk than SOD fraud. To paraphrase the classic TV show, the stories are true, but the names (commodities) have been changed to protect the innocent (and the author).

SOD Fraud A major appliance manufacturer had a profitable repair depot in which appliances within and beyond warranty would be received from customers and repaired, renovated, and returned. If the units were beyond repair, they would be scrapped and the units replaced with a rebuilt or new unit. The man running the repair depot was technically adequate, but the consensus of management was that he was not bright and required a lot of hand-holding as to how to perform the required system transactions. In his position, he would perform receiving transactions (from customers), inventory transactions (scrapping units and issuing components), and shipping transactions (to customers). Well, he was dumb as a fox, running a side business selling refurbished units. The process was simple. He created a false scrap transaction for a unit that he would refurbish and sell to some of the company's customers at discounted prices. Since he was in control of all the required transactions, no one in the organization suspected the fraud until the Saturday afternoon that a senior manager came into the office to catch up on some work and caught him loading a truck with several units. It was estimated that he was reaping $50,000 per year in his venture. The company did not want the embarrassment and effort to pursue a criminal prosecution and terminated him via a layoff.

HSOD Fraud   A major automotive accessory manufacturer purchased a great deal of coiled aluminum. This could be procured by actual net weights or by a theoretical minimum weight (TMW) calculation. Using the TMW calculation, the buyer typically pays a small premium but is assured of only paying for the TMW and not actual and higher net weights of materials. The head of operations made a deal with the company's largest supplier to defraud the company by charging for more weight than received. It required her to manipulate the purchasing, receiving, and accounts payable processes. She convinced a naïve and inexperienced buyer that the POs to the supplier were in TMW and, therefore, did not need to be weighed upon receipt. The truth is that TMW purchases should have been weighed and the TMW calculations verified by determining the length of coils. In turn, the buyer instructed the receiving department not to weigh coils because they were TMW. The head of operations helped her cause by preventing the purchase of an electronic scale large enough to weigh the great majority of coils. Receiving was instructed to enter the weights on the packing lists as the actual net weights, so AP and finance had no reason to suspect fraud. A consultant was hired by the company president to revamp the organization. Unfortunately for the head of operations, she had a background in buying TMW and suspected fraud. She verified it by weighing the smaller coils that the electronic scale could accommodate. Every coil was 7% to 10% underweight. The calculated fraud was over $1 million per year and had been in place for five years. It took the organization over a year, substantial management effort, and legal fees to remove the operations manager with an early retirement package.

Conclusion

If preventing HSOD conflicts is essential, why have auditors failed to address it? Getting through the initial Section 404 audits was a top priority, and it included measures to address SOD conflicts. Introducing the need for HSOD may seem like overkill and a daunting task because it is more complex and is not easily handled with current questionnaires and testing procedures. Unfortunately, this will not save an organization when something goes wrong. The types of errors and fraud that SOD addresses are small potatoes when compared to the potential pain from mistakes and wrongdoing at higher and more sophisticated levels of an organizational hierarchy.

Auditors are lulled into a false sense of security because they are not addressing HSOD issues. In many cases, senior managers and auditors may not be aware of the hierarchical SOD conflicts that exist in their organizations. Obviously, all duties report to one individual at the top of the hierarchy pyramid, but not all conflicts need to be resolved by segregating duties until they reach a C level. The question is how high the segregation should continue to provide adequate process controls while balancing the needs for operational efficiencies.

BEST PRACTICES IN SOFTWARE TOOLS TO ENFORCE SOD

Most organizations have relied on manual internal and external audits to address SOD violations. The problems are obvious. The process is labor intensive, and nothing can prevent reoccurrences of violations after the audits end, and the auditors move on or depart.

Best practices will include software tools that create a matrix of SOD violations and detect them when they occur. More robust software solutions will include detection and prevention capabilities. Since many organizations will require certain users to hold responsibilities that are in conflict with one another, a best practice software solution will provide the ability to control SOD violations as follows:

- Prevent the violation completely with an audit trail.
- Allow the violation with an approval process and audit trail.
- Allow the violation with business rules and audit trail.

This flexibility is critical in today's business environment with cradle-to-grave buyer/planners or in smaller operations in which one person must wear multiple hats. An example would be a small purchasing organization in which a buyer is required to create suppliers in the supplier master. SOD can be maintained by creating a workflow approval in which all supplier additions and changes are approved by a manager in finance. Another example would include changes in supplier tax identification numbers. All such changes would be controlled by a business rule requiring a reason code by the person requesting the change. In all cases, there would be a complete audit trail.

ENDNOTES

1. This concept is courtesy of Jag Padala, Vice President of Engineering, LogicalApps.
2. Parts of this section copied with permission from the publisher from "Hierarchical Segregation of Duties," by Anthony Tarantino, *Cutter IT Journal,* 7:22, December 2004.

CHAPTER 27

Best Practices in Internal Controls: Case Studies

ITEM/PARTS MASTER CONTROL CASE STUDY

Most compliance regulations require an enterprise to provide an assertion that an item is properly classified, described, and disclosed in its financial statements. To this end, proper control of item or part masters is critical. An item master is a listing of all the goods and services used in the manufacturing, distribution, and sales process. An item master typically contains the following information: item number, description, unit of measure, cost, source of supply, and any relevant supplier numbers as a cross-reference.

The problem arises from the creation of redundant item numbers for basically the same items whether they are components, subassemblies, or finished goods. This is a nearly universal problem in almost all enterprises even with the best controls over item masters.

In this case study, a mid-sized medical equipment company with facilities on the west and east coasts had acquired various product lines and had consolidated their manufacture and distribution in its east coast facility. Each of the product lines came with existing item masters, bills of material, engineering drawings, and manufacturing processing documentation. These data were merged into one enterprise resource planning (ERP) database.

Therefore, the same item commonly had been listed under four or five item numbers. Unfortunately, no visibility existed for the redundancy, which meant the pain of simultaneous excess inventories and shortages. The most obvious example of this came to light with a simple and standard item: twist ties used to bundle together electrical wiring harnesses. Of course, it came to light during a crisis in which one of the five manufacturing/product lines, which all used the twist tie, came to a halt due to a shortage of twist ties.

The materials manager was new to the facility and scrambled to expedite a delivery from the supplier. He was about to authorize the paying of a premium, when one of the old hands on the manufacturing floor came to his rescue. The old hand informed him that the same twist tie was in stock under other item numbers.

By walking the production floor and physically checking the other manufacturing lines, he found the same or equivalent twist ties in stock in four other locations. Checks of the item master revealed twist ties meeting the same form, fit, and function. The twist ties were in stock under five different item numbers, purchased from five different suppliers, at five different prices. Most embarrassing, one of the five was in stock as an obsolete item and being written off at the direction of the financial auditors. So, there was no need to order more twist ties. Cleaning up the item master and consolidating the redundant item numbers generated a major cost savings. Excess inventories were reduced and a major price reduction was negotiated with a primary supplier who was offered much greater volumes than in the past.

As mentioned earlier, this is a nearly universal problem but can be typically addressed by the following action items:

- Adopt a standardized commodity coding system such as the United Nations Standard Products and Services Classifications (UNSPSC). The UNSPSC is a hierarchical classification, having five levels. Each level contains a two-character numerical value and a textual description. With the exception of the order of the segment level (that can be used to distinguish between products and services), all hierarchies are insignificant. The order in the family, class, and commodity is not significant and the order of the words in a title does not imply hierarchy or importance. If the UNSPSC does not drill down to enough detail, it is advisable to add further levels.
- Adopt a standardized protocol for item descriptions. Just pick one and stick to it. There are government specifications to support this process.

- Once a standardized commodity code and standardized item master are adopted, apply them to all exiting items and add them to all new items going forward. Software is available to help in automating this process. Otherwise, this can be a very labor-intensive effort. Rationalizing items by on-hand values, transaction volumes, etc., can prioritize the attack.
- Form a value engineering team to analyze items within the same commodity codes and the same descriptions for duplications or the same form, fit, and function.
- Eliminate the redundant items using an engineering change process that cross-references the old item numbers. (In some cases, the old item number will need to be retained, if it is a spare or repair.)
- For items with the same form, fit, and function, charter the value engineering team to standardize on one item. These efforts will typically be self-funding and will generate significant returns.
- Create an ongoing maintenance program. This problem will never go away completely.

The return on investment (ROI) from these efforts can be high. The identification of redundant items can generate price reductions through increased volume discounts. Inventories are reduced as items are cross-referenced and/or duplicates merged under one item number. Value engineering teams can identify and eliminate items with overlapping form, fit, and function. This has the largest ROI potential of all.

SUPPLIER MASTER CONTROL CASE STUDY (COURTESY OF KOTI ANCHA)

The Problem

A high-tech company with a global presence and several locations within the United States had no controls in place to define and maintain its supplier master. Different sites across the globe defined and maintained the supplier master and, thus, created and maintained duplicate supplier records. When it was time to negotiate a contract with Grainger, an MRO supplier, extracting the spend data was difficult as Grainger was defined five different ways and some products were procured at different prices.

Grainger presents an especially difficult problem since it is commonly known as W.W. Grainger or simply Grainger. The same supplier can be listed as Inc., Incorporated, Corporation, or Corp. Another common problem is to list a supplier's PO Box one time and a street address the next time. So, redundancy can easily occur. Because of the W.W. Grainger versus Grainger listing, this redundancy is especially difficult to find.

Each site that used Grainger had its own purchase agreement and pricing based on the volumes specific to that site. Similar products were being procured at different prices.

Commodity codes were inconsistently used and, thus, spend analysis was a nightmare. This is one example, and this was the case with several suppliers and several commodities.

So, no one within Grainger knew the total spend. Even the personnel at Grainger would have had a difficult time determining the total. Of course, it was not in Grainger's interest to let its customer know the extent of the purchase volumes, as the customer would then have increased leverage with which to negotiate price reductions. Global agreements for a few commodities could have saved the company significant dollars and contributed to the bottom line.

The Solution

The company launched an initiative to standardize the commodity codes used in its procurement system and put controls in place to stop "commodity code proliferation." The company consolidated the supplier master so there was only one supplier record for each supplier. Different supplier sites could be maintained based on business needs. Dunn & Bradstreet (D&B) could be used to consolidate the supply base, thus enabling accurate reporting and providing better leverage for negotiating future contracts. Internal commodity codes were mapped to UNSPSC codes to report spend data. The company identified key commodities and negotiated global agreements that resulted in significant savings, and reduced active supplier master records and put controls in place to define and maintain supplier records.

The Benefits

- Reduced purchase prices with greater volume discounts and global sourcing agreements, significant savings to the bottom line
- Reduced maintenance thus reducing maintenance costs
- Accurate reporting
- Improved supplier performance

SPEND VISIBILITY AND CONTROL CASE STUDY (COURTESY KOTI ANCHA)

Spend visibility and control is essential for running a successful supply chain organization. Supply management personnel should be able to report on spend accurately and in a timely manner to assist in activities like sourcing, budgeting, and forecasting future spend. If an organization cannot accurately record and report the spend in terms of commodity, supplier, and timeframe it will fail in controlling the spend.

A large high-tech global company, which designs and manufactures its products, uses several procurement systems for procuring direct and indirect material. Though the procurement process is distributed around the globe by site/location, the payment process is centralized by region and consolidated for reporting purposes in the United States.

The Problem

The company used five different procurement systems (different software products or separate installations of the same software which made them unique) to facilitate the procurement process across its manufacturing and research and development (R&D) facilities worldwide. There were no process controls in place to maintain master data like suppliers, items, and commodity codes. This inherently resulted in duplicate suppliers being defined along with item numbers and commodity codes. Most of the time items were not classified and assigned to the proper commodity code. Commodity codes were defined in the respective procurement systems as needed and were mapped inconsistently to general ledger (G/L) accounts. Reporting was a challenge and never accurate. Reporting on spend by commodity was inaccurate as most of the spend fell into the category of Miscellaneous. This was the case for direct and indirect purchases. In instances where commodity codes were used, they were mapped to different G/L accounts based on the procurement system they were using and type of reporting they were used to. Non-catalog requisitions were used to procure material for manufacturing and R&D purposes, which bypassed the controls put in place in the form of "Approved Suppliers List."

The Solution

The company embarked on an initiative to standardize the procurement processes by replacing all the different procurement systems with a single global instance of an e-procurement system that integrated with the ERP system from the same software vendor. In phase I, the company addressed the indirect side of the business and was successful in rolling out a global e-procurement system where the commodity codes were standardized and mapped to the correct G/L accounts and were centrally maintained. Supplier catalogs were used wherever possible, which resulted in reduced maverick spend and accurate reporting. The purchasing approval process was consistently enforced and was easy to control. Phase II of the initiative was to deal with the direct side of the business by categorizing the items in the item master and clean up the supplier master.

SALES AND PURCHASE ORDER CONTROL CASE STUDY

A medium-sized division of a global corporation built and sold various flight and missile hardware for the National Aeronautics and Space Administration (NASA), the U.S. military, and commercial aircraft manufacturers. It used one legacy ERP system which included customer and sales order management. The ERP system prevented entering the same order number twice but could not prevent or flag poor sales order and PO management. Each presented its own unique problems.

Poor maintenance of sales orders can have some dramatic effects on the validity of sales order backlog. In this example, sales orders were not maintained adequately as to promise ship dates and remaining quantities. The typical result was to overstate sales order backlog. In some cases, orders would be shipped incompletely, and the customer would close the order with the remaining balance left open in the customer service system. The most significant issue was the lack of realistic promise ship dates. The company had a poor record of shipping customer orders on time to meet promise dates. Rather than being proactive and notifying customers that their orders were going to be late and providing new commitments dates before the fact, customers would have to call when promised orders had not shipped as promised. These calls would trigger a reactive response in which the customer was promised a new date, many times an unrealistic date. Worse yet, the new promise dates were not always entered into the customer service system.

All these issues exist on the supplier side as well. Just as poor maintenance of customer order dates frustrates efforts to provide valid sales order backlog data, poor maintenance of purchase order dates frustrates efforts to provide valid cash flow requirements, to plan production, and to make valid commitments to customers.

The solution to both problems is the same, regular and robust maintenance of promise dates and not a reactionary approach of waiting until dates are missed before taking action. Management of the company took the approach that historical or past due commitment dates would not be tolerated. This should not be confused with capturing the original promise date. Most ERP, CRP, and supply chain management (SCM) systems have a field to capture original commitments, which can be compared with current promise dates. The delta between the two dates is the measure of customer service.

The telltale metric here is to run open order reports capturing orders with historical or past due dates. In the first pass at correcting the problem, the customer service and purchasing departments took the path of least resistance and effort: they rescheduled all the past due orders to the next week. Few of them bothered to verify the validity of the dates. So for the metric to work, open orders for close-in periods need to be compared with historical averages of actual shipments for customers and suppliers.

The company did not tolerate its customer service and purchasing personnel playing games with due dates. Supervisors were instructed to make spot checks with customers, suppliers, internal customers, and users of the data to verify if the dates were valid. The supervisors met with their direct reports to review the reports on a regular basis. The company started to track the performance for each customer service and purchasing department member.

In summary, historical or past due dates cannot be tolerated in a customer order or PO system. Each creates problems related to maintaining valid process controls: invalid sales order backlog, invalid cash flow requirements, and reduced operational execution. The cures are as follows:

- Reports capturing historical and close-in promise dates against actual history
- Spot checks with suppliers, external customers, and internal customers/users
- A no-tolerance policy for historical/past due promise dates or arbitrarily rescheduling dates
- Publishing sales and purchase order date maintenance
- Making the maintaining of valid promise dates a KPI and part of the employee review process

FINANCIAL VS. ACTUAL INVENTORY ACCURACY CASE STUDY

A large domestic manufacturer of vending machines had a problem with physical control of inventory. Poor inventory accuracy created the double miseries of excess inventories and parts shortages. The company had an ongoing cycle counting program to maintain high inventory accuracies via a system-generated schedule of spot inventory counts and adjustments of particular items. In the program, the cycle counter would look for an item in its designated warehouse or shop floor location; the location was captured in the legacy ERP system. If the item was found in an adjacent location and the quantities matched, it would designate that as a "hit," meaning accurate inventory. Vending machines require a great deal of low-cost, but high volume, hardware items: bolts, screws, washers, plastic components, labels, and steel stampings.

The company used a rudimentary ABC classification of inventory which guided the cycle counting program. The company used an ABC classification based on dollar demand for items generated through ERP system requirements. The legacy ERP system in place supported inventory classifications based on dollar requirements, units requirements, dollars on hand, and units on hand. In the weeks before a physical inventory, the company would change and accelerate its cycle counting program so it would be based on dollars on hand. In this way, it could minimize the risk of an inventory writedown by verifying that high dollar items in the system were correctly valued.

A typical ABC classification stratifies inventory based on the classic Pareto 80/20 rule. Applied to inventory, it means that 80% of the value or on-hand balances of inventory will be found in 20% of the items. History has shown this to be almost always true. Using the ABC stratification of inventory based on manufacturing resource planning (MRP) and ERP (MRP/ERP) demand, the cycle counting program consistently documented inventory accuracies over 95%, not world-class or best practice but pretty good by most manufacturing benchmarks and standards.

The chief financial officer (CFO) and auditors struggled in understanding how these supposed inventory issues were disrupting operations and causing excesses when the results of their physical inventories showed a close match between actual dollar totals and book or system dollar totals. The auditors in particular struggled in explaining the discrepancies in their commentaries. From a financial perspective, it did not make sense. The financial numbers always matched, and the cycle counting program showed consistently high levels of inventory accuracy.

The company hired an independent consultant with many years experience in industrial manufacturing. He was tasked to solve the inventory problem. He had faced similar problems in the past. The solutions were as follows:

- The cycle count program was changed so that a "hit," meaning inventory was accurate, was only allowed if the item was in its exact location as captured in the ERP system. Cycle counters may have been able to find items by wandering the floor, but busy stock clerks did not have the time to search for an item. If it was not in its location, they would move on to the next item.

■ The cycle counting methodology was changed from counting items based on their dollar demand to items based on their unit demand. The problem was obvious. The company needed to improve its inventory accuracy for the high-volume, but low-value items that made up over 80% of their item master.

■ The cycle counting program was expanded from one dedicated person to two, with the warehouse supervisor taking on the role of analyzing inventory problems as part of a root cause analysis. In the past, the inventory would be adjusted, but the problem was not evaluated with corrective actions to prevent its reoccurrence. In many cases, the problem was caused by bill of material (BOM) inaccuracies which caused inventories imbalances when automatic issuing techniques were employed, known as back-flushing or post-deduct issuing.

■ The biggest change and improvement was to develop a supplier managed inventory (vendor managed inventory or VMI) program for low-cost hardware items. The consultant consolidated over 20 suppliers down to one primary and one secondary VMI provider. The VMI provider moved inventory to its point of use and used simple visual controls, known by its Japanese name of *Kanbans*.

The results were impressive. Because the VMI provider had the great majority of the company's hardware business, prices were reduced by 10% to 15%. Inventory levels improved from months to less than a week. Because the warehouse was no longer burdened with hundreds of low-cost hardware items, inventory accuracies increased as shortages were greatly reduced.

The SOX implications are clear. Section 404 calls for the control of assets. Poor inventory accuracy creates the double pain of paying premiums to expedite items needed due to shortages along with excess inventories for other items. Poor inventory accuracy hurts the ability to execute production, distribution, and shipping, which reduces customer service levels.

AFTER-THE-FACT POS CASE STUDY

A global high-tech manufacturing company had significant issues with after-the-fact POs even though their policies clearly stated that only the purchasing department could make purchase commitments. After-the-fact means that various employees outside of the purchasing department would contact suppliers and order goods and services because they could not wait until their requisitions were approved and processed into POs by the purchasing department, a process that usually took at least a week or two. The company had manufacturing and engineering facilities in several companies, most operating on a 24-hour-per-day basis and often on weekends. There was a great deal of procurement for expense goods and services.

When employees were confronted with violating company policy, the typical response was that they could follow the policy and let the facility come to a halt, or they could keep the facility running. In many cases, this was no exaggeration and a valid argument. Of course, there were abuses by managers, typically by higher-level directors and vice presidents, who believed that policies did not apply to them. For obvious political reasons, the heads of purchasing did not want to risk alienating these executives, especially when they were so slow in processing requirements.

The company's purchasing departments had a system for rush or emergency purchasing requirements, but this still took a few days to process under the best of conditions. Worse yet, the purchasing department had always given expense procurement a low priority, with few long-term agreements in place. The company had a petty cash system in place to handle low-value items. There was no use of purchase or supplier cards and no Internet procurement system even though the company owned the Internet procurement module as part of their ERP system.

The company engaged a large consulting company to attack this and other procurement-related issues. A senior-level consultant with many years of procurement and supply chain expertise evaluated the situation and instituted the following changes:

- The senior-level consultant found the petty cash system to be outdated and ineffective, only working for items that could be purchased from the local hardware or office supply stores. As a first step, a system of purchasing cards was instituted. A purchasing card was assigned to certain employees with a legitimate need to procure ad hoc and emergency goods and services. The latest generation of purchasing cards can block purchases for specific commodities, so, for example, the maintenance foreman could not order airline tickets. Typically, a monthly statement was received, reconciled by the employer, and approved by the employees' supervisor with budgetary responsibility. The company's ERP system supported an electronic approval workflow in which the purchase card invoice was routed first to the employee and then to the appropriate supervisor. This reduced AP and purchasing involvement.

- The next phase was to conduct a strategic sourcing effort to rationalize the expense/indirect supply base, standardize goods and services, and then source and negotiate. The goal was to reduce the number of suppliers to one primary and one secondary partner working under long-term agreements. Wherever possible, the purchased items would be rationalized and reduced. The best example and success story was in office supplies. The number of office supply providers was reduced and the types of items standardized: one standard stapler, paper cutter, sharpener, etc. The savings averaged over 15% and ranged from office supplies to scientific test equipment.

- The final part of the solution was to take the fruits of the strategic sourcing effort and apply them to an Internet procurement system, the one they owned. All repetitive items were placed into electronic catalogs, internally maintained and supplier maintained. Between the two systems of catalogs, users could search, shop, and buy thousands of items. In some cases, the supplier catalogs were restricted to show only preferred items.

The result of these three actions was the near elimination of after-the-fact POs, cost reductions averaging 15%, the freeing up of valuable purchasing time to pursue value-added activities, and the improvement of service levels to requestors.

While after-the-fact POs are a problem, they are a symptom of a much bigger problem: poor control of and services levels for expense procurement on the one hand and high administrative and purchase costs on the other. The SOX implications are clear: after-the-fact purchase orders demonstrate an unacceptable level of control over assets.

CHAPTER 28

Best Practices in Compliance Project Management

COMMON COMPLIANCE PROJECT ELEMENTS

There are common elements in managing compliance projects based on a Committee for Sponsoring Organizations-like (COSO-like) framework. Here are some common elements worth considering as a best practice:

- Obtain executive-level approval for program and supporting projects to document planning assumptions and decisions, facilitate communication among all the various stakeholders, and document approved scope and schedule baselines.
- Create a program with deliverables that include all business processes and key control activities that have significant impact on the organization's financial information.
- Identify all critical business processes and a hierarchy of business processes.
- Identify business owners for each business process and the acceptance by the owners of the requirements to ownership.
- Identify risks and develop risk mitigation strategies.
- Automate the process for the quarterly review of significant financial accounts to determine whether any new accounts fall within the defined materiality threshold.

- Complete a detailed quality assessment review and clean up all business-level key controls documentation.
- Verify that no key controls are missing.
- Ensure all significant risks to financial reporting are matched to key controls.
- Document all embedded systems application controls.
- Design and pilot an operational effectiveness testing methodology; test all key controls and revise control ratings based on their operational effectiveness.
- Document all internal processes for managing outsourced and third-party activities. This should include the assurance that the third parties have created and are maintaining the appropriate documentation, which confirms their internal control environment is effective.
- Identify any new control gaps arising from the quality assessment review and operational effectiveness testing and ensure remediation action plans are in place.
- Conduct and document operational effectiveness testing. Dry run the year-end internal controls assertion process.
- Establish a team that will be accountable for managing the processes that sustain your company's compliance.
- Formalize a process for periodically updating changes to significant financial statement line items.

COMPLIANCE PROJECT CHECKLIST

What follows is a basic checklist that can be helpful in planning and executing a compliance project:

- Create a Basic Plan Project
- Select Members for a Compliance Steering Committee
- List All Key Processes and Prioritize by Their Level of Risk and Auditor Findings
- Select the Nature and Format for Documentation
- Evaluate and Select Compliance Softwares—Tools and Solutions
- Select and Communicate the Documentation Control Process

- Review Project Plan and Approach with Internal and External Auditors
- Evaluate the Assess Control Environment
- Identify Corporate Governance and Management Controls
- Evaluate the Current State of Information Technology (IT) Controls
- Evaluate the Current State of Application and General Controls
- Identify the Owners of the Applicable IT, Application, and General Controls
- Conduct a Pilot for a Key IT and Business Process
- Document and Test Controls for the Selected Key IT and Business Processes
- Modify Approach, Methodology, and Resources Based on Pilot Results
- Review Pilot Results with Compliance Steering Committee
- Conduct Full Project
- Modify Approach, Methodology, and Resources Based on Project Results
- Summarize Documentation and Testing Results

COMPLIANCE PROJECT ROLES AND RESPONSIBILITIES

A best practice would include defining and communicating the roles and responsibilities of the key players in the compliance process, and then obtaining a complete buy-in by the owners of each.

Chief Financial Officer (CFO)

Provide overall project management standards and methodology to business and process owners as to

- Perform Process Flow Documentation
- Perform Risk and Controls Identification
- Test Controls
- Perform High-Level Quality Control Review Evaluation
- Provide Periodic Status Reporting and Monitoring to Executive-Level Steering Committee

CFO/Finance

- Provide Program and Project Management for SOX Team
- Review Financial Statement Accounts and Determine if Significant
- Perform Process Identification for Significant Financial Statement Accounts
- Arrange and Schedule Process Review Sessions and Communicate Requirements to Participants
- Facilitate Process Review Sessions
- Prepare Risk and Control Matrix Process Documentation
- Monitor Completion of Process Flow Documentation, Walk-through, and Testing Documentation
- Monitor Resolution of Control Deficiencies
- Report on Project Status to SOX Program Management Officer (PMO)
- Obtain Finance and Process Owner Signoff of Processes

Business and Process Owner

- Provide Support to Finance in the Process Identification
- Support SOX Project Team in Gathering Initial Documentation of Process Flow
- Attend and Participate in the Process Review Validation Sessions
- Validate Final Process Flow Documents and Risk and Control Matrix
- Assist Internal Audit with Walkthrough and Testing of Controls
- Resolve Any Major Control Deficiencies
- Provide Process Owner Signoff

Internal IT

- Provide Support to Finance in the Process Identification
- Support SOX Project Team in Gathering Initial Documentation of Process Flow
- Attend and Participate in the Process Review Validation Sessions
- Verify Process Flow Documents and Risk and Control Matrix Relating to the IT Portion of the Process

- Assist Internal Audit with Walkthrough and Testing of Controls
- Support Operations in Resolving Any Major Control Deficiencies

Internal Audit

- Assist in Gathering Initial Process Flow Documentation for First Process Review Session
- Attend and Participate in the Process Review Validation Sessions
- Update Process Flow Documentation Based on Process Review Sessions.
- Conduct Walkthrough of Process Flow and Key Controls
- Prepare Walkthrough Documentation
- Prepare Test Plan and Perform Testing
- Submit Test Results to Management

SIX SIGMA APPROACH

Six Sigma is growing in acceptance as a best practice in project management and has initially been applied to manufacturing and distribution environments. Leading organizations have extended its use to a wide variety of projects which have in common the need to solve a problem that can be addressed in a three- to six-month timeframe and in which the outcome is quantifiable. Six Sigma can and should be applied to compliance, especially to projects for addressing significant deficiencies, material weaknesses, and compliance automation. While this may seem like a stretch or the overhyping of yet another buzz concept, it is a very natural extension of a tried and proven best practice in project management.

Common misconceptions are that Six Sigma is a statistical and quality program best applied to repetitive manufacturing environments. While Six Sigma uses statistics and will improve quality, it is better described as a project management approach for improving controls in a process, specifically reducing the variation in a process.

The solution to a Six Sigma project comes from performing a root cause analysis rather than relying on intuition. This is not to say that Six Sigma practitioners do not have a great deal of intuition as to where the solutions lie. Six Sigma attacks a problem in which the solution is not known, needs to be resolved in fairly short timeframe, and the results are quantifiable. Does this sound like a material weakness or significant deficiency?

Six Sigma project experts are classified by a system developed for Asian-based martial arts in which a white belt is a beginner, a green belt is an intermediate practitioner, a black belt is an expert, and a master black belt is a guru. Like the martial arts, Six Sigma black belts and master black belts are expected to teach and mentor lower-level belts.

Six Sigma applies a variety of technical and nontechnical tools in project management. The nontechnical tools will rely on the soft skills of project leaders, which ironically can be more challenging than statistical methods required by many of the technical tools. What follows is a brief overview of a few of both and their applicability to compliance projects:

Nontechnical Tools

- **Stakeholder Analysis**—Determines and evaluates key internal control process owners and influencers, and the gap between their current state and desired end state to resolve a given compliance problem.
- **Planning and Influence Chart**—Identifies key internal control stakeholders, their resistance to improving an internal control process, the reasons for their resistance, and a strategy to resolve their resistance.
- **Threat and Opportunity Matrix**—Identifies the threats if the internal control problem is not improved and the opportunities if the internal control problem is resolved. Both the threats and opportunities must be quantifiable and need to be prioritized so as to not overwhelm the project.
- **Payoff Matrix**—Evaluates the cost versus benefits of improving internal controls. It helps to prioritize the effort around those controls with the largest benefits with the lowest amount of effort required.

Technical Tools

- **Fishbone or Cause and Effect Diagramming**—It is a form of structured brainstorming to solve a compliance problem. It encourages team members to contribute because of the simple graphical format.

- **Process Map**—Creates a current state picture of internal control process flows. It starts with the inputs from suppliers (both external and internal) and ends with the outputs to customers (both external and internal).
- **Histogram**—Measures continuous data (as opposed to static data) in a graphical format that displays the number of times an event is observed in a set of observations. It is popularly referred to as a bell-shaped curve of common cause variation, but also captures bimodal special cause variation, and other outcomes.
- **Pareto Chart**—Measures discrete data. This is counted data yes/no, on/off, go/no go, etc. Originated by the Italian economist, Vilfredo Pareto and popularized by Joe Juran, it measures the number of times a given event occurs. It is a very attractive means of identifying the significant few internal controls generating the greatest number of problems—the 80/20 rule.

The application of Six Sigma to compliance may be a new concept, but offers a cost effective and proven project management approach to tackle tough problems. The alternatives are to rely on expensive external resources or force the improvement project on managers not trained or conditioned in effective project management. Leading organizations are aggressively training Six Sigma black belts in finance and other nonmanufacturing areas. Applying them to solving compliance problems will become a best practice in the coming years.

CHAPTER 29

Best Practices in
Governance and Ethics

A *BusinessWeek* cover story on downsizing the chief executive officer (CEO) describes the change in corporate governance philosophy from the bubble years when CEOs were motivated by carrots such as huge stock option packages. Now we face what Home Depot's founder Kenneth G. Langone calls the dilemma of being "the best-governed, worst-managed" corporations in the world in which executives will be too risk averse to make smarter but more courageous decisions. This could happen if boards and management are in an adversarial relationship with their CEOs. While Mr. Langone has a valid point, this may be an overreaction to efforts to rein in white-collar corruption that has caused so much grief.[1]

Let's begin with the obvious: White-collar corruption and fraud are as old as humankind and not likely to ever disappear. A less obvious notion is that corruption and fraud are a way of life in much of the world and that not everyone engaging in these activities is evil or sinister. Kickbacks and bribes are institutionalized in many areas of the world and are required to facilitate change. Changing this behavior will be a long-term and painful process. Ironically, much of the efforts to improve governance and ethics target processes performed by lower-level managers and have little to do with most of the fraud and wrongdoing committed in most organizations.

The large majority of fraud and wrongdoing documented in the last several years is committed at executive levels. Rarely does one read of fraud and wrongdoing orchestrated by senior or middle managers. Even rarer are examples of fraud by lower-level or technical resources. This is not to say that safeguards are not needed at all levels of an organization, but it does suggest that the large sums of spending to improve internal control are not likely to achieve their goals without a change at the executive level.

The simplistic best practice is to hire and promote only ethical executives and managers. Since the great majority of executives are inherently ethical, the environment that fostered so much corruption needs to be addressed. In short, it was caused by what has been called the imperial CEO, with huge compensation schemes tied to short-term stock price increases over the organization's long-term viability. The imperial CEO's accomplices in this process were anemic and lazy boards of directors and chummy relationships with their public auditors and legal firms with obvious conflicts of interest.

Consultants love the term "tone at the top" to describe the environment needed to promote good governance and ethics. The problem is that many CEOs surround themselves with a team of like-minded people who start to believe their own propaganda. Harold Innis called this a bias of communications, in which contrary opinions are seen as career limiting. So, here are some basic best practices to promote good governance and ethics:

- **Create a Chief Compliance Officer (CCO):** It is critical that the CCO does *not* report to the chief financial officer (CFO) or CEO since they are often the culprits in many of the most infamous breakdowns in ethics. The CCOs should report directly to the board of directors who have created and vigorously enforce the CCO's charter along with a realistic budget.
- **Create a Process of Ethics:** Creating a code of ethics is only the beginning. All employees, consultants, and subcontractors need to receive annual training and then sign a code of ethics which includes a clear and realistic course of action for whistleblowers. The process must include whistleblower access and protections. Good practices include enforcing regular vacations and job rotations as a means to uncover wrongdoing.
- **Clean Up the System and IT Mess:** We are paying the price for following years of McKenzie advice to decentralize operations, and years of mergers and acquisitions done on the cheap. The result is that the average organization is run with a hodgepodge of disparate financial and operating systems. Typically, this was

not the fault of IT professionals, who often sought to standardize and improve systems but could not demonstrate a quick return on investment (ROI). No matter how dedicated and honest the senior management, such a heterogeneous mess will never foster good governance.

- **Use Compliance Software to Improve Internal Control:** Though solutions are emerging quickly and others are under construction, some elements are a must. Documentation management solutions are well established and a must. Fewer than 20% of organizations have auditor tools that support the Committee of Sponsoring Organizations (COSO) and Control Objectives for Information and Related Technology (COBIT) processes. These solutions have become mature enough to justify their deployment even if they are throwaway solutions that will only be in place for two to three years. Finally, software exists that automates internal control enforcement and monitoring with electronic workflow, access, and update controls. These solutions are evolving quickly and are worth a look.

- **Do Not Hide Behind U.S. or Local Generally Accepted Accounting Principles (GAAPs):** Granted that GAAP is an accounting standard and not an auditing standard, but so much corruption has been perpetuated while following U.S. GAAP, its limitations should be obvious. This rules-based approach creates loopholes by permitting companies to use alternate accounting methods while still complying with the rules. Even after Enron and the collapse of Arthur Andersen, the accounting profession has failed to address the limitations of GAAP, and it took the draconian solution of SOX to tighten controls. Many local GAAPs are less stringent than the new International Financial Reporting Standards (IFRS) or GAAP. So, executives should be forewarned that following GAAP will not keep them out of jail. Whether the IFRS GAAP with its principles-based approach will do much better than GAAP remains to be seen. At least, it will provide a level playing field from country to country.

- **Steer Clear of Off-Balance Sheet (OBS) Ploys:** If you are wondering why, ask Enron's Kenneth Lay, who followed the advice of the best and brightest and who faces spending the rest of his life in jail. Many of these ploys had the effect of spending stockholders' money to mislead them.

- **Take a Conservative Approach to Revenue Recognition:** Many companies have been forced to restate earnings after regulators challenged aggressive revenue recognition schemes. Over the long haul, these schemes would probably not have made much difference in earnings.
- **Find a Better Solution Than Stock Options:** Stock options are the poster child for many of the most notorious scandals of the 1990s. In spite of advice from the Financial Accounting Standards Board (FASB) to expense stock options, few have done so. There has to be a better solution to create incentives for executives and managers based on long-term growth and profitability.
- **Invest in Internal Audit:** Many organizations have treated the internal audit as a necessary evil and have grossly understaffed and underbudgeted the process. One commonly reads of examples of billion-dollar organizations with several operating divisions staffed by only two to five internal auditors. A best practice is to look at internal audit as a self-funding process with a great ROI. It deserves the best and brightest in any organization. They are the eyes and ears of the CEO and must be strong enough to be on the same level as external auditors.
- **Create a European Union Version of U.S. SOX:** While the SEC and the accounting profession made some major mistakes in their efforts to improve internal controls, there is a very valid requirement for a process of attesting to the viability of internal controls. A system that makes allowances for the size of an organization makes sense as long as investors can clearly see that smaller firms do not meet the same level of controls as larger firms. The EU can learn from the hard lessons learned in the United States to formulate a workable system of regulations.
- **Create a European Union Version of the SEC:** While the efforts to develop a global GAAP using the IFRS are a major move forward, it is difficult to see how it will succeed without a strong regulatory agency to enforce the rules. The huge U.S. scandals demonstrates that self-regulation is doomed and that it took the combination of mandatory controls and a strong enforcement agency to promote compliance.
- **Promote Complete Transparency in Executive Compensation:** Shareholders continue to express major complaints about the lack of transparency in compensation for corporate officers and

senior executives. Many compensation packages contain stock options, and perks that are not visible to investors and amount to major financial obligations for years to come, GE's Jack Welch being the most famous example. The SEC has proposed new regulations, but they do not go far enough as to the information provided or the number of senior managers covered. Ironically, executive compensation continues to rise at a greater level than the profitability of their organizations. So much for performance-based compensation.

■ **Promote Good Governance:** It sounds corny, but good governance is good business. Organizations with good governance and high ethical standards will win over the long haul and enjoy a competitive advantage in attracting and retaining investors and supporters, especially in a global marketplace.

ENDNOTE

1. "Downsizing the CEO," *Business Week*, April 25, 2005.

CHAPTER 30

Costs *versus* Benefits and the Business Reaction

COST ESTIMATES

In its final rulings, the SEC attempted to estimate the direct costs for internal and external resources in complying with the Sarbanes-Oxley Act (SOX). Part of this is to comply with the Paperwork Reduction act. These estimates were unrealistically low and only spoke to a very narrow area of financial reporting. It is hard to imagine even a small to medium company complying with Sections 401, 404, and 409, with the addition of less than one full-time equivalent (FTE) internal resource, and less than one-half of one FTE external resource. This is roughly how their original estimations project out. When operational controls are included, a realistic projection of internal and external resources will be five to ten times higher for the first year, and there is scant evidence that costs fell in year two for most firms.

The SEC also offered an estimation of the ratio of internal versus external resources: "We estimate that 75% of the burden of preparation is carried by the company internally and that 25% of the burden of preparation is carried by outside professionals retained by the company at an average cost of $300 per hour." A few thoughts on why this may be unrealistic:

- Few companies have much fat left in their corporate finance departments.

- U.S. SOX will require a very specialized expertise, at least initially.
- There will be a host of operational and security issues that will need to be resolved quickly.

The fixes to these problems will not be cheap or quick and will require a consolidating and streamlining of many disparate systems and processes, and an upgrading and expansion of management to digest the data and report in a manner to comply.

The U.S. SOX cost estimates also continue to rise. Here are examples of the changes in cost estimates:

- **July 2004:** PricewaterhouseCoopers' (PWC) Management Barometer reports that: "Despite complaints by some companies about the increased costs and regulatory burden imposed by Sarbanes-Oxley, most respondents, 56 percent, said their company does not track and report internally on the costs of Sarbanes-Oxley and other compliance programs. Forty-one percent do track such costs." This finding is hard to understand. If the costs of compliance are such a burden, why not track and publish them? One reason could be that it would open an organization to unfavorable publicity and scrutiny, especially within a given industry and among competitors.[1]
- **July 2004:** James Flannigan, the distinguished business journalist for the *LA Times,* warns that SOX will accelerate the merger and acquisition trend as small enterprises struggle in complying in a regulatory environment that makes few concessions to smaller enterprises. He notes a survey by the Chicago law firm of Foley and Lardner, which predicts the annual cost of being a public company will increase from $1.3 million to $2.5 million. This is quite disturbing considering that small enterprises create more jobs and are far more entrepreneurial and innovative than large enterprises.[2]
- **August 2004:** Paul Grant, writing in an AccountancyAge.com, August 2004 article, "Sarbanes-Oxley costs soaring," that actual costs are 60% higher than estimates made only six months earlier, says, "The average cost for a company in the survey rose from $1.93m in January to $3.14m in July . . . . The rises have resulted from a 109% increase in internal costs, a 42% rise in external costs and a 40% jump in auditor's fees. Employees hours

spent on Sarbanes-Oxley compliance have also risen from 12,265 to 25,667 over the last half year." These findings are very consistent with other surveys over the last year—estimates of costs continue to rise each quarter or so.[3]

■ **November 2004:** AMR Research predicts that SOX spending will reach $5.8 Billion in 2005 with one third of companies expecting to pay more in 2005 than 2004. "When people first started down the SOX compliance path, they treated it as a one-time project," says John Hagerty, Vice President of Research at AMR Research. "Even though the November 15th deadline will soon pass, companies realize compliance is an ongoing issue and are investing to make processes repeatable, sustainable and cost effective." Over the next year, AMR Research estimates expenditures will occur in four key areas. They include:

- 42% on internal labor / headcount
- 29% on outsourced services
- 28% on technology
- 1% on other

AMR Research has also identified the technology markets to directly benefit from spending. The top five spending priorities in technology supporting SOX compliance in 2005 are:

- Document and record management
- Business process management to integrate disparate business systems
- Applications compliance management software, which will document, monitor, and manage compliance processes
- Enterprise and financial application suites to standardize the compliant business practices for financial transparency

"Technology will play an increasingly significant role in the integration of SOX compliance initiatives into business processes," says Hagerty. "Of equal importance is the consulting necessary to implement these technologies and establish best practices."

AMR's research also found the following SOX compliance facts:

- 33% of companies say the risk of noncompliance is driving their investment.
- 81% of companies have an operational solution plan in place to add to or improve it.

- 98% say 2004 spending has been higher or at the level anticipated.
- Spending on SOX is 42% of overall IT compliance budgets.[4]

■ **December 2004:** Oversight Systems in its "The 2004 Oversight Systems Financial Executive Report on Sarbanes-Oxley," reports that 79% of the over 200 financial executives surveyed believe they have stronger internal controls due to SOX efforts. The report also notes that 57% describe their company's SOX compliance as a good investment for stockholders; 79% say they have stronger internal controls after complying; 74% say their companies realized a benefit from SOX compliance. When asked to identify the benefits from SOX, the survey reports that:

- 46% say SOX ensures the accountability of individuals involved in financial reports.
- 33% say SOX compliance decreases the risk of financial fraud.
- 31% say they have reduced errors in their financial operations.
- 27% say SOX provides improvements in the accuracy of financial reports.
- 25% say SOX empowers the board audit committee by providing it with deeper information.
- 54% say they spent more than originally projected.
- 63% describe their SOX compliance as "difficult" or "very difficult."
- 37% say SOX increased shareholder value because investors know they operate as an ethical business.
- 25% report that SOX boosts shareholder value by building overall confidence in the market.
- 33% say SOX compliance created a cost burden that suppresses stock prices.
- 14% feel that SOX decreased their ability to pay out dividends because compliance expenses are a significant drain on earnings.

As part of the survey, respondents were also asked to define their feelings toward SOX legislation. Of the group, 52% say Congress had good intentions when it passed SOX, but the costs of compliance were not fully considered. Thirty-eight percent say SOX was Congress's overreaction to the unethical behavior of a few executives, and 28% say the market requires regulations like SOX to boost investor confidence in the market's integrity. Only

13% say the benefits of SOX outweigh the costs of complying while 25% say the costs of complying with SOX outweigh the benefits (respondents could select all that applied).[5]

■ **February 2005:** Steven Taub, writing in CFO.com, reports that Sarbanes-Oxley—also known as the "Accountants Full Employment Act"—has led to a doubling of audit fees by the Big Four accounting firms, according to a study by Corp. Executive Board. Increase examples: PWC = 134%, KPMG = 109%, E&Y = 96%, Deloitte = 78%. Taub also referenced a study by the *Financial Times* that found 43 surveyed companies spent an average of $5 million to $8 million to comply with SOX last year. Taub goes on to show the changes in surveys by the CFO Executive Board (part of the Corp. Executive Board) of 60 member companies. At the beginning of 2004, participants most often responded that they expected their Section 404 fees to account for between 20% and 60% of their total financial-statement audit fees. At the end of 2005, for 58% of the participating companies, that ratio has reached 60% to 120%. For 2005, nearly three-quarters of respondents are projecting Section 404 fees to range between 20% and 80% of their total financial-statement audit fees.[6]

■ **March 2005:** Steven Taub, in CFO.com, reports "Nearly half of the large companies surveyed said they are spending more than $10 million to document their internal controls, certify their financials, and comply with other provisions of Sarbanes-Oxley." The nation's largest companies have found that Sarbanes-Oxley compliance costs have surged in the past year, according to a new survey from the Business Roundtable. In the survey of 106 companies, 47% report spending more than $10 million to document their internal controls, certify their financials, and comply with other provisions of Sarbanes-Oxley. Last year only 22% reported spending over 29%. Another 29% estimated their costs at between $6 million and $10 million.[7]

■ **October 2005:** The *Wall Street Journal* cites a Foley and Lardner survey that the average annual cost of being a public company in fiscal 2004 more than tripled since Sarbanes-Oxley was passed, to $3.4 million, with audit fees representing about a third of total costs. "According to the study, which based its conclusions on an analysis of proxy statements from more than 700 public companies, audit fees for companies in the Standard & Poor's Small-Cap 600 index surged an average of 84% in fiscal 2004, following increases of 17% in 2003 and 34% in 2002. Similarly, fees at S&P Mid-Cap 400 companies jumped 92% for 2004, while fees at S&P 500 companies rose 55%."[8]

While much has been written about the large financial burden U.S. SOX is imposing on most companies, what has not been captured in these estimates is whether these will be recurring costs or are higher for the first year as companies ramp up compliance efforts. Many companies are paying high initial costs due to years of neglect and lackluster internal control efforts. The problems are more pronounced in some industries than others. High-technology companies tended to underinvest in their internal audit function and are now having to greatly expand these efforts.

Initial compliance efforts have been labor intensive and manual for the most part. The market is responding quickly with software tools to automate risk management, document management, and security enforcement at the database and application level. Companies are learning from their year-one efforts and will benefit from a great deal of cleanup activities.

Risk and compliance management tools virtually unknown a few years ago will be the norm going forward. The key will be to compare year-two and year-three costs with those incurred as part of the mad rush to comply in 2004. If the ISO certification programs of the 1990s are any example, costs will drop dramatically after the first year or two.

BENEFIT ESTIMATES

So much for the costs of U.S. SOX and other compliance initiatives. Are there any benefits in this, or is this simply an additional cost of doing business and payment for the sins of the high flying 1990s?

It is true, small enterprises will bear a larger burden with the SEC making so few concessions to their size. The December 2005 recommendations for the treatment of microcap and small companies will ease the burden, but do not remove the liability that CEOs and CFOs face. It will take longer for companies to go public, but they will be stronger and more viable than in the past. The quality of initial public offerings should improve substantially over the high flying 1990s, which will increase investor confidence.

U.S. SOX and other COSO-based compliance initiatives will provide enhanced financial and operational visibility in a timely manner. It will expose problems and opportunities earlier. Company managers, analysts, and investors will all benefit. Company managers will be able to make better decisions more quickly. Depending on their abilities, it can make the difference in heading off major disasters. Analysts and investors will benefit from a much clearer picture of a company's business practices and processes.

Beyond compliance requirements, the efforts to improve internal controls are based on sound business principles, such as improved efficiencies, improved decision making, and to reduce intentional and criminal fraud and unintentional errors. Joseph Wells in his 2004 book, "The Corporate Fraud Handbook: Prevention and Detection," cites a survey of 30,000 members of his antifraud association. Based upon their personal experience and general knowledge, his members estimate losses to fraud and abuse represent 6% of gross revenues. Applied to the U.S. Gross Domestic Product of $10 trillion this would result in $600 billion in losses.[9]

Global economic forces will mandate improvements in internal controls. Investors are going to reward enterprises which are viewed as champions of robust internal controls and punish those which are not. Improved internal control efforts, which can cut fraud and errors by even a small percent, can be a self-funding process and provide a strategic competitive advantage by:

- Reduced Risk of Material Deficiencies and Weaknesses
- Reduced Losses from Intentional Fraud and Unintentional Errors
- Reduced Anti-Fraud Enforcement Costs
- Improved Investor and Regulator Confidence
- Higher Analyst Ratings Translating Into Improved Share Prices

While there is an ongoing and very healthy debate as to how to improve internal controls, there is little debate as to the need to improve internal controls. The common elements in U.S. SOX, OMB A-123, Canada's 52-109 and 52-111, the UK's Turnbull Guidance,

Base II and Solvency II, and much of the OECD's Principles, include requirements or recommendations to:

- Identify risks to financial reporting and develop risk mitigation strategies.
- Ensure all significant risks are matched to manual and automated controls.
- Design and pilot an operational effectiveness testing methodology.
- Test all key controls and revise control ratings based on their operational effectiveness. This includes monitoring, detecting, and enforcing controls.
- Automate the process for the quarterly review of significant financial accounts to determine whether any new accounts fall within the defined materiality threshold.
- Identify any new control gaps arising from the quality assessment review and operational effectiveness testing, and ensure remediation action plans are in place.
- Complete a detailed quality assessment of all business controls documentation and verify that no key controls are missing.
- Document all embedded systems application controls.

Initial reactions have been mixed within the business community. According to AMR Research, 80% of CIOs believe SOX will require changes in their information technology and application infrastructure, but are unsure how SOX will affect their companies.

The reaction is also evolving. In 2003 most of the emphasis was on the financial impact. In 2004 there was a growing emphasis on the operational and IT impact. There is a growing awareness that CPOs and CIOs will need to take a very proactive role, and are not likely to survive assuming that SOX is a financial matter.

PWC, in its July 2004 Management Barometer, notes that "by a margin of nearly two to one, large U.S. companies have made compliance with the Sarbanes-Oxley Act part of their regular corporate governance approach and have integrated it with other regulatory activities . . . . The survey of senior executives at U.S.-based multinational companies found that: 64 percent say their company's senior management and board of directors see Sarbanes-Oxley as one of many steps in a larger corporate governance initiative, while 30 percent say it is simply a goal to be achieved. Six percent are uncertain.

62 percent report Sarbanes-Oxley is integrated with their other corporate regulatory compliance processes, but 34 percent say it is not. Four percent are uncertain."[10]

In the same issue of the Management Barometer, PWC's Dan DiFillippo, Partner and U.S. Practice Leader, Governance, Risk and Compliance, states: "Integrating the requirements of Sarbanes-Oxley compliance into ongoing corporate governance and regulatory activities, rather than managing compliance with the law as a separate task, offers the potential for improved business performance in both the short and long term . . . . Given the early outcry about Sarbanes-Oxley's added costs, it's surprising that most companies do not document and track this expense . . . . However, many companies have only recently begun to understand the types of costs and value associated with compliance efforts. We expect more aggressive monitoring as companies examine the effectiveness of their compliance approach."[11]

PWC's Management Barometer's July 2004 survey found that "79 percent of senior U.S. executives say their company must make improvements in order to comply with Section 404 of Sarbanes-Oxley, which requires companies to file a management assertion and auditor attestation on the effectiveness of internal controls over financial reporting. Among areas needing remediation:

- Financial processes 55%
- Computer controls 48%
- Internal audit effectiveness 37%
- Security controls 35%
- Audit committee oversight 26%
- Fraud programs 24%"

PWC's Management Barometer's July 2004 survey also found that "93 percent of U.S. executives expect their company to launch process improvement initiatives to streamline future Sarbanes-Oxley compliance. Among areas cited:

- Financial reporting 63%
- Risk identification and assessment 61%
- Risk mitigation 55%
- IT security strategy and implementation 55%

- Internal audit 55%
- Compliance management 54%
- IT oversight and operations 45%"

An October 2005, *CPA Journal* article cites a survey by Financial Executives International (FEI) of 217 public companies with average annual revenues of $5 billion to evaluate the cost versus benefits to SOX Section 404. The consensus of the survey is that the costs have outweighed the benefits:

- About 55% of all respondents believe Section 404 provides investors with greater confidence in its financial reporting.
- Over 80% of larger companies (over $25 billion in annual revenues) agree.
- But almost all companies (94%) believe the costs of compliance exceed the benefits.
- Many companies agree with focus on internal controls, but criticize the approach as too detailed and bureaucratic.[12]

CONCLUSION

This text began in the fall of 2003 as research for my first article on the Sarbanes-Oxley Act for the Institute for Supply Management. Several articles, web seminars, and speaking engagements followed, including articles with a technical perspective for *Cutter IT Journal* and with a financial perspective for *Accounting Today.* The problem was how and when to cut off the research for the book. The events that are unfolding show no sign of slowing to the point that one can confidently predict exactly what the global compliance landscape will look like in the next few years.

The spring 2005 rulings by the SEC and PCAOB are a good example. Under mounting pressure from foreign and small filers that the U.S. SOX was far too costly for the benefits derived, the SEC has substantially reduced the number of key controls that will require testing. It could mean a reduction of 40% to 50% in internal and external audit fees. The December 2005 recommendations to exclude microcap companies altogether from Section 404 and permit small companies to perform their own audits is the most recent example, which will have a profound effect on a large majority of U.S. public companies.

But the basic thrust of the movement to improve internal controls around standardized methodologies is undeniable. Global markets will impose themselves in all regions and industries and compel the adoption of globally accepted accounting, audit, and IT standards. Organizations will look for proven best practices in business and technology processes to ease the pain and cost of compliance and to provide a competitive advantage.

We conclude by offering two cautions. They come from Miyamoto Musashi (1584?–1645), arguably the greatest samurai swordsman in Japanese history. In his "Book of the Five Rings," he describes key concepts in sword fighting that many have adapted to business strategy. Miyamoto warns against taking a hard focus on the point of your opponent's sword. The reason is simple. The attack will never come from that point. (Being on a college fencing team, I can assure you this is true.) For most U.S. organizations, the point of the sword has been Section 404 of the Sarbanes-Oxley Act. Miyamoto recommends taking a soft focus to expand your peripheral vision. The soft focus will mean looking at 404 as only one part of a comprehensive global compliance process. Ironically, even within U.S. SOX, the lack of attention to Section 401, off-balance sheet arrangements, is surprising, given their terrible abuse that was the foundation of Enron.

Miyamoto also warns against having a favorite weapon—a samurai must master equally all of the weapons at his disposal. Having a favorite weapon can lead to disaster when you are forced to fight with your least favorite weapon. Good compliance and improved internal controls will only come by using all the weapons at your disposal as well. This means using a wide variety of accounting, audit, business process, and technology improvements on your road to global compliance. There is no single or simple fix. It is not a project but a continuous process. Those who master it best will be victorious over their opponents—something Miyamoto could relate to, since he was never defeated in 60 engagements.

Hopefully this handbook has assisted in providing a high-level introduction to most of the initiatives underway and some of the best practices in internal controls to support them.

ENDNOTES

1. PricewaterhouseCoopers, Management Barometer, July 14, 2004.
2. James Flannigan, *LA Times,* July 11, 2004.
3. Paul Grant, Sarbanes-Oxley Costs Souring," AccountancyAge. com, August 2004.
4. John Hagerty, AMR Research, November 11, 2004.
5. Oversight Systems, "Oversight Systems Financial Executive Report on Sarbanes-Oxley," December 2004.
6. Steven Taub, CFO.com, Feb. 11, 2005.
7. Steven Taub, CFO.com, March 18, 2005.
8. Deborah Solomon, "At What Price?" *Wall Street Journal,* October 17, 2005.
9. Joseph Wells, *The Corporate Fraud Handbook: Prevention and Detection,* John Wiley & Sons, 2004.
10. PricewaterhouseCoopers, Management Barometer, July 14, 2004.
11. Dan DiFillippo, PricewaterhouseCoopers, Management Barometer, July 14, 2004.
12. *The CPA Journal,* "The Sarbanes-Oxley Act Improves Investor Confidence, But at a Cost," October 2005.

Frequently Asked P2P Questions[1]

Q: What are customer and supplier collaboration portals and how do they support compliance efforts?

A: Customer and supplier collaboration portals are an electronic means to transmit orders, change orders, forecasting, and inventory information between and among trading partners. Newer versions of supplier collaboration portals can share forecast and inventory information among multiple tiers of trading partners. The numbers of transactions can total over one million per month for very large organizations when enabled for thousands of customers and suppliers. They support compliance efforts by standardizing and automating the means of transmission in an efficient, secured, and auditable electronic format. They typically support a range of technologies from simple web-based access to true B2B using EDI or XML.

Q: Do the examples of segregation also apply to P-cards?

A: Purchase, or P-Cards, and Supplier/Ghost, or S-Cards are used to reduce the use of petty cash, lower purchasing and accounts payable processing costs and efforts, and eliminate the need for after-the-fact purchase orders, while providing excellent service to their users. Segregation of duties (SOD) can be enforced by having two levels of approval for the monthly statements: the budgetary departmental supervisor and a separate approval by finance.

Q: Regarding HSOD, what about dropping supplier masters? If you drop that from the HSOD is it still a problem? In other words, let's say the director still has responsibility for Receiving and Purchasing but not Supply Master. What if the VP is responsible for all?

A: This question relates to the example of segregation of duties (SOD) in which the following functions are shown as in conflict: purchasing, receiving, inventory, and supplier master. A hierarchical segregation of duties (HSOD) conflict could exist if users with these individual responsibilities all report to the same supervisor or manager. Dropping the supplier master would help reduce the conflict potentials, but most auditors would argue that receiving and purchasing responsibilities are a major conflict on an SOD level, but would probably approve their reporting to the same higher level managers—the higher the better.

Q: In regard to SOD, if you are limited and have the same person doing inventory control, purchasing, and receiving, can having an approval hierarchy within those roles satisfy SOX?

A: Using standardized approval hierarchies with a clear audit trail would always be advisable. The higher the approval process, the better. Adding watchers of the approval process in finance would also reduce the chance of errors and fraud.

Q: If a small company has a group of two responsible for both buying and receiving, can they act as "receiver" on each others' orders and have that be considered adequate segregation of duties?

A: This would not be advisable in that both people would have both purchasing and receiving capabilities. There is no easy or systematic means to restrict them from receiving their own purchase orders. Most ERP systems do not provide an auditor-friendly capability to monitor such an arrangement.

Q: Regarding the Master Supplier List, should Purchasing be allowed to add a new supplier to the database and/or the ability to modify it without some sort of approval?

A: Purchasing should be restricted from the supplier master without compensating controls (e.g., review and approval by accounts payable). A best practice would be to segregate supplier maintenance from those performing purchasing, invoice matching, and approval. The fewer people involved with supplier maintenance, the better. This will also improve the odds of applying a consistent naming convention and preventing supplier redundancies. In smaller organizations where one person must wear both hats, an approval workflow process should be in place where a higher level person in an accounts payable approves each new supplier and each supplier change.

Q: How can a procurement group reduce its supplier base if they don't control supplier masters?

A: Many organizations that have advertised impressive reductions in their supplier base have actually only eliminated suppliers with no activity over some extended period of time. The idea is to rationalize purchase spend by commodities, select a primary and alternate supplier for each commodity, develop strategic relationships supported by contracts, and eliminate the spend with other suppliers. The key metric here is that 75–90% of spend is among an ever decreasing number of suppliers. Of course, cleaning up the supplier master to eliminate redundancies and those with no activities is also a very worthwhile effort.

Q: How does poor planning and forecasting create a SOX violation? I understand why it is a poor business decision, but how is it a SOX violation?

A: At the heart of internal controls is the means to maintain fundamental segregation of duties. Many of the SOD efforts attempt to reduce fraud and errors. Providing reviews and approvals of production plans and forecasts outside of supply chain is even more critical in maintaining SOD and providing good checks and balances. Ironically, there are typically very tight controls over all purchase activities, but few systematic controls over forecasts and planning, which drive spending. As a result, a $100 PO will get a formal review and approval process, but a $100 million forecast or production plan may only be informally reviewed and approved, and then by no one outside of supply management.

Q: Would you clarify what an "event" is when event management tools were referred to under best practices in documenting internal controls?

A: Event management tools provide an electronic workflow and approval flow to facilitate the handling of extraordinary events. These events could rise to the threshold of a SOX Section 409 material event requiring the filing of an 8-K form. With only four days to respond to and report on material events, an event management tool will help to standardize, automate, and speed the process as to who is in the communication and decision process. An alternative to event management tools is to customize the electronic workflows that are imbedded in most major ERP systems. This is typically not a simple process.

Q: You recommend Item Master segregation from the Supply Chain. Where should responsibility reside?

A: The item or material master should be segregated from most all departments, not just supply chain. In manufacturing companies, this could be restricted to an engineering or document control group that has no purchasing, inventory, sales, or order management responsibilities or capabilities. An alternative is to use a technology solution which restricts access to various fields within the item master. The problem is that most ERP systems do not permit selected access to master level data. Once a user is in, they may be able to update all fields.

Q: Is my company responsible for internal controls for processes we have outsourced?

A: Yes. A company that has outsourced a process that is normally handled internally, and that may impact financial reporting, is responsible for assessing the viability of the controls around the process. This can be handled in two ways. If the process is closely controlled by the company, it may want to use its own auditors to audit the process. In other cases, the company can request that the outsourced service provider submit an SAS 70 form. An SAS 70 is an internationally accepted means for auditors to validate process controls for an outsourced process.

Q: What types of breakdowns in internal controls would create a material event or material weakness?

A: There have been hundreds of material weaknesses declared under Section 404 of U.S. SOX since the fall of 2004, and they have been caused by a wide variety of problems. Ironically, very few have been caused by SOD, inventory, or supply chain events. A material write down is the most obvious example of a supply chain activity that would cause a material weakness.

Q: Why is it important to automate the enforcement of internal controls?

A: Without automated enforcement of internal controls and business rules, there is nothing to prevent violations from occurring after the auditors have signed off and departed. If a violation then occurs, the audit firm and the company both face major problems in that both have certified that adequate controls are in place. Automating the enforcement of internal controls is also a good way to reduce both internal and external audit costs in that manual controls will typically require a much greater level of testing than automated controls.

Q: Why do I need a document management tool as part of good internal controls?

A: Document management tools are widely available as stand-alones or part of ERP systems. They provide the means to secure and control documents including access and revision controls, with notifications and alerts when a document is checked out or revised. There is nothing more basic in internal controls than documenting controls. Doing this without document controls is not a viable option.

Q: How can a small company deal with segregation of duty conflicts when one person typically wears many hats?

A: If a conflict exists because of the small size of an organization, it should be reported to internal and external auditors as a potential area of risk. Part of the reporting should include measures to mitigate the risk of one person with duties that may be in conflict with each other. This should include management review and approval of the relevant transactions and processes. It should also include a complete transaction audit trail.

Q: What types of reports would purchasing need to create to support SOX and related compliance initiatives?

A:
- Purchase orders without an approved requisition
- Supplier shipments consistently out of receiving tolerance
- Purchase orders with historical or past due dates
- Purchase orders where payment date is less than the "payment terms"

- Supplier quality performance
- Percentage of spend with preferred, approved, certified suppliers
- Purchase price to standards variances and invoice to PO variances

Q: What is needed from our suppliers that we need to keep on file in case of audits?

A:
- Supplier qualification and certification records
- Electronic and hard copies of contracts and purchase orders
- Supplier performance history—on-time, quality levels, etc.
- EH&S-related material, RoHS-related material, MSAs

Q: What will we need to include in customer and supplier contract terms to cover ourselves?

A: It is more important to demonstrate that you have standardized your terms and conditions and have a process in place for reviewing, approving, and communicating changes in Ts and Cs. One suggestion would be to consider adding verbiage that mandates suppliers to maintain valid due dates and quantities and builds in penalties and/or rewards for the accuracy of this data.

Q: Do all items need to be under a contract? Or are some items, such as services, exempt?

A: There is nothing in the SEC final rulings covering Section 401a, 404, or 409 of U.S. SOX mandating all purchased goods and services under contract. Good practice under U.S. SOX and all related compliance regulations would suggest that long-term agreements with strategically sourced business partners are highly desirable and a major advantage over short-term POs with a variety of suppliers that have not been strategically sourced.

Q: How can I enforce segregation of duties within an ERP system?

A: Several software solutions are available to document responsibility or function incompatibilities. Some of these applications actually enforce segregation of duties by preventing conflicts at a role or responsibility level. Others go further and enforce segregation of duties within shared screens, by locking down master level data attributes and enforcing approval processes for key data changes.

Q: What is the effect of inventory inaccuracies with regard to SOX?

A: The physical and logical control of assets is a cornerstone of Section 404. Poor inventory accuracy is major evidence of poor internal controls and typically translates into the double dilemma of excess inventories and critical part shortages. Even if financial balances are fairly constant (i.e., the negative and positive adjustments balance each other out), actual on-hand inventories need to be accurate to maintain viable operations.

Q: What is the impact of "after-the-fact" POs on public companies?

A: This is a very obvious example of an out-of-compliance situation. Creating a purchase order after the receipt of an item should be completely prohibited. Violations in well run companies are not tolerated. A variety of means are available to accommodate the need for emergency procurement. Many enterprises have used petty cash in the past and are now issuing purchase and/or supplier cards to cover ad hoc purchasing activities. Leading enterprises are using Internet procurement solutions with emergency requisitioning provisions in which approval workflows are still in place. One way to monitor this situation is to run reports in which the invoice date predates the PO date.

Q: What is the best way to handle slow-moving inventory?

A: In general it is a good business practice to first identify slow-moving or obsolete inventory, take the appropriate reserves against it, and then dispose of it when appropriate.

Q: What is the dividing line between small and large firms?

A: In December 2005, SEC recommended a major change in its definition of small companies, with the creation of a three tiered approach. The first tier is made up of microcap companies representing the bottom 1% of market capitalization—or about $100 to $125 million—and would be exempt from U.S. SOX 404 provisions altogether. The second tier is made up of small companies with a capitalization representing about 6% or under $700 million.

Q: Will SOX Section 404 and related compliance initiatives impact a company's contract management and purchase order control systems?

A: Contract management and purchase order controls will also fall under the OECD Principles, Basel II, and all SOX-related initiatives. Both U.S. SOX Section 401a, covering off-balance sheet obligations, and U.S. SOX Section 404, covering process controls, may apply. Section 401a requires capturing time-phased contractual requirements—such as year 1, year 2, etc. Section 404 will apply as well. A company will want to demonstrate that it has the proper controls over contracts and purchase orders including creation and change order approvals, maintenance, record retention, plus standardized terms and conditions that have legal department review and approval. Section 409 could come into play as well. If contract or PO cancellations create significant charges, an 8-K filing may be required.

Q: If a company with operations and business units throughout the country makes purchases of capital property and supplies, and such purchases are made and controlled separately by the different business units, would the formation and utilization of a centralized "purchasing company" improve SOX compliance?

A: Any activity to standardize processes in a more efficient and auditable manner will improve a company's operations and in turn improve the ability to comply with SOX. The Institue for Supply Management (ISM) has used the term "virtual centralization" to describe a process of using cross-functional teams and e-business tools to achieve centralized efficiencies while maintaining a decentralized organization.

Q: What questions should be included in an RFP/RFI for supplier selection that will enable assessment of that supplier's conformance to SOX and other compliance regulations?

A: Are they tracking their U.S. SOX or related compliance costs and what do they estimate those costs to be? Do they foresee any major problems in compliance? Ask if they would be willing to share the documents they provided to their auditors. Who is their audit company and who is doing their professional services to correct audit deficiencies?

Q: Is there a published list of all the companies that are required to comply with the SOX Act?

A: All publicly traded companies need to comply with U.S. SOX. Check the SEC's EDGAR database. It has a listing of all companies and their filings, and you can conduct searches for specific companies. Visit www.sec.gov/edgar/searchedgar/webusers.htm.

Q: Are Supplier Masters and Item Masters a consideration for SOX implications?

A: Most definitely. U.S. SOX Section 404 demands that internal processes and controls be in place to deter fraud and theft. If there are limited or weak controls as to who can set up and maintain Suppliers and Items, this is would constitute a material deficiency and possibly a material weakness.

Q: Within the supply chain process, what should be considered standard key controls?

A: For Section 401a, any process that captures time-phased purchase commitments and applicable terms and conditions should be considered key. This should include early termination, cancellation, or restocking charges. For Section 404, any process that controls a company's assets should be considered key. To name a few: the physical and logical identification and control of inventory, timely and accurate transactions capturing the movement and consumption of assets including inventory.

Q: How can I assure myself that segregation of duty (SOD) conflicts do not occur after the auditors have departed?

A: Most all audits today include testing for conflicts in segregation of duties. Examples would include a buyer with accounts payable or supplier master access. There is a rising demand for software tools that will automate the detection and prevention of SOD conflicts on a continuous basis. The next generation of these tools will hopefully also look for conflicts in an organization's hierarchy. Examples would include a purchasing supervisor who has subordinates with purchasing and accounts payable responsibilities.

Q: What purchasing commitments are included in off-balance sheet obligations? The documentation I have seen is confusing.

A: The SEC's final ruling on U.S. SOX Section 401 discusses off-balance sheet obligations and early termination/cancellation charges, but did little to answer this question. The SEC issued a further clarification with its 2005 "Report and Recommendations Pursuant to Section 401(c) of the Sarbanes-Oxley Act." One possible interpretation is that off-balance sheet obligations would *not* include purchase agreements that can be canceled in their entirety without paying early termination or cancellation charges. It *would* include any cancellation and early termination charges associated with those purchase agreements. Unfortunately, the SEC did not clarify the early termination/cancellation issue with its 2005 Report and Recommendation. It would be advisable to request clarification from your internal and external auditors. Anecdotal feedback suggests that there is no clear consensus among audit firms on what is covered. The safe bet would be to list all material or major purchase commitments in the tabular format specified by the SEC. The argument for listing all major purchase agreements is that while a company could legally cancel all these agreements, doing so would have a devastating impact on its ability to run its business and remain profitable. Material would depend on the size of an organization, but would include those that could affect financial results.

Q: What are the evidencing requirements of SOX?

A: The primary requirements are a signature and a date by both the preparer and the reviewer. The signature can be either an actual signature, initials, or electronic identification and accomplishes two things. First, it specifically identifies who performed the activity or the review or at least is accepting responsibility for having performed the activity or review. Second, it documents that there was a separation of duties between who performed the action and who performed the review. The date provides evidence that the activities (action *and* review) were done timely.

Q: How long must a control be in place to be used in SOX testing?

A: A control should typically be in place for 90 days for there to be reliance on it from a SOX perspective. For new, more efficient controls introduced in the system, this means there should be parallel controls utilizing the old controls until the new controls have been in place for 90 days and have passed the subsequent testing.

Presenting both an opportunity and a challenge for supply managers, SOX points to the need to identify, measure, and plan for handling operating vulnerability as it might impact financial performance. A thorough understanding of the intricacies of this Act is essential to today's successful supply chain management.

Q: Does SOX affect foreign companies doing business in the United States?

A: Foreign companies are not directly impacted by SOX unless they have securities registered with the SEC or are listed on a U.S. stock exchange and thus required to file periodical reports with the SEC. The deadline for foreign and small company filers has been pushed out one year to mid-2007. This was caused by very strong criticism that Section 404 imposed too great a financial burden and threats by foreign filers to de-list from the American stock exchanges.

Q: Within the procure-to-pay process, what are examples of key controls that will need to be tested by internal and external auditors?

A: Internal and external auditors will typically want to see that there is a three-way match among purchasing, receiving, and supplier invoicing documentation. They will also want to see assurances that no one individual has the ability to control all three of these processes as this would be a clear violation in segregation of duties. They will also want to see assurances that controls over the supplier master are in place.

Q: What have you seen in the market as far as public companies converting to privately held? Should this be a case for concern for the sourcing community?

A: There is a great deal of interest in SOX among privately held companies since their bankers and insurers are starting to put pressure on them to comply on a voluntary basis. While there has been a lot of talk about U.S. and UK companies going private to avoid the internal controls provisions of U.S. SOX, the actual numbers are very limited. The SEC has delayed until mid-2007 the compliance dates for small and foreign filers, reducing the need to take action.

Q: Is there a universally accepted definition or guidelines in terms of percent or dollars for "material" events such as percent of sales, inventory levels, etc.?

A: Material is typically used to indicate an event that impacts financial reporting. So an inventory write down of $100,000 may not be considered material in a billion-dollar enterprise, but would be material in a smaller company.

ENDNOTE

1. Copied with permission from the publisher, Institute for Supply Management™, "Sarbanes Oxley—Your Questions Answered," by Anthony Tarantino, Inside Supply Management™, February 2005, Vol. 16, No. 2, page 6.

Links to Referenced Organizations and Documents

- AICPA, Evaluating Process/Transaction-Level Exceptions and Deficiencies:
  - www.aicpa.org

- Anthony Tarantino's web site:
  - AnthonyTarantino.com

- ASX 10 Principles:
  - http://www.aar.com.au/corpgov/asx/prin.htm

- Basel II:
  - http://www.emcc.eurofound.eu.int/content/source/a0003.html

- COBIT:
  - http://www.isaca.org

- COSO and ERM:
  - www.coso.org

- Form 8-K:
  - http://www.sec.gov/about/forms/secforms.htm

- IFRS and International Accounting Standards Board:
  - http://www.iasb.org/

- ISACA IT control objectives for Sarbanes-Oxley:
  - www.isaca.org

- ISO7799:
  - www.iso.org

- OECD:
  - www.oecd.org

- PCAOB, Auditing Standard No. 2, An audit of internal control over financial reporting performed in conjunction with an audit of financial statements:
  - www.pcaobus.com

- SEC, Frequently Asked Questions, Management's Report on Internal Control Over Financial Reporting and Certification of Disclosure in Exchange Act Periodic Reports:
  - www.sec.gov

- SEC, Rule 33-8238, Management's Report on Internal Control Over Financial Reporting and Certification of Disclosure in Exchange Act Periodic Reports and SEC, Rule 33-8392, Management's Report on Internal Control Over Financial Reporting and Certification of Disclosure in Exchange Act Periodic Reports:
  - www.sec.gov

- Solvency II:
  - http://www.cea.assur.org/cea/v2.0/posi/uk/detail.php?position_id=260

- UK's Turnbull Guidance:
  - www.frc.org.uk/corporate

- U.S. Government Printing Office, The Sarbanes-Oxley Act of 2002:
  - www.gpoaccess.gov

Glossary of Terms

Balance Sheet: According to the SEC, a balance sheet portrays an issuer's financial position at a point in time. Its basic components include: assets, which are probable future economic benefits obtained or controlled by a particular entity as a result of past transactions or events; liabilities, which are probable future sacrifices of economic benefits arising from present obligations of a particular entity to transfer assets or provide services to other entities in the future as a result of past transactions or events; and equity, which is the residual interests in the assets of an entity that remains after deducting its liabilities.

Basel II: In June 2004, The Central Bank governors and the heads of bank supervisory authorities in the Group of Ten (G10) countries published a new framework for capital adequacy called "The International Convergence of Capital Measurement and Capital Standards: A Revised Framework." This is commonly known as Basel II since the meetings took place in Basel, Switzerland. The first Basel Accord, published in 1988, set standards for capital requirements because banking regulators understood that weaknesses in internal controls presented major risks to banking on a global level.

California AB 1386: It is the first legislation in the United States to require businesses and government agencies, beginning in July 2003, to notify consumers if hackers gain access to computer databases that contain unencrypted personal information such as credit card numbers, pass codes needed for use of personal accounts, Social Security Numbers (SSNs), or drivers' license numbers. Mass identity thefts have become commonplace over the last two years with major incidents reported by ChoicePoint, LexisNexis, CitiBank, DSW, the Federal Deposit Insurance Corporation (FDIC), and Visa International. The number of thefts is approaching 100 million. California AB 1386 is bound to spawn similar U.S. federal legislation and there is growing international concern that regulations will be required in an industry that has been largely self-regulated and incapable of preventing mass identity thefts.

Certification of Financial Results: Section 302 of the U.S. Sarbanes-Oxley Act of 2002 (SOX) requires a company's management, with the participation of the principal executive and financial officers (the certifying officers), to make the quarterly and annual certifications with respect to the company's Internal Control over financial reporting. The act also directs officers to take responsibility for "establishing and maintaining internal controls" and to "have evaluated the effectiveness of such controls as of a date within 90 days prior to the report, and have presented in the report their conclusions about the effectiveness of their internal controls based on their evaluation as of that date."

COBIT: Control Objectives for Information and Related Technology, COBIT was developed as a standard for good information technology (IT) security and control practices that provides a reference framework for management, users, and IS audit, control, and security practitioners. COBIT was issued by the IT Governance Institute and is increasingly internationally accepted as good practice for control over information, IT, and related risks. Its guidance enables an enterprise to implement effective governance over the IT that is pervasive and intrinsic throughout the enterprise. In particular, COBIT's Management Guidelines component contains a framework responding to management's need for control and measurability of IT by providing tools to assess and measure the enterprise's IT capability for the 34 COBIT IT processes. The tools include performance measurement elements (outcome measures and performance drivers for all IT processes); a list of critical success factors that provides succinct, nontechnical best practices for each IT process; and maturity models to assist in benchmarking and decision making for capability improvements. (Source: Information Systems Audit and Control Association (ISACA).)

COSO: Committee of Sponsoring Organizations. In 1985, the Treadway Commission, a private sector initiative, was formed to study American financial reporting systems. COSO was formed to make recommendations on how companies and auditors might identify and attack fraudulent financial reporting. The group consists of the American Institute of Certified Public Accountants

(AICPA), the American Accounting Association, Financial Executives International, the Institute of Management Accountants, and the Institute of Internal Auditors. The SEC references COSO in its Section 404 final ruling. COSO's report attempted to standardize the definition of internal control. COSO provides a framework for risk management and regulatory compliance. Gartner Group's Lane Leskela noted that SOX standards are "clearly consistent with the Committee of Sponsoring Organizations (COSO) framework for regulatory compliance and risk management. COSO requires risk assessments, a control-based environment, control-based activities, information and communication procedures, and a monitoring mechanism for the control environment."

COSO II—Enterprise Risk Management (ERM): COSO, an independent, nonprofit, and private sector initiative, was originally published in the late 1980s and is widely accepted as the framework for risk management and internal control for SOX and related compliance regulations. In late September 2004, COSO released its anticipated Enterprise Risk Management—Integrated Framework (COSO II), which describes the essential components, principles, and concepts of ERM.

Code of Ethics: The SEC in its final ruling on Section 406 defines a code of ethics as "written standards that are reasonably designed to deter wrongdoing and to promote: honest and ethical conduct, including the ethical handling of actual or apparent conflicts of interest between personal and professional relationships; full, fair, accurate, timely, and understandable disclosure in reports and documents that a registrant files with, or submits to, the Commission and in other public communications made by the registrant; compliance with applicable governmental laws, rules and regulations; the prompt internal reporting to an appropriate person or persons identified in the code of violations of the code; and accountability for adherence to the code."

Control Environment: According to PriceWaterhouseCooper's (PWC's) White Paper: "Sarbanes-Oxley Act: Section 404 Practical Guidance for Management" (July 2004), "the control environment sets the tone for the organization, influencing the control consciousness of its people. This component is the foundation for all other components of internal control, providing discipline and structure. The control environment encompasses the following factors: Integrity and ethical values (including code of conduct and anti-fraud programs); commitment to competence and development of people; management's philosophy and operating style; organizational structure; assignment of authority and responsibility; human resources policies and procedures; and participation by those charged with governance (as required by the PCAOB, participation involves, among other things, the Board of Directors' assessment of the effectiveness of the audit committee)."

D&O Insurance Policy: Directors and officers of both public and private corporations are fiduciaries in the EU, United States, and other countries, and as such, may face both civil and criminal liabilities for acts they perform on behalf of the corporation. Companies often provide directors and officers with insurance coverage called a Directors' and Officers' Insurance Policy (D&O Policy), which generally covers their potential liability for defense and settlement costs. D&O Insurance has become much more vital with the growing number of litigations against board members who in the past were rarely held accountable.

Extensible Business Reporting Language (XBRL): This is an attempt to create an Internet-based global reporting language. Its adoption should help to facilitate the movement toward a global Generally Accepted Accounting Principles (GAAP) based on the International Financial Reporting Standards (IFRS) and improved internal control under SOX and the Organization for Economic Cooperation and Development (OECD) Principles. The spotty history of efforts to create industry-specific and process-specific XML standards would suggest that this will be a difficult task and will be a long-term effort.

Federal Financial Management Improvement Act (FFMIA): The U.S. Federal Financial Management Improvement Act of 1996 (FFMIA) builds upon and complements the Chief Financial Officers Act of 1990 (CFO Act), the Government Performance and Results Act, and the Government Management Reform Act. The FFMIA requires that federal agencies conform to the government-wide standard general ledger (G/L), comply with all applicable federal accounting standards, establish financial management systems that support full disclosure of federal financial data (including the full costs of federal programs and activities), include an auditor's statement regarding compliance with these provisions, and establish a remediation plan for areas of an agency not in compliance with these requirements. The FFMIA and Federal Managers' Financial Integrity Act (FMFIA) are part of the U.S. federal government's efforts to improve internal control under the Office of Management and Budget (OMB) Circular A-123, the federal government's version of SOX.

Federal Managers' Financial Integrity Act (FMFIA): The FMFIA requires U.S. federal agencies to annually provide a statement of assurance regarding the effectiveness of management, administrative and accounting controls, and financial management systems. Core to FMFIA is maintaining integrity and accountability in all programs and operation.

Foreign Corrupt Practices Act of 1977 (FCPA): The FCPA is referenced in the SEC's final ruling on Section 404. The FCPA was originally enacted after a series of scandals involving questionable or illegal payments by U.S. firms to foreign government officials overseas and by revelations that some of this money had returned to the United States in the form of political contributions. The FCPA was influenced by the Treadway Commission and the COSO framework which it created. Before SOX, the FCPA has been the single most important anticorruption driver for U.S. companies. It prohibits U.S. firms and foreign companies listed on the New York Stock Exchange (NYSE) from giving anything of value, such as a payment, gift, or bribe, to induce a foreign government to enter into a contract or business relation. Enforced by the SEC and the U.S. Department of Justice (DOJ), the FCPA has resulted in fines of US$69 million against General Electric Co. in 1992 and US$25 million against Lockheed Martin Corp. in 1995. In 2003, according to the *Wall Street Journal*, the DOJ launched a far-reaching FCPA investigation into mid-1990s business deals in Kazakhstan involving Mobil Oil Corp. and three other oil companies. A former Mobil executive has pleaded guilty to money laundering in connection with the investigation. In 1998, the United States passed legislation expanding the scope of the FCPA to bring its provisions into accord with the OECD Convention. In 2001 and 2002, eight criminal cases and six civil cases were brought under the FCPA against seven corporations and 13 individuals, including two officials of an international financial institution who acted as intermediaries for bribes of foreign officials.

Financial Statement Assertions: The AICPA's Statement on Auditing Standards No. 31 (SAS 31): Evidential Matter provides a logical framework for designing audit procedures. The framework is built around five financial statement assertions. The first three assertions—existence or occurrence, completeness, and valuation—address if accounts contain valid entries that are recorded accurately. The last two assertions—rights and obligations and presentation and disclosure—focus on if the entity's legal rights and obligations are presented properly and described adequately in the financial statements.

Generally Accepted Accounting Principles (GAAP): GAAP refers to a set of widely accepted accounting standards used to standardize financial accounting of public companies. It was established by the Financial Accounting Standards Board (FASB), which was created in 1973, replacing the Accounting Principles Board and the Committee on Accounting Procedure of the AICPA before it. Currently, most countries have their own versions of GAAP. There is now a movement by the IFRS to create a global GAAP. Over 7000 European Union (EU) companies now file financial results using their local GAAP and the new IFRS GAAP.

Gramm-Leach-Bliley Act (GLB): The U.S. Gramm-Leach-Bliley Financial Modernization Act of 1999 imposes financial privacy requirements on financial institutions, including insurers, and requires companies to give consumers privacy notices that explain the institutions' information-sharing practices. In turn, consumers have the right to limit some sharing of their information. The Federal Trade Commission (FTC) is charged with enforcing the act in situations where federal and state banking agencies and the SEC are not the controlling agencies.

Health Insurance Portability and Accountability Act (HIPAA): The HIPAA was enacted in 1996, but requirements were not published until 2003 and went into effect on April 20, 2005. HIPAA created new requirements to protect patient data and impose civil and criminal penalties for violations of the act. AMR Research estimates the 225 companies that participated in its survey spent $3.7 billion on HIPAA compliance. Civil penalties range from $100 per violation to $25,000 per year per violation. Criminal penalties range from $50,000 to $250,000 and one to ten years in prison. Administrative safeguards account for more than half of the provisions and involve a risk analysis, assign responsibility to an information security officer, train employees, and document security procedures such as data backup and disaster recovery. Physical safeguards include means for workstation disposal, media reuse, and securing areas where Electronic Protected Health Information (EPHI) may be stored. The technical safeguards spell out system authentication, encryption and decryption of data, and transmission of EPHI within and outside an organization. Paper-based records are also covered by HIPAA. HIPAA is based on a number of existing IT standards such as International Organization of Standards (ISO) 17799 and COBIT.

IFRS (International Financial Reporting Standards)—Global GAAP: Effective January 1, 2005, all EU companies that have shares traded on any EU regulated market will be required to prepare consolidated financial statements in accordance with IFRS. The FASB and the International Accounting Standards Board (IASB) are committed to working with each other and converging U.S. accounting standards and IFRS, with the ultimate goal being one set of high-quality global accounting standards, a Global GAAP.

Internal Controls: The internal control over financial reporting has been defined by the SEC to include a process to provide reasonable assurance regarding the reliability of financial reporting and the preparation of financial statements for external purposes in accordance with GAAP. This includes those policies and procedures that pertain to the maintenance of records that in reasonable detail accurately and fairly reflect the transactions and dispositions of the assets of the company; that provide reasonable assurance that transactions are recorded as necessary to permit preparation of financial statements in accordance with GAAP; that receipts and expenditures of the company are being made only in accordance with authorizations of management and directors of the company; and that provide reasonable assurance regarding prevention or timely detection of unauthorized acquisition, use, or disposition of the company's assets that could have a material effect on the financial statements.

ISO 17799: First published in 2000, it is a voluntary and internationally accepted ISO standard defining a "code of practice" comprising statements of good practice for information security management, and superseded British Standard BS7799 Part 1, first published by the British Standards Institute (BSI) in 1995. ISO 17799 is an international standard and thus not tied to a particular country's legislation. A number of countries have adopted localized variants of the standard but, in most cases, these are simple translations of ISO 17799.

Item or Parts Master: A database containing all the items or parts that an organization buys, builds, distributes, and sells. These include goods and services. Typically, an item master includes a description, unit of measure, unit cost, lead time, supplier or customer cross-referenced items, and any applicable engineering, design, or specification documentation. Robust controls over item masters are vital to any organization in maintaining internal controls.

Material Events: Material events are changes in the financial or operating condition of a company, which have been interpreted by the SEC to include the following: a change in control; a significant acquisition; a bankruptcy; a termination of a material agreement not made in the ordinary course of business; a termination or reduction of a business relationship with a customer that constitutes a specified amount of the company's revenues; and the creation of a direct or contingent financial obligation that is material to the company.

Material Weakness: A material weakness is a single significant deficiency or a combination of significant deficiencies that creates the possibility that a material misstatement of the annual or quarterly financial statements will not be prevented or detected.

Nonprofits: Designated as public interest entities by the International Federation of Accountants, these are organizations that have significant public responsibility. Examples of nonprofits include charitable organizations, museums, libraries, private schools, colleges, universities, labor organizations, churches, and hospitals.

OECD Principles: The Organization for Economic Cooperation and Development (OECD) describes itself as "a group of 30 member countries sharing a commitment to democratic government and the market economy. With active relationships with some 70 other countries . . . it has a global reach . . . . The OECD plays a prominent role in fostering good governance in the public service and in corporate activity. It helps governments to ensure the responsiveness of key economic areas with sectored monitoring." The OECD Principles are similar to the SOX in attempting to improve internal control but differ in using a guidelines approach versus the mandatory regulation approach with SOX.

Off-Balance Sheet (OBS) Arrangements: OBS arrangements are defined by the SEC as guarantees that may be a source of potential risk to a company's future liquidity, capital resources, and results of operations, regardless of whether they are recorded as liabilities. The SEC has ruled this may include "contracts that contingently require the guarantor to make payments to the guaranteed party based on another entity's failure to perform under an obligating agreement (e.g., a performance guarantee)."

PCAOB: The Public Company Accounting Oversight Board (PCAOB) is chartered to oversee corporate governance, financial reporting, disclosure, and auditor standards. The PCAOB has the responsibility to oversee and investigate the audits and auditors and has the authority to sanction firms and individuals for violations. Accounting firms that audit public companies must register with the PCAOB and pay registration/annual fees. It is empowered to inspect registered accounting firms' operations regularly. The PCAOB has international authority over foreign accounting firms that "prepare or furnish" an audit report involving U.S. registrants.

Risk: According to Steve Weil, CISSP, CISA, "risk is the likelihood that a specific threat will exploit certain vulnerability, and the resulting impact of that event. Risk analysis, the starting point in an overall risk management process, is a systematic and analytical approach that identifies and assesses risks and provides recommendations to reduce risk to a reasonable and appropriate level." Risks are assessed on an inherent and a residual basis. Inherent risk management, sometimes called gross or absolute risks, assesses the consequence and likelihood of a risk occurring before any controls are taken into account. Residual risk management, sometimes called net or controlled risks, assesses the consequence and likelihood of a risk occurring after any controls are taken into account.

Statement on Auditing Standards No. 70 (SAS 70): This is an internationally accepted independent auditor's report of a service provider's control activities, which generally include controls over IT and related processes. In an age of extensive outsourcing and global organizations, service organizations and service providers must demonstrate they have adequate controls and safeguards when they host or process data belonging to their customers. Section 404 will put even greater emphasis on SAS 70 Reports. There are two types of Service Auditors' Reports: Type I and Type II. A Type I report describes the service organization's description of controls at a specific point in time. A Type II report includes the service organization's description of controls and includes detailed testing of the service organization's controls over a minimum six-month period. In a Type I report, the service auditor will express an opinion on (1) whether the service organization's description of its controls presents fairly, in all material respects, the relevant aspects of the service organization's controls that had been placed in operation as of a specific date and (2) whether the controls were suitably designed to achieve specified control objectives. In a Type II report, the service auditor will express an opinion on the same items noted above in a Type I report and (3) whether the controls that were tested were operating with sufficient effectiveness to provide reasonable, but not absolute, assurance that the control objectives were achieved during the period specified. (Source: Mark Stebelton, SOX Solutions Product Manager, Logical Apps.)

Securities and Exchange Commission (SEC): The SEC is chartered with interpreting the provisions of SOX via a series of final rulings, findings, and enforcements. Founded in 1934, the SEC defines its role as requiring "public companies to disclose meaningful financial and other information to the public, which provides a common pool of knowledge for all investors to use to judge for themselves if a company's securities are a good investment . . . . The SEC also oversees other key participants in the securities world, including stock exchanges, broker-dealers, investment advisors, mutual funds, and public utility holding companies . . . . Crucial to the SEC's effectiveness is its enforcement authority. Each year the SEC brings between 400–500 civil enforcement actions against individuals and companies that break the securities laws."

Small Company: Small companies were initially defined by the SEC for purposes of the Sarbanes-Oxley Act as those with a public float under $75 million. (Public float is the number of common shares of an issuer, or the market value of the number of shares, that are available for trading by the public. Shares held by corporate insiders or affiliated companies are not included in the public float.) Due to major criticism from U.S. small businesses, the SEC has delayed its SOX compliance date until July 2007. In December 2005, SEC's Small Company group has recommended a major change in its definition of small companies with the creation of three-tiered approach. The first tier is made up of microcap companies representing the bottom 1% of market capitalization or about $100 to $125 million. Under the December 2005 plan, they would be exempt from U.S. SOX 404 provisions altogether. The second tier is made up of small companies with a capitalization representing about 6% or under $700 million. This is estimated to represent about 7000 public companies in the United States. These companies would be allowed to perform their own audits, free of external auditors.

SOX, SOA, or Sarbox: The U.S. Sarbanes Oxley Act of 2002 (SOX), which is technically called the Public Company Accounting Reform and Investor Protection Act of 2002. It is named after Democratic Senator Paul Sarbanes of Maryland and Republican Congressman Michael Oxley of Ohio. Some pundits have also called Sarbanes-Oxley the Accountants' Full Employment Act.

Supplier or Vendor Master: A database containing a listing of all the suppliers or vendors for a company. (The term supplier is now typically preferred over vendor by supply chain professionals and the Institute for Supply Management.) It typically includes billing, shipping, payment, tax IDs, and banking information.

Timely Notification: Interpreted by Section 409 as four working days from the time that a company's management becomes aware of a material event. The SEC requires the use of an 8-K form to declare material events including material weaknesses.

White-collar Crime: The corrupt business practices of individuals in powerful positions, especially corporate leaders and government officials. The term was first coined by Edwin Sutherland in 1939 at the American Sociological Society's annual meeting. His argument is still widely embraced today that corporate and governmental officials regularly commit crimes that are as destructive to society as those of violent blue-collar criminals. Until the era of Enron, white-collar crimes were typically never punished as severely as blue-collar crimes. The massive fraud of the 1990s, and the resulting financial loss to millions of investors, fundamentally changed society's attitude toward white-collar criminals. White-collar criminals can expect to face harsh civil and criminal penalties from zealous prosecutors who see their convictions as a means to advance their political careers.

Index

8-K Form, US SOX Section 409, 38,
115, 119, 29

A.R.C. Morgan, 123
Accountancy Age, 51, 52, 101, 105
Accounting Principles Board (APB),
130, 297
Opinion No. 2 , 130
Accounting Today, 275
Accounts Payable (AP), 165, 228
Accounts Payable Super User,
Segregation of Duty Issues, 229
Accounts Receivable (A/R), 228
Acxiom, 76
Adelphia Scandal, xiv,111, 119
Advanced Technology Attachment
(ATA),137
After-the-Fact Purchase Orders,
Internal Control
Considerations, 253
Ahold Scandal, 118
Alan L. Beller, Securities and Exchange
Commission, 49
American Accounting Association, 47,
294
American Depository Receipts (ADRs),
50
American Institute of Certified Public
Accountants (AICPA), 47, 107
American Sociological Society, 303
Ancha, Koti, xvii ,245, 246
Anderson, Curt, 110, 119
Anti-Deficiency Act, 61
Application Controls, 60, 61, 255, 273
Assets, Derivative Considerations, 17
Federal Government's
Approach to, 56
Federal Government's
Control Over, 60

Federal Government's Laws Over, 65
Lease Considerations, 12, 14–15
OBS Considerations, 11
Purchase Order Considerations , 10
SAS 31 Existence Considerations, 148
SAS 31 Presentation and Disclosure
Considerations, 150
SAS 31 Rights and Obligation
Considertions149–150
SOX Section 401 Treatment of ,
5–12
Turnbull Guidance Treatment of, 86
Use of RFID to Control, 145
AstraZeneca International, 51
ASX Corporate Governance Council,
79, 89, 200, 212, 216, 223
ASX Corporations Act, 207–210, 214,
215, 216, 222
ASX Listing Rules, 207–210, 214,
215, 216, 222
ASX
Principle 1: Lay solid foundations
for management and
oversight, 200
Principle 2: Structure the Board to
Add Value, 202
Principle 3: Promote Ethical and
Responsible Decision-
Making, 208
Principle 4: Safeguard Integrity in
Financial Reporting, 210
Principle 5: Make Timely and
Balanced Disclosure, 214
Principle 6: Respect the Rights of
Shareholders, 215
Principle 7: Recognize and Manage
Risk, 216
Principle 8: Encourage Enhanced
Performance, 219

Principle 9: Remunerate Fairly and
Responsibly, 221
Principle 10: Recognize the
Legitimate Interests of
Stakeholders, 225
Auditing Internal Controls, 147, 177
Australian Accounting Standards
Board (AASB), 223
Australian Stock Exchange (ASX),
79, 200
Principles, 200–225
Automated Controls, 46, 139,
273, 282

Back Flushing, Internal Control Issues
In Using, 51
Balance Sheet, Definition, 292
Bank of America Corp., 118
Barkley, Tom, 73, 78
Basel Accord, 71, 292
Basel Committee, 71
BASF (BF), 50
Basil II, Internal Controls for Banking,
71–74
BearingPoint, 96–99, 105
Beller, Alan L., 49
Benchmarking, OECD Principles
Approach, 93, 293
Benefits of Compliance, 271
Bill and Hold Sales, Revenue
Recognition Issues, 171
Bill of material (BOM), 251
BoardSource, 40, 43
Bondi, Enrico, 118, 120
Bonds News, 118, 120
Brady, Nick, 94, 95
British Standards Institute (BSI), 299
Burns, Judith, 46, 48
Burt, Anne, 228
Business Roundtable, 270
Business Week, 50, 52, 261, 265, 241

Cadbury Schweppes (CSG), 50
California's AB 1386 (SB 1386), 292
Canada's 105–109, 82, 272
Canada's 105–111, 82, 83
Cancellation and Restocking Charges,

Off Balance Sheet
Considerations, 2
Capital Leases, Off Balance Sheet
Considerations, 12
Carney, Beth, 50, 51, 52
Category A Material Weakness,
Moody Designation, 122
Category B Material Weakness,
Moody Designation, 122
Certification of Financial Results, 293
CFO Executive Board, 270
CFO.com, 112, 119, 121, 123, 124,
139, 146, 270, 277
Chief Compliance Officer (CCO), 262
Chief Executive Officers (CEOs),
27, 65
Chief Financial Officer Council
(CFOC), 54
Chief Financial Officers (CFOs), 27,
36, 41, 65, 102
Chief Financial Officers Act of 1990
(CFO Act), 53, 295
Chief Information Officer (CIO),
188, 273
ChoicePoint, 76, 292
Circular A-123, OMB, 55, 56–67, 296
Citigroup Inc., 110, 118
City of San Diego, 66
Civil Penalties for Non Compliance,
65, 297
Clark, Elizabeth, 136, 137, 138
COBIT, 36, 190–199, 263, 290, 293,
298
Code of Ethics – US SOX Section 406,
32–34, 39, 40, 262, 294
Code of Federal Regulations (CFR),
136
Combined Code on Corporate
Governance, 72, 103, 125, 139,
190, 263, 294
Committee of Sponsoring
Organizations (COSO), xiv, 21,
25, 28, 30, 31, 46, 48, 55, 58,
72, 73, 82, 86, 125, 139, 178,
179, 180, 182–184, 190
Committee on Accounting
Procedure, 297

Committee on Smaller Public
    Companies, 45, 48
Company-Level Controls, 122
Completeness, One of Five General
    Audit Assertions, 107, 148, 297
Compliance Tools and Softwares, 135,
    255, 140–141, 263
Computer Security Act of 1987, 185
Computer World, 29, 31
Confederation of British Industry
    (CBI), 50
Confucius, xi
Contingent Liabilities, 8
Contingent Off Balance Sheet
    Obligations, 1–9, 11, 14,
    18–19, 37, 129
Contractual Obligations
    Off Balance Sheet Considerations,
        6–7, 10–12, 14
    Treatment as a Liability, 11
Control Activities, Internal Control
    Component
Control Environment, Internal Control
    Component under COSO, 26,
    27, 55, 58, 59, 72, 75, 82, 122,
    151, 191, 255, 256, 294, 295
Control Matrices in Auditing, 28
Control Objectives for Information
    and Related Technology
    (COBIT), 190, 263
Convention on Combating Bribery of
    Foreign Public Officials in
    International Business
    Transactions
Convention on Corruption, 117, 120
Coopers & Lybrand Consulting, 122
Corp. Executive Board, 270
Corporate Governance Council. See ASX
    Corporate Governance Council,
    9, 89, 200, 212, 216, 223
Corporate Governance Reform Task
    Force, 94, 95
Corporate Governance Services, 94
Corporate-Wide, 232
Corporations Act. See ASX
    Corporations Act, 206,
    208–211, 221–223

COSO I , 183, 190–194
COSO II - Enterprise Risk
    Management , 178, 190–193,
    294
Cost of Compliance, 276
Council of Europe, 116–117, 120
    Criminal Law Convention, 117, 120
Cox, Christopher, 1,101
Criminal Law Convention, 116,
    117, 120
Criminal Penalties
    Within the European Union (EU),
        xv, 34, 42, 52, 109–111, 297,
        303
    Non Compliance, 109–119, 297
    Under US GLB, 116
    Under US HIPAA, 115
Cross-Enterprise Issues in
    Compliance, 179
Crowe, Chizek, and Company, 112
Customer Relationship Management
    (CRM), 22
Cutter IT Journal, 146, 241, 275

Data Protection Act of 1998, 115
Delisting, Issues Relating to US SOX ,
    37
Delivery Has Occurred or Services
    Have Been Rendered, Revenue
    Recognition Condition, 25,
    127, 128
Deloitte & Touche, 118, 270
Department of Commerce, 67
Department of Labor, 33
Derivatives, Asset Considerations, 17
Derivatives, Off Balance Sheet
    Considerations, 5–9, 17
Detective Controls, 24
Difillippo, Dan, 274, 277
Division of Corporate Finance, 266
Document Management Softwares and
    Tools, 29, 140, 144, 165, 282
Document Retention Under US
    HIPAA, 57
Documentation of Internal
    Controls, 28
Donald T. Nicolaisen, US SEC, 14, 49

Donaldson, William H., xiv, xv, 1, 50
Doss, Michael,122
Dow Jones Newswires46, 48, 140, 146
DSW, 292
Dun & Bradstreet (D&B), 245

Ebbers, Bernard, 111
E-business, 231, 285
E-commerce, 129
Electronic Data Gathering, Analysis,
    and Retention (EDGAR), 35
Electronic Data Interface (EDI)35, 38,
    103, 285
Electronic Funds Transfer (EFT), 159
Electronic Protected Health
    Information (EPHI), 70, 298
Email, Compliance Documentation
    Issues, 77, 163, 168, 170, 216
End-of-Life, Compliance Issues, 23, 144
End-User, 60
Enron, 19, 33, 42, 47, 66, 100,
    109–110, 114, 150, 216, 302
Enron Scandal, 19, 33, 150
Ensure Systems Security, COBIT
    Control Guidance, 192, 195.
    197, 199
Enterprise Resource Planning (ERP),
    22, 36, 61, 141, 166, 231, 242
Enterprise Risk Management (ERM),
    178, 294
Environmental Health and Safety
    (EH&S), 283
E-Procurement, 247
ERP System Crashes, US SOX Section
    409 Considerations, 36
European Anti-Fraud Office (OLAF),
    118
European Commission (EC), 100
European Commission's Financial
    Services Action Plan (FSAP) , 74
European Union (EU), xii, 50, 67, 96,
    106, 117, 190, 297
European Union (EU) Convention on
    Corruption, 117
Event Management Software Tools,
    29, 144, 178, 181, 280–281

Events – Risks and Opportunities in
    ERM, 180, 183
Evidencing Requirements Under US
    SOX, 287
Existence, One of Five General Audit
    Assertions148, 169, 203, 204,
    211, 217, 219, 224–225, 231,
    297
Extensible Business Reporting
    Language (XBRL), 102, 295
Extensible Markup Language (XML),
    102, 144

Fannie Mae Scandal, xii, 112, 119
Federal Computer Week, 53, 67
Federal Deposit Insurance Corporation
    (FDIC), 292
Federal Financial Management
    Improvement Act of 1996
    (FFMIA), 65, 295
Federal Financial Services Supervisory
    Authority, 75
Federal Managers' Financial Integrity
    Act of 1982 (FMFIA), 68,
    295–296
Federal Trade Commission (FTC), 76,
    296
Financial Accounting Standards (FAS),
    27
Financial Accounting Standards Board
    (FASB) , 100–101, 264,
    297–298
Financial Executives International,
    47,275, 294
Financial Reporting Council, 85, 89–90
Financial Services Action Plan (FSAP), 74
Financial Times, The, 101, 270
Flannigan, James, 267, 277
Flow Charts in Auditing, 150
Foley and Lardner, 43, 268, 271
Foreign Companies Under Sarbanes-
    Oxley Act, 49–51, 100, 288, 297
Foreign Corrupt Practices Act of 1977
    (FCPA), 296
Form 8-K, US SOX Section 409, 38,
    115, 119, 29

Gartner Group, 294,
General Electric Co., 296
General IT Controls, 190
General Ledger (G/L), 148, 229,
    247, 295
General Ledger Super User,
    Segregation of Duty
    Considerations, xv, 6–7, 52, 74,
    100, 150,
Generally Accepted Accounting
    Principles (GAAP), xv, 6–7, 52,
    74, 100, 150, 295, 297
Global GAAPv11, 96–105, 264,
    297, 298
Global Risk Regulator, 73
Government Accountability Office
    (GAO), 57
Government Management Reform Act,
    65, 296
Government Performance and Results
    Act, 65, 296
Gram-Leach-Bliley Financial
    Modernization Act of 1999
    (GLB), 76, 78, 297
Grant, Paul, 51, 52, 267, 277
Grant Thornton, xiv, 118
Green Book, 57, 68
Group of States Against Corruption
    (GRECO), 117
Group of Ten (G10), 71, 292
Guidance for Directors on the
    Combined Code (Turnbull
    Guidance), 85, 89, 292
Gupta, Parveen, 21, 122

Hagerty, John, 268, 277
Half, Robert, 43
Health Insurance Portability and
    Accountability Act (HIPAA) ,
    69–70, 137, 297
HealthSouth Corp., xiii, 111
Hedge Accounting of
    Derivatives, 17
Hierarchical Segregation of Duties,
    237, 241, 279
    and Fraud, 236, 241, 279

HIPAA, Health Insurance Portability
    and Accountability Act, 69–70,
    137, 297
Home Depot, 161, 261

IFRS, Impact on IT Requirements
    xv.36., 74, 96–105, 263–264,
    289, 295–298
ImClone, xiii
Income Tax Act (Canada), 85
Independent Sector, The, 40, 43
Indirect vs. Direct Selling,
    Revenue Recognition
    Considerations, 131
Information and Communication,
    Internal Control Component
    under COSO, 26, 28, 58, 60,
    183, 294
Information System Security Officer
    (ISSO), 188
Information Systems Audit and
    Control Association
    (ISACA), 293
Information Technology (IT), xv,
    60, 132, 173, 185, 190, 231,
    256, 293
Information Technology Management
    Reform Act of 1996, 185
Information-Sharing, 76, 298
Initial public offering (IPO), xiii, xv
Innis, Harold, 262
Institute for Supply Management
    (ISM), 30, 275, 289, 302
Institute of Internal Auditors, 47,
    227, 294,
Institute of Management Accountants,
    47, 294
Inter-American Convention Against
    Bribery (IAC), 91
Internal Audit, 39–47, 69, 140, 147,
    183, 193, 213, 217–218, 226,
    257, 271, 274–275
Internal Controls
    Auditing of, 147–177
    Definition of, 26–27
    Impact of Outsourcing on, 106–107

Improvements
  with ASX 10, 79–90
  with Basel II , 71–78
  with GLBA, 76–77
  with HIPAA, 69–70
  with OECD Principles, 91–95
  with OMB-A123, 53, 68
  with Solvency II, 74–75
  with US SOX Section 404,
    21–31
Internal Controls Best Practices
  Case Studies,242, 253
  COBIT, 194, 199
  ERM, 178–179
  in Segregation of Duties, 228–241
  Mapping COSO to COBIT to
    PCAOB, 190, 193
  NIST 800-30, 185, 189
  SDLC, 185–189
  Using ASX-10 Principles, 200–227
International Accounting Standards
  (IAS), 27
International Accounting Standards 39
  (IAS 39), 98
International Accounting Standards
  Board (IASB), 100, 298
International Convergence of Capital
  Measurement and Capital
  Standards (BASEL II), 71
International Federation of
  Accountants, 299
International Financial Reporting
  Standard (IFRS), 2, 50, 75, 96,
  105, 264, 295, 298
International Organization for
  Standardization (ISO), xii
International Sales, Revenue
  Recognition Considerations, 132
Internet Sales, Revenue Recognition
  Considerations, 133
Inventory Write Offs, Internal Control
  Considerations, 23
ISO 17799, 298, 299
IT Governance Institute, 293

Jones, Sir Digby, 51
Jorgenson, Mary Ann, 123

Journal of Property Management, 29
JP Morgan Chase & Co.,110

Kanban, 251
Kazakhstan, 296
Kostigen, Thomas, 100–101, 105
Kozlowski, Dennis, 111

Langone, Kenneth G., 261
Later Supplier Deliveries, US SOX
    Section 409 Considerations, 35
Laursen, Eric, 139
Lay, Kenneth, 109, 263
Lease Agreements, Off Balance Sheet
    Considerations, 2
Leech, Tim, 73, 77, 122
Lehigh University, 121
Leone, Maria. 121, 123, 124
Leskela, Lane, 294
Lewis, Elliott, 76, 292
LexisNexis, 76, 292
Liabilities
  As Contingent Off Balance Sheet
      Obligations, 8
  As Off Balance Sheet Obligations,
      3–10
  Contingent, 8
  Contractual Obligations
      Governing, 6
  Derivative Issues, 17
  Lease Issues, 14–15
  Purchase Order Issues, 9
  SAS 31 Existence Considerations,
      148
  SAS 31 Presentation and Disclosure
      Considerations, 150
  SAS 31 Rights and Obligation
      Considerations, 149–150
  SEC Treatment of Under Section
      401, 3–5
Liabilities v. Equity, 8
Lion Bioscience (LEON), 50
Listing Rules. See ASX Listing Rules,
    206, 209, 214, 215, 222
Lockheed Martin Corp., 296
Loftus, Peter, 140, 146
Logical Apps, xvii

Long Term Purchase Agreements, Off
Balance Sheet Considerations, 2
Los Angeles Times, The267, 277

Maastricht Treaty, 116
Manage the Configuration, COBIT
Control Guidance, 193, 199
Manage Third-party Services, COBIT
Control Guidance, 194
Management Barometer, PWC, 267,
273, 274, 277
Management Discussion and Analysis
(MD&A), 5, 10, 84, 129
Mandatory Regulations, 53
Manual Controls, 45, 139, 282
Manufacturing Resource Planning
(MRP), 250
Mapping COBIT to COSO I and
COSO II, 190–193
Marsh & McClennan, xiii
Material Events, 20, 35, 142, 145,
281, 288, 299, 303
Material Weakness14, 24, 27, 36,
45–46, 55, 64–65, 82, 85,
121–125, 143, 146, 250–251
Mencius, xi
Michael Oxley, US Congressman,
xiv, 302
Mickly, Paul, 40, 114, 119
Mintz, Robert, 110
Mobil Oil Corp., 296
Moody's Investors Service, 121, 122
Multi-Lateral Instrument 52–111, 82,
84, 89, 273
Musashi, Miyamoto, 276

Narratives in Auditing, 28, 141,
151, 171
National Aeronautics and Space
Administration (NASA), 248
National Banking and Securities
Commission, 73
National Institute of Standards and
Technology (NIST), 185, 187, 189
National Institute of Standards and
Technology (NIST), 185,
187–189

National Whistleblower Center, 33, 34
Network Magazine, 138
Neveling, Nicholas, 101, 105
New York Stock Exchange (NYSE), 296
Nicolaisen, Donald T., 14, 49
NIST 800-30, 185–189
Non Traditional Business Models and
Revenue Recognition , 129
Nonaccelerated Fliers, 49, 50
Non-Profits, US SOX Considerations,
xii, xv, 40, 43
Non-Public Companies, 41
Not-For-Profit Organizations, 41

OBS Obligations, Purchase Orders,9–10
Occupational Safety and Health
Administration (OSHA), 33
OECD Convention on Combating
Bribery , 91, 92, 116
OECD Principles, 52, 91–95 231, 299
Off-Balance Sheet Arrangements, US
SOX Section 401, 1–20, 115,
276, 300
Office of Administrative Law Judges
(OALJ), 33
Office of Civil Rights, 69
Office of Management and Budget
(OMB), 53, 296
Off-the-Books, 92
OMB Circular A-123, 53–68, 273
One-Size-Fits-All, Approach to
Auditing, 44, 79, 94
Ontario Securities Commission, Multi-
Lateral Instrument 52–111,
82–83, 272
Operating Leases, Off Balance Sheet
Considerations,2 6,7, 12, 13
Order Management Super User,
Segregation of Duties
Considerations, 229
Organization for Economic Co-
operation and Development
(OECD) , 91–95
Out-of-Balance Batches, 175
Outsourcing, Compliance
Considerations, xv, 67, 76,
106–107,

Oversight Systems, 269, 277
Oxley, Michael, xiv, 302

Padala, Jag, 241.
Paisley Consulting, 122
Paperwork Reduction Act of 1995, 216
Pareto 80/20 rule, 260
Parmalat, xi, 118, 120
Patriot Act, 145
PCAOB, 39, 46, 79, 147, 190–193, 276, 291, 295, 300
Perera, David, 53, 67
Performance and Accountability Report (PAR), 64
Period End, 28, 146, 157
Persuasive Evidence of an Arrangement, Revenue Recognition Considerations, 125, 126
Physical and Logical Controls of Assets, Internal Control Considerations, 284, 288, 296
Pillar 2 of Basel II, Internal Control Considerations, 72
Pillar 2 of Solvency II, Internal Control Considerations, 75
Poor Inventory Accuracy, US SOX Section 409 Considerations, 249–250
Poor Item Master Control, Internal Control Considerations, 23, 243
Poor Purchase Order Visibility, Internal Control Considerations, 247–248
Post Deduct Issuing, Internal Control Issues, 251
Presentation and Disclosure, One of Five General Audit Assertions, 148, 297, 150
President's Council on Integrity and Efficiency (PCIE), 54
Preventative Controls, 135, 141
PriceWaterhouseCooper (PWC), 29–31, 42–43, 52, 102, 267, 270, 273–275, 294

Principles of Corporate Governance, OECD, 92–93
Principles-Based Guidelines to Compliance, 92, 263
Privacy Notice under GLB, 76, 297
Privately Held Companies, US SOX Considerations, 39–43
Process of Ethics, 262
Procure-to-Pay Super User, Segregation of Duty Considerations, 230
Product Lifecycle Management (PLM), 144
Program Management Officer (PMO), 257
Public Company Accounting Oversight Board (PCAOB), 39, 45, 79, 147, 190–191, 291, 295, 300
Public Company Accounting Reform and Investor Protection Act of 2002, xiv
Purchase Card (P-Card), 253
Purchase Orders, Off Balance Sheet Considerations, 9–10
Purchase Orders as OBS Liabilities, 9–10
Purchasing Super User, Segregation of Duty Considerations, 230

Questionnaires in Auditing, 140, 152, 154, 156, 160

Radio Frequency Identification (RFID), 145
Real Time Issuer Disclosure, US SOX Section 409 Considerations, 35–39
Real Time Reporting of Material Changes, Definition, 37
Recognition of Intercompany Accounts, Internal Control Considerations, 22
Refco Scandal, 47
Remediation Matrices in Auditing, 175, 176
Request For Information (RFI), 40

Request For Proposal (RFP), 40
Restriction of the Use of Certain
    Hazardous Substances (RoHS),
    283
Return on Investment (ROI), 244–245,
    263–264
Revenue Recognition, 129–134, 264
Rigas, John, 111
Rigas, Timothy, 111
Riggs Bank, xiii
Rights and Obligations, One of Five
    General Audit Assertions, 9, 11,
    14, 149, 150, 297
Risk, Definition of, 183, 186
Risk and Control Matrices in Auditing,
    150, 257
Risk Assessment, Internal Control
    Component under COSO, 26,
    27, 55, 59, 179
Rittenberg, Larry, 46, 47
Roosevelt, Teddy, xiii

SAB 101, 125–127, 129
SAB 104, 126–128
Safe Harbor Protection by the SEC, 115
Sarbanes, Paul, xiv, 302
Sarbanes-Oxley Act of 2002 (SOX)
    Certification of Financial Results,
        293
    Control Environment, 294
    Section 302, 293
    Section 404 , 21–30, 41, 47–52, 72,
        90, 107, 128, 147, 281
    Small Company Treatment Of, 301
SAS 31
    Existence Considerations, 148
    Presentation and Disclosure
        Considerations, 150
    Rights and Obligation
        Considertions 149–150
SAS 70, xv, 107–108, 301
Scrushy, Richard, 111–112
SDLC, 185–189
Section 401, Off-Balance Sheet
    Arrangements Under US SOX,
    1–9

Section 404, Internal Controls Under
    US SOX, 21–30, 41, 47–52, 72,
    90, 107, 128, 147, 281
Section 406, Code of Ethics Under US
    SOX, 32–40, 263–265
Section 409, Real Time Reporting of
    Material Changes Under US
    SOX, 35–39
Section 744, Basel II, 72
Section 745, Basel II, 72
Section 751, Basel II, 72
Section 752, Basel II, 72
Section 8, OECD Principles, 92
Section 802, Data Retention
    Requirements under
    US SOX, 136
Section 806, Whistleblower Protection
    under US SOX33, 119
Securities and Exchange Commission
    (SEC), 100–103
Securities Exchange Act of 1934, 34
Security Rule, HIPAA, 69, 70
Segregation of Duties (SOD), 24, 142,
    174, 228, 240
Segregation of Duties Fraud, 238–239
Segregation of Duties over Time, 233
Seller's Price to the Buyer is Fixed or
    Determinable, Revenue
    Recognition Condition, 128
Shared Services, Segregation of Duty
    Issues, 231–232
Siemens, 50
Significant Deficiencies, 146, 299
Single Act and the Maastricht
    Treaty, Criminal Penalties
    in the EU, 116
Six Sigma
    A Best Practice in Compliance
        Project Management,
        258–260
    Non Technical Tools, 259
    Technical Tools, 259
Small and Medium Size Enterprises
    (SMEs), 96
Small US Companies Impact from US
    SOX, 44–47, 49, 279, 302

Solvency II, 74–75
South Sea Bubble Scandal, xi
Special Purpose Entities (SPE)100
Spitzer, Eliot, xii, 112
Spreadsheet Errors and Controls, 22, 29, 31
Springer, Linda, 53, 67
Squire Sanders, 123
Staff Accounting Bulletin (SAB), 125
Standard & Poor's (S&P), 94, 271
Standard Sales Contracts, Internal Control Considerations, 24
Statement of Accountant Standard 31 (SAS 31), 148–150, 297
Statement of Auditing Standards 70 (SAS 70) xv, 107–108
Stebelton, Mark, xvii
Super Users, 229, 238
Supplier Collaboration Portals in Compliance, 278
Supplier/Ghost Card (S-Card), 168–169, 172–173
Supply Chain Management (SCM), 230, 258, 288
Sutherland, Edwin, 302
Swartz, Mark, 111
Symonds, Jon, 51
System Development Life Cycle (SDLC), 185, 188

Taub, Stephen112, 123, 270
Taylor, Jim, 66
The Enron Effect, Off Balance Sheet Considerations, 8, 19
Three-Way Segregation of Duties, 231, 233
Time Warner, 111, 119
Tone-at-the-Top, 182, 262
Treadway Commission25, 44, 47, 184, 293, 296
Turnbull Guidance
Turnbull Guidance, Guidance for Directors on the Combined Code, 85–86, 89–90, 291
Tyco, xii, xiv, 111, 119
Type I SAS 70, 107, 301
Type II SAS 70, 107, 301

U.S. Department of Justice (DOJ), 296
U.S. Rehabilitation Act (Section 508), 143
UK Listing Authority's Listing Rules, 88
United Nations Standard Products and Services Classifications (UNSPSC), 243, 245
U.S. Federal Control Activities, OMB A-123, 55
U.S. Federal Control Environment, OMB A-123, 56, 272
U.S. Federal Risk Assessment, OMB A-123, 56
U.S. Federal Standards for Internal Controls, OMB A-123, 56, 272
U.S. Gramm-Leach-Bliley Financial Modernization Act (GLB), 76–78, 116
U.S. SOX Impact on Foreign Companies, 49–50, 100, 288, 296
U.S. SOX Impact on Privately Held Companies and Non–Profits, 39–43

Valuation, One of Five General Audit Assertions, 297
Value–Added Resellers (VARs), 130, 131
Vendor Managed Inventory (VMI), 2, 251
Visualization Controls, 141–143
Voluntary Compliance, 41, 74, 94

Wall Street Journal, The, xii, 66, 68, 73, 78, 177, 270, 277, 296
Walsh, Campion, 74, 78
Washington Business Journal, 114, 119
WebCPA, 51–52
Weil, Steve, 69–70, 300
Wells, Joseph, 272, 277
Whistleblower Protection, 33–34
White–Collar Crime, 261, 303
Wholly Owned Subsidiary, 207
William Donaldson, US SEC Chairman, xiv, xv, 1, 50

Workflow, Electronic141, 143–144,
165, 234, 237, 241, 253, 263,
280–281
World Com, 110

XBRL, 102–104
XML, 102

Y2K, Comparisons to US SOX, xii